AN INTRODUCTION TO
SOCIAL PLANNING IN
THE THIRD WORLD

A Wiley Series

SOCIAL DEVELOPMENT IN THE THIRD WORLD
Textbooks on Social Administration, Social Policy, and
Sociology in Developing Countries

General editor
JAMES MIDGLEY
Department of Social Science and Administration
London School of Economics and Political Science

AN INTRODUCTION TO SOCIAL PLANNING IN THE THIRD WORLD
D. Conyers, *University of Nottingham*

THE SOCIAL DIMENSIONS OF DEVELOPMENT
Social Policy and Planning in the Third World
M. Hardiman and J. Midgley, *London School of Economics and Political Science*

SOCIAL RESEARCH IN DEVELOPING COUNTRIES
Edited by **M. Bulmer**, *London School of Economics and Political Science*, and
D. P. Warwick, *Harvard Institute of International Development*

Further titles in preparation

AN INTRODUCTION TO SOCIAL PLANNING IN THE THIRD WORLD

Diana Conyers

Institute of Planning Studies
University of Nottingham

1807 1982

JOHN WILEY & SONS
Chichester · New York · Brisbane · Toronto · Singapore

Library of Congress Cataloging in Publication Data:

Conyers, D.
  An introduction to social planning in the Third World.
  Includes index.
  1. Underdeveloped areas—Social policy.
  I. Title.
  HN980.C68   361.6′1′091724   80-14717
                                  AACR2
  ISBN 0 471 10043 9 (Cloth)
  ISBN 0 471 10044 7 (Paper)

British Library Cataloguing in Publication Data:

Conyers, Diana
  An introduction to social planning in the Third World.
  1. Underdeveloped areas—Social policy
  I. Title
  361.6′1′091724   HN980
  ISBN 0 471 10043 9 (Cloth)
  ISBN 0 471 10044 7 (Paper)

Photoset by Paston Press, Norwich
Printed in United States of America

*The great thing in this world is
not so much where we are but in
what direction we are moving.*

OLIVER WENDELL HOLMES

CONTENTS

TABLES

FIGURES

PREFACE

There has been a growing interest in the social aspects of planning in both developed and developing countries in recent years. This has resulted in the emergence of a discipline known as social planning, the appointment of social planners in planning offices and on planning teams, and the introduction of courses on social planning at univerisities and professional training institutions.

The rise of social planning has also led to the publication of a number of textbooks on the social aspects of planning. However, most of these books are oriented towards the conditions and needs of the developed nations of Western Europe and North America and so are of limited relevance to the Third World. There is, therefore, a need for more material on social planning in the Third World and it is hoped that this book will help to meet this need.

The book is intended as an introductory text on social planning for use in universities and professional training institutions in the Third World or in courses on the Third World taught in universities in developed countries. It is designed primarily for use at undergraduate level or in professional post-experience or in-service training programmes. However, it could also be used as an introductory text at postgraduate level, especially in courses where social planning is taught as a subsidiary subject rather than as the main focus of the course. It adopts a practical rather than a theoretical approach to social planning and should, therefore, be particularly useful for students who are already involved in development planning in the Third World, or may become involved at some time in the future.

It is impossible in a book of this length to cover all aspects of a field as wide as social planning or to cover individual aspects in any depth. It should therefore be emphasized that it is, as its title suggests, only an introduction to the subject. However, in order to assist readers to pursue particular topics in more depth, a fairly extensive guide to further reading is included at the end of each chapter.

The decision to write this book arose as a result of my involvement in the design and teaching of social planning courses at the University of Papua New Guinea and for overseas students at the Institute of Planning Studies at the University of Nottingham, and I would like to acknowledge the help and encouragement which I have received from colleagues and students in both these institutions. Much of the material incorporated here, including most of the case studies, is based on my wider experience in development planning in Tanzania, Papua New Guinea, and Zambia over the last 13 years, and I would also like to thank the many people with whom I have worked in these countries who have thus contributed indirectly to the content of this book. Finally, thanks are due to Colin Lewis, cartographer in the Department of Geography at the University of Nottingham, who drew the maps.

DIANA CONYERS

Nottingham, April 1981

PART ONE

THE NATURE OF SOCIAL PLANNING

CHAPTER 1

WHAT IS SOCIAL PLANNING?

Many changes occurred in the field of development planning during the 1970s, and one of the most significant was the increasing emphasis placed on the 'social' aspects of planning. Most countries of the Third World now acknowledge to a greater or lesser extent the importance of social goals and aspirations and the need to take social factors into consideration when planning development programmes and projects. This has resulted in the rise of a discipline and a profession commonly referred to as 'social planning'.

The rise of social planning is reflected in the employment of a new type of planner and the adoption of new planning techniques. A considerable number of national planning agencies now have a special social planning section or positions specifically earmarked for social planners, and there is an increasing demand for social planners in interdisciplinary planning teams. Social planning is also taught at universities and training institutions in developed and developing countries, both as a component of general courses in sociology, social administration, or planning and, increasingly, as a course in itself. This book is intended to provide an introduction to the scope, methods, and organization of social planning in developing countries.

Although few people involved in development planning would dispute the fact that social planning has become an important discipline in its own right, many people would find it difficult to define what it actually involves. This is hardly surprising because social planning is a rather vague term which is used to cover a wide range of activities. In an attempt to find out what it does involve, let us begin by considering what we mean by 'planning'.

What is planning?

There are probably almost as many definitions of planning as there are plans. In order to give some idea of the variety which exists, a few are quoted here:

Planning is . . . in essence, an organised, conscious and continual attempt to select the best available alternatives to achieve specific goals. (Waterston, 1965, p. 26)

Whatever else we may have in mind when we talk about planning, we must certainly be thinking about decision-making. The implication is that there is a better way of going about decision-making, by allowing it to take into account more data about events, or outcomes which are further off into the future. (Schaffer, 1970, p. 29)

1

Planning is the exercise of intelligence to deal with facts and situations as they are and find a way to solve problems. (J. Nehru, quoted in Waterston, 1965, p. 8)

Planning can be referred to as 'the art of getting future things done'. (Beenhakker, 1980, p. 22)

[Planning is] the rational application of human knowledge to the process of reaching decisions which are to serve as the basis of human action. (Sociedad Interamericana de Planification, quoted by Waterston, 1965, p. 8)

It is not within the scope of this book to consider the advantages and disadvantages of alternative definitions or to study the history or methodology of planning in any detail. However, a brief discussion of these issues is necessary at this point in order to ensure that, when we mention the word 'planning' in subsequent chapters, there is no doubt about the way in which it is being used.

As a starting-point, we may note that most definitions of planning—including those quoted above—imply that planning involves making decisions, or choices, about how best to use available resources to achieve particular aims or objectives some time in the future. The term 'resources' is used in this context to include natural resources, manpower (sometimes called human resources), capital resources (buildings, plant, equipment, etc.), and finance.

While accepting this broad interpretation of planning, some qualification is needed for our present purpose because this broad definition includes a very wide range of activities. The farmer who has to decide what crops he will grow next year, given the resources available to him, is planning. The 'physical' planner who prepares a design for a new housing area in the city or the layout of a village settlement scheme is planning. And decisions made by a national planning agency or a ministerial committee to increase the proportion of government revenue spent in the rural areas or to give priority to the less developed parts of the country are planing decisions.

Every form of planning has some social aspects or implications, and so it could be claimed that social planning should encompass the whole range of planning activities. However, in this book we shall be particularly concerned with the kind of planning which is employed by governments or other agencies to bring about general social and economic change; this kind of planning is usually known as *development planning*. The use of this term may be clarified by quoting from a survey of development planning in a number of countries published by Albert Waterston in 1965. Waterston explains that, for the purposes of his survey:

Countries were considered to be engaged in development planning if their governments were making a conscious and continuing attempt to increase their rate of economic and social progress and to alter those institutional arrangements which were considered to be obstacles to the achievement of this aim. (Waterston, 1965, p. 27)

New approaches to development planning

It is not enough, however, merely to say that our concern is with development planning, since there is more than one approach to development planning. We indicated earlier that the growth of social planning was only one of many changes in development planning which have occurred in recent years. These changes may be divided into two broad categories. Firstly, there have been changes in the *scope* or *content* of development planning, which can in turn be attributed to changes in the concept of development itself. In the immediate post-war period, when development planning first became a major focus of attention, development was seen primarily in economic terms, and the achievement of economic growth was thus the main focus of development planning. However, development is now seen in much broader terms, involving a complex of social, political, and environmental—as well as economic—factors. Consequently, development planning has also become a much more complex process, with a wide range of goals and objectives.

It is this very significant change in the goals of development planning, and therefore in its scope or content, which is largely responsible for the rise of social planning in its present form; and we shall be examining the implications of this in much greater depth elsewhere in the book. At this point, however, it should be noted that it has broadened the scope of development planning in other directions as well. For example, planners are now much more concerned with environmental issues, such as pollution and energy control, and with the relationship between politics and planning.

The second type of changes which have occurred may be described as changes in the *methodology* of development planning. These changes have arisen mainly as a result of increasing concern about past performance in planning—and in particular about the frequent occurrence of a very large gap between plan goals or targets on the one hand and actual achievements on the other. We shall examine the implications of these changes for social planning in appropriate chapters, particularly in Chapter 9 which is concerned with the methods and skills used in social planning; while anyone wishing to obtain additional information of a more general nature is referred to the guide to further reading at the end of this chapter. However, it is necessary to look briefly here at the impact they have had on the general concept of development planning.

The main effect has been that planning now tends to be viewed not as an isolated activity but as part of a complex process of 'development', which involves a number of related activities, including:

(i)   the identification of general goals or objectives;
(ii) the formulation of broad development strategies to achieve these objectives;
(iii) the translation of the strategies into specific programmes and projects;
(iv) the implementation of these programmes and projects; and

(v) the monitoring of their implementation and their impact in achieving the stated goals and objectives.

In other words, the interrelationship between 'policy-making', 'planning', and 'implementation' is emphasized, to the extent that one cannot distinguish clearly where one ends and another begins. When we talk about 'planning' in this book, it is in this sense that we are regarding it.

This concept of planning has a number of more specific implications. Firstly, it means that planning in the sense used here involves much more than merely producing a *plan document*. In the early days of development planning the importance of a plan document tended to be overemphasized, to the extent that planners put most of their effort into producing an impressive document and, once this was done, considered that they had achieved their objective. More recently, however, it has been generally recognized that producing a plan document is much less important than ensuring that plans are implemented. Colin Leys, in an attempt to define a new concept of planning, maintains that the main value of the conventional plan document is merely in 'providing politicians with a magic book to brandish at political meetings or at consultations with aid donors' (Leys, 1972, p. 75).

This does not mean that it is unnecessary to record plans and proposals in written form or to have some sort of plan document. What it means is that, firstly, a plan should be regarded as a tool for implementers rather than the end-product of the work of the planners, and secondly, that its preparation should not be regarded as the only—or the most important—activity of the planners. We shall look at the implications of this for social planning later on; at this point it is merely necessary to note that when we refer to 'planning' and 'plans', we do not merely mean the preparation of plan documents.

Secondly, in this book planning is regarded as a continuous process, not merely something which is done every now and again. In the early approaches to development planning, plans were usually prepared for fixed periods of time—five-year plans being particularly popular. Planners put a great deal of effort into the preparation of each plan, but planning activity then ceased, or at least declined, until it was time to produce the next plan. In contrast, more recent approaches emphasize the importance of continuous monitoring and revision of plans. We shall see in Chapter 9 that in many countries this has resulted in the preparation of annual plans linked into the budgeting system, while some countries have adopted a system known as 'rolling plans', in which the plan is extended each year and so never actually comes to an end.

Thirdly, this concept of planning has important implications with regard to the concept and role of the planner. In this book we shall use the word 'planner' to refer very broadly to anyone involved in some sort of planning activity; not merely someone who works in a specialized planning ministry or the planning section of a ministry, or someone whose position is officially classified as a 'planner'. Furthermore, we shall emphasize the fact that anyone who is actually employed as a 'planner' must work very closely with others involved in the overall process of development, including politicians, administrators, and the community at large. We shall discuss this in much more detail later, particularly in Chapter 10, which considers the organizational framework required for social planning.

Let us summarize briefly the main points made about planning so far. Firstly, while recognizing that the term 'planning' may be used to refer to a very wide range of decision-making activities, we have declared that our main concern in this book will be with what is generally called 'development planning'. Secondly, we have emphasized that there have been many changes in the content and methods of development planning. The conventional approaches to development planning consisted basically of the preparation of plan documents specifying proposals for the achievement of economic growth over a fixed period of time. However, when we refer to development planning here, we have in mind a much more complex and continuous process of decision-making, designed to bring about a wide range of social, economic, environmental, and political change. Furthermore, when we use the word 'planner', we are referring to anyone involved in this decision-making process. With this concept of planning in mind, let us now look at the other half of our subject and consider what is meant by the word 'social'.

The definition of 'social'

Like 'planning', the word 'social' is used very widely and with very many different meanings. We can group these various uses into five main categories. In the first category, which is very common in everyday usage but does not help to define social planning, the word 'social' is associated with entertainment or leisure. For example, we talk about a person's social life or the need for more social activities in a particular community. Social planning may, of course, include planning for the provision of social facilities, in this sense of the term—such as a national park or children's playgrounds—and it recognizes the importance of leisure; however, it means much more than that.

The second way in which the word 'social' is used is as the antonym of 'individual'. In this case, the word suggests a group of people and is associated with terms such as 'society' and 'community'. It has the implication that a group is more than just the sum of a number of individuals, and so what is good for the individual may not necessarily be good for the group as a whole. We therefore talk about doing something for the *social good*, meaning for the good of the community or society as a whole. This usage is particularly common among economists, who often use expressions such as the *social benefits* of a project, meaning the benefits to society. In social planning this interpretation of the word 'social' is reflected in a concern with communities, particularly community participation in planning and decision-making and concepts of community development.

The word 'social' is also used in a rather more general sense of concern or involvement with people, as opposed to 'things'. For example, in everyday language a social (or sociable) person is one who enjoys being with other people and 'social relations' is a term used to refer to the relations or interactions between people. This use of the word has had some influence on the meaning of social planning, in the sense that social planning may be very loosely defined as planning which involves or concerns people. However, although this definition points us in the right direction, since social planning is particularly concerned with people, it is not sufficiently precise because all forms of planning are concerned directly or indirectly with people in some way or other.

Another definition of the word 'social', and one which is more helpful in defining social planning, can again be explained by the use of antonyms. In this case, 'social' is used as the antonym of 'economic'; for example, social development is contrasted with economic development and the social benefits of a project are compared with the economic benefits. Unfortunately, although these terms are often used as if they were clearly definable and mutually exclusive, they are not—as one soon discovers if one tries to define exactly what is meant by 'social' and 'economic' in this context.

We shall not attempt here to consider the many different interpretations of the word 'economic', since it is used in about as many ways as the word 'social'. In this context, however, it is used in a relatively narrow sense to imply an association with money, production, or physical output. In contrast, 'social' suggests something non-monetary or not contributing directly to production, particularly something related to the general quality of human life. Thus, for example, the economic benefits of the construction of a road through a rural area might include increased agricultural production, lower costs for transporting goods in and out of the area, employment in small-scale commercial activities along the road, and so on; while the social benefits may be better access to health services, a wider range of goods for sale in local stores, or easier communication with friends and relatives.

However, it is very difficult to define the two terms more precisely and, in many cases, the two are so closely and complexly interrelated that it makes little sense to try to do so. Thus, in the above example, providing employment in small-scale commercial activities will also have social benefits for those people so employed, since the extra income they thus earn may be spent on social goods or services, such as entertainment, better food, children's school fees, or beer-drinking. Similarly, better access to health services may have indirect economic benefits since a healthier population is likely to be able to work harder and so produce more.

In spite of the difficulty of defining 'social' and 'economic' precisely, it is this use of the term which is very often implied when one talks about social planning. In this sense, social planning means taking into account factors other than purely economic ones—such as an increase in output or income or the relative costs of alternative courses of action—when making decisions. To return once again to the example of the road project, if only economic factors were taken into account, the road would be built if the anticipated economic benefits—in the form of increased production, lower transport costs, and so on—exceeded the costs of constructing the road; furthermore, the planners would choose a route which maximized these benefits and minimized the construction costs. However, if social factors were also taken into consideration, the road might be built even if the economic benefits were unlikely to exceed the costs, and an alternative route might be chosen in order to, for example, serve a larger number of people or provide more direct access to a health centre. This use of the terms 'economic' and 'social' will become clearer when we examine other examples of social planning, particularly in Chapters 4 and 5, which consider the social aspects of planning development programmes and projects.

Finally, there is one other use of the term 'social' which is again rather vague, but has had an important impact on the evolution of social planning as a discipline. This is the concept of 'social' as meaning something to which people have some intrinsic right or entitlement as members of society. For example, one might say that people have a *social right*—or are *socially entitled*—to such things as equality of opportunity, adequate food, clothing and shelter, freedom of speech, justice, or participation in government by the right to vote. What things are actually considered to be social rights varies considerably according to the goals or standards of the individuals claiming them and the societies in which they live. However, the word 'social' in this case indicates something which is of value for its own sake, rather than as a means of achieving some other objective.

We shall look in more detail at some of the implications for social planning of this concept of the term 'social', with particular emphasis on concepts of social equality and social justice, in Chapter 2. However, we should mention here that the word 'socialism' is closely associated with this usage of the word 'social', since socialism is particularly concerned with notions of equality and distribution. But it should be added that this does not mean that *social planning* is the same as *socialist planning*. Social planning may be an important component of socialist planning and social planning may be socialist in nature; but the terms are not synonomous.

The reader should not be too concerned if at this point he—or she—feels more confused than ever about the meaning of the term 'social'. He must accept that it has many different meanings and, although these meanings are interrelated, they cannot be used interchangeably. One important implication of this is that anyone using the word 'social' should take care to clarify the particular sense in which he is using it. For example, if he is talking about 'social goals', does he mean goals set by society rather than by individuals, goals which cannot be measured in economic—and particularly monetary—terms, or goals which are part of a set of intrinsic rights?

In view of the many different uses of the word 'social', it is hardly surprising that there are many different, although related, interpretations of the term 'social planning'. These various interpretations will hopefully become clearer when we look at different forms and dimensions of social planning in this book. At this point, however, we may—perhaps at the risk of some overgeneralization—summarize the discussion so far by suggesting that social planning is concerned in very general terms with planning for and by people and, somewhat more specifically, with the 'non-economic' aspects of development and the attainment of certain intrinsic rights and objectives (especially those related to equality) and with people's direct involvement in the processes of planning and development.

The rise of social planning

The term 'social planning' was first used in the developed nations of Western Europe and North America, where it originally referred predominantly, if not entirely, to planning for the provision of social welfare services. And although it is now usually interpreted much more broadly in these countries, to many people in the 'western' world social planning is still closely associated with social welfare planning.

What do we mean by social welfare planning? Like so many other terms with which we are concerned, it may be used in a number of ways. The United Nations, in a report on social welfare planning published in 1970, concludes that:

For planning purposes, the field of social welfare can be defined as a body of organized activities which are basically meant to enable individuals, groups, and communities to improve their own situation, adjust to changing conditions, and participate in the tasks of development. These activities, requiring special skills in social diagnosis, human relations, and informal education among others, can be differentiated for instance from the body of health services or from the basic facilities available for formal education and vocational training. (United Nations, 1970, p. 65)

This definition is rather broad and vague. The United Nations acknowledges this but believes that it reflects the many different interpretations of social welfare which exist. However, it also points out that in the past the term was often used in the more restricted sense of:

a body of activities designed to enable individuals, families, groups and communities to cope with the social problems of changing conditions (United Nations, 1970, p. 53)

It lists a number of specific services which were included in an earlier United Nations review of welfare services, conducted in 1959. These are:

family counselling, parent education, day-care services, child welfare services, care of the aged, rehabilitation services for the disabled or for the offenders, services for migrants and refugees, group activities for young people, medical social work, school services, community centres and social services related to housing projects. (United Nations, 1970, p. 53)

This group of activities is sometimes known as 'social work' or 'social welfare work' and it is associated with the employment of a special cadre of staff, usually called 'social workers', who are specially trained to provide these kinds of services.

It is this rather narrower concept of social welfare services which was originally identified with social planning in western developed nations. In other words, social planning was viewed mainly as planning the type of services listed above. It was, in particular, concerned with the translation of government policies regarding the provision of assistance to socially disadvantaged individuals or groups into specific programmes for the provision of such services.

The fact that social planning was, and in some cases still is, viewed in such terms in these countries reflects two significant features of 'western' society. Firstly, it reflects the relatively important role of the state in providing such services. Although the extent of assistance provided by the state varies considerably from one country to another—and in countries like the United Kingdom is also partially dependent on which political party is in power—it is generally accepted that the state has a significant role to play in this respect.

Secondly, it reflects the fact that the developed nations of Western Europe and North America do not normally practise development planning, in the sense in which we defined the term earlier. In other words, they are engaged in a comprehensive and continuous effort to bring about calculated changes in the nature of their society and economy. Planning is a much more haphazard or piecemeal affair, in which there is little or no attempt to coordinate the planning activities of various sectors or fields of activity into some sort of overall 'plan'. Consequently, there has been a tendency to confine social planning to planning activities which are more obviously 'social', notably social welfare services.

In the Third World, however, the situation is rather different. In the first place, the role of the state in providing conventional social welfare services is much more limited and tends to focus on different kinds of activities. This is partly because many of the social problems from which the need for such services arises, occur less frequently in developing countries, since they are problems which are associated with the structure of the population and the mode of life in the developed nations, and partly because 'welfare services' are more likely to be provided within the traditional social structure, without the need for government intervention.

For example, it is seldom necessary in a developing country for the state to play a major role in caring for the aged, partly because the age structure of the population is such that there are fewer old people but also because old people are usually cared for by their own families. Similarly, services for physically or mentally handicapped are less important because handicapped children are less likely to survive through infancy since they are particularly vulnerable to the many childhood ailments and, if they do survive, they are normally cared for by the community. There is also less demand for services such as psychiatric care and marriage counselling, since the problems which they are designed to tackle tend to be associated with urbanization and westernization.

This does not mean that there is no demand for this type of welfare service. There is a demand, and in most Third World countries it is increasing with the spread of urbanization, the breakdown of traditional social structures, and the greater stress of 'modern' life. However, the demand is still much less than in the western world and tends to be concentrated in the major urban areas.

The limited demand for conventional welfare services has resulted not only in the fact that they absorb a smaller proportion of national resources than in developed countries but also that the concept of 'social welfare' has tended to be extended to cover a variety of other related activities. In particular, there is much more emphasis on a wide range of activities which are often referred to as 'community development' or even more broadly as 'social development'. In many countries social welfare workers have been encouraged to engage more in community development activities, and in rural areas community development has tended to be established in place of more conventional welfare work. Furthermore, a 'community development approach' is often advocated in a wide range of developmental activities. This broadening of the concept and scope of 'social welfare' is reflected in the United Nations definition quoted above and we shall be looking at some of its implications later, particularly in Chapter 6, which looks briefly at the concept of community development and alternative types of community development programme.

The second important difference between the Third World and the countries of North America and Western Europe concerns the role of development planning. In most countries of the Third World development planning has become a major focus of activity since the Second World War, and more particularly since individual nations have attained political independence. Consequently, planning generally means more than the implementation of ad hoc government policies in various sectors in a piecemeal fashion; it usually involves the preparation of comprehensive plans for all aspects of social and economic development.

The result of these differences is that in the Third World social planning does include planning for the provision of conventional social welfare services; but this has never been more than a very small part of it. It also includes planning for a much wider range of social welfare activities—as suggested in the 1970 United Nations definition of social welfare planning—and it includes many other activities designed to bring about broad social change and development as part of a process of comprehensive development planning.

The rise of social planning in the Third World in the last decade or so can, therefore, be attributed not to any increase in the importance of social welfare services as such, but to the move to broaden the scope of development planning by placing much more emphasis on social change and the achievement of social goals. We have already indicated this earlier in the chapter and we shall be looking at its implications for specific aspects of social planning in subsequent parts of the book. However, at this point it may be useful to examine how these changes in the scope of development planning have actually occurred.

The growing interest in the social aspects of development, and therefore development planning, can probably be traced back to the early 1960s, when it was gradually realized that many plans were not implemented successfully because of 'human' or 'social' factors. Plans to introduce new food crops failed because the farmers did not like to eat the new food; family planning programmes were ineffective because for many reasons—including the wish to have children to look after one in old age—people preferred to have large families; efforts to commercialize livestock production were handicapped by the traditional social or prestige value attached to livestock—India's problem of the 'sacred cow'; the introduction of small-scale industries failed because people did not have the 'right' attitude (that is, a western commercial attitude) to business; and so on. Many other examples could be quoted.

At first such cases prompted a negative reaction among many of those responsible for planning development programmes. They were generally economists or technicians whose main concerns were with maximizing output, minimizing financial costs, introducing more up-to-date and cost-effective modes of operation, and other such developments. Their response tended to be to complain that 'the people' were hampering their development efforts. One writer on social planning, Raymond Apthorpe, has described this realization in the following terms:

There is the recurring tendency for development studies at the present time to explain the failure of predominantly economic development plans (as most plans are), by invoking the following reason. There must have been a troublesome knob on the development machine, marked 'the human factor' which was twiddled wrongly, inadequately or not at all, and therefore, somehow, 'the non-economic variables' were left out of account. Economic planners are alluding here to the proper studies of sociologists, social anthropologists, political scientists, community development specialists, penologists, etc. etc.—(Apthorpe, 1970, p. 7)

However, as this quotation suggests, a more positive approach gradually emerged. Firstly, the planners began to realize that plans were unlikely to be implemented successfully unless the 'non-economic variables' were taken into consideration. This meant that information about social conditions, needs, and attitudes must be obtained, the people likely to be affected by the proposed development should be consulted, and policies and programmes should be modified on the basis of the information thus obtained.

Secondly, and somewhat later, there emerged the realization that the social aspects of development should be regarded as justifiable ends in themselves. For example, the provision of social services, such as education and health, is important in its own right, not only as a means of increasing the productivity of the labour force. And objectives such as a general improvement in the 'quality of life' or an increase in equality, justice, participation, or other basic social rights, must be taken seriously and weighed up against the more conventional economic objectives.

It is the combination of these two changes in attitude among planners and policy-makers—the realization that social factors must be taken into account if plans are to be successfully implemented and the acknowledgement that social goals are important as ends in themselves—that have been largely responsible for the emergence of social planning in its present form in the Third World. It should be mentioned that similar changes have also influenced the concept and scope of planning in the developed nations of Europe and North America; but their impact has been less dramatic and less pronounced, mainly because of the lack of any form of comprehensive development planning and the continued preoccupation with the provision of social welfare services.

Fields of social planning

Enough has already been said about the definition and origins of social planning to indicate that it is a very broad concept covering a wide range of planning activities. As a basis for discussing social planning in this book, these activities may be grouped into three broad fields:
  (i) planning social services;
 (ii) taking account of social priorities and considerations in development planning; and
(iii) ensuring popular participation in planning.
This division is not intended to be definitive and the student of social planning will find that every author has his own classification system. For example, Apthorpe (1970), in his introduction to a collection of essays on social development and planning, suggests nine types of social planning. However, it will be found that most of the types identified by Apthorpe, and by other authors, can be grouped into the three main categories used here. These three categories have been chosen because they tend to reflect the main kinds of activity in which social planners in developing countries are likely to become involved. It is hoped that this division will therefore be particularly meaningful to those directly involved in social planning in the Third World.

In this section we shall look briefly at each of the three fields of social planning defined above, as a basis for more detailed discussion of each field in Part Two of the book. Before doing so, however, we should mention two possible interpretations of social planning which are not specifically discussed here. These are population planning and planning to achieve social reform.

In some books on social planning one will find that population planning is included as part of social planning. Apthorpe, for example, mentions it as a rather specialized form of social planning (Apthorpe, 1970, p. 17). In some respects this seems a logical deduction, since population planning is obviously concerned with people. However, it involves a rather different approach to people than that adopted in the kinds of social planning which we have encountered so far. Moreover, it requires specialized demographic skills. Consequently, in most countries population planning is the responsibility of a special unit or section. General social planners are likely to be closely involved in many population planning exercises, particularly in the less demographic aspects of population planning—such as studies of rural–urban migration; but they are not usually directly or solely responsible. For these reasons, population planning is not discussed in detail in this book, although its importance in development planning is fully recognized.

Some writers also include planning to achieve social reform—that is, a change in the structure of society—as a specific field of social planning. We shall discuss the role of the social planner in relation to the formulation of social policy and the achievement of social reform in some depth in Chapter 2. At this stage we shall merely state that we prefer to regard it as a particular approach to all aspects of social policy formulation and social planning, rather than as a specific field of social planning. The implications of this should become clearer in Chapter 2.

(i) *Planning social services*

The most straightforward use of the term social planning refers to planning the provision of services which are primarily of a social rather than an economic nature; that is, services which contribute to the social well-being of the population rather than to the development of the economy.

This interpretation of social planning can be traced back to its original association, particularly in the developed world, with planning social welfare services. This rather narrow definition of social planning has since been extended to include other social services, such as education and health services, housing, water supply, and the provision of recreation facilities. In fact, in most developing countries welfare service planning is much less important than planning some other services, such as education and health, which absorb a much larger proportion of national resources and raise major policy and planning issues.

The classification of such services as 'social' requires some explanation since, in most cases, they have both an economic and a social component and in some cases it is not easy to differentiate the two. Thus, education affects economic development through the provision of skilled manpower as well as being of social benefit to the people who receive the education. Similarly, the improvement of domestic water supplies in rural areas can contribute to increased agricultural production—by improving the health of the labour force and making more time available for productive activities other than fetching water—as well as make life generally easier and more pleasant for the rural population. However, since the services have very obvious social implications, while the economic implications tend to be more indirect, they are generally classed as social services and, therefore, fall within the social planner's area of responsibility.

Chapter 3 examines in some detail the process of planning social services, including a discussion of which services are normally included in this category, the type of policy issues involved, and the organizational structure required. It will be seen that a number of common issues arise when planning most social services. These include issues related to the distribution of services between different regions and social groups and questions regarding the appropriate quality or level of services to be provided, bearing in mind particularly the fact that resources are limited and a choice often has to be made between 'quantity' and 'quality'. It will also be noted that the main responsibility for planning specific social services usually rests with a particular government ministry or department—such as a ministry of education, health, or social welfare. Examples will be drawn from a variety of social services, but with particular emphasis on education and health planning, since these two sectors play a particularly important role in most countries.

(ii) *Taking account of social priorities and considerations*

A less straightforward form of social planning is concerned with the complex interaction of social and economic factors in the development process, and more specifically with the need to give adequate attention to social goals and social considerations.This aspect of planning has become particularly important during the last decade or so, reflecting—as mentioned earlier—the gradual realization that social factors must be taken into account in any development programme and that social development is an important goal in itself.

This form of social planning is practised at two rather different levels: as part of the process of formulating overall policies and plans at the national level (or, in some cases, at regional level) and as part of the planning of individual projects, especially major economic development projects.

At the national level social planners become involved in a variety of activities. They assist in the formulation of social policies—for example, policies to combat urban crime or to tackle the problem of unemployed school-leavers—and in the preparation of programmes to implement them. They monitor changes in social conditions and have to forecast the social changes which are likely to occur as a result of national policies, such as a decision to produce a particular crop on state farms rather than by smallholder production, or devise procedures to ensure that social considerations are taken into account in all new departmental programmes or projects. This form of social planning is discussed in much more detail in Chapter 4.

At the project level the role of the social planner is somewhat more easily defined, but still involves a fairly wide range of activities. In most cases, his task is to assess the social aspects or social implications of a project which is primarily economic in nature, and to ensure that steps are taken to minimize social disruption and provide necessary social services. The projects include major natural resource development projects (such as mining or lumbering), the provision of infrastructure—for example, a road or a dam, and large-scale industrial projects. The process of planning such projects is discussed in detail in Chapter 5, using three case studies which illustrate different kinds of project.

There are a number of common issues which arise at both the national and the project level, and it is for this reason that the two have been grouped together here under the heading of taking account of social priorities and considerations. The most important common issue is the preoccupation with the interrelationship between social and economic factors. What proportion of resources should be devoted to the achievement of social as opposed to economic objectives? How does one identify forms of economic development which also maximize social benefits—or at least minimize social costs? What does one do if social and economic objectives are in direct opposition to each other? These are very complex and very sensitive questions and they are further complicated by the fact that, as we have already noted, the social and economic aspects of any development programme are very closely interwoven and it is not possible to define either term precisely.

Arising from the interrelationship of social and economic factors is the related issue of how one defines and measures social objectives and benefits. The problem is twofold. Firstly, what criteria does one use to measure social benefits or social change? For example, if one wants to know whether social conditions have improved in an area as a result of, say, a new agricultural policy, what does one look for? Secondly, there is the difficulty of actually measuring social aspects of change. It is usually much easier to measure the economic benefits of a project than the social benefits.

A third issue of importance in this form of social planning is a procedural or organizational matter. Unlike the planning of social services, this type of social planning cannot be easily allocated to particular ministries or departments. It is not usually practicable to create a ministry of 'social priorities'—or even 'social development'—which has specific responsibility for ensuring that social factors are taken into account in all aspects of development. One must therefore look at alternative arrangements, such as the location of social planners in a national planning agency or in planning teams engaged on specific projects.

(iii) *Ensuring popular participation in planning*

The realization that many plans were not implemented because insufficient attention had been given to social factors affected the planning process in two ways. Firstly, as already indicated, it encouraged the employment of social planners specifically responsible for studying the social aspects of any programme or project. And secondly, it also led to more direct participation in planning by ordinary people. The planners realized that the people who are going to be affected by a particular development project should be involved as much as possible in the planning stages, partly to ensure that detailed information on social conditions and needs is obtained and partly to encourage a sense of involvement in, and commitment to, the project by the people.

The move towards more popular participation in the planning process has occurred in both developed and developing countries. However, it could perhaps be argued that participation is particularly important in the developing world, since there is a tendency for people to be less accustomed to social change and therefore more apprehensive of it and for the social and cultural gap between planners and people to be greater. Furthermore, in many developing countries the desire for more participation in planning is also associated with a general feeling, often related to the achievement of political independence, that people should be more involved in decision-making as a basic social right.

Participatory planning is the subject of Chapters 6 and 7. Chapter 6 looks in more detail at its advantages and examines the different ways in which effective participation may be encouraged, while Chapter 7 considers the problems which are likely to arise in any form of participatory planning and their implications for the social planner.

Social planning as a discipline

So far we have tended to emphasize the diversity of social planning activities, and in the previous section we identified three significantly different fields of social planning. However, it has also been assumed throughout this chapter that there is some relationship between these various activities which justifies their inclusion under the general heading of social planning and which explains the existence of social planning sections within ministries, the recruitment of professional staff who are officially classified as social planners, courses on social planning at universities and training institutions—and books, such as this, on social planning.

In other words, we have assumed that there is a common body of thought behind the various types of social planning and that they share a common methodology and organizational framework. These issues are pursued in other chapters. The thought processes underlying the concepts of social development and social planning are explored further in Chapter 2, before we go on in Part Two to look in more detail at specific fields of social planning. Then in the last part of the book, we again consider social planning as a whole when we examine its methodology and organization. Chapter 8 considers the information needs for social planning, while Chapter 9 examines the application of a number of general planning methods and skills to social planning. And finally, Chapter 10 looks at the organizational framework, including such issues as the role and location of the social planner and his interaction with others involved in the process of development planning.

The Third World

Finally, in this introductory chapter some comment is needed regarding the geographical scope of this book and the use of the expression 'Third World' in relation to social planning. It is intended that the concepts, principles, and methods discussed here will be applicable in most countries of the so-called Third World which practise any form of development planning. There is no particular reason for choosing the term 'Third World' in preference to any of the other names commonly used to describe this particular group of countries, except that it is, perhaps, at the time of writing one of the most universally acceptable terms. Other names—which include 'developing countries', 'less developed countries', 'low-income countries', and most recently 'the South' (a term popularized by its use in the 1980 Brandt Commission report (Independent Commission on International Development Issues, 1980) which examined the relationship between 'the North' and 'the South')—are at times used interchangeably with the term 'Third World' in this book.

The extent to which any general concepts and methods can be applied across the wide range of countries included in the general category of 'the Third World' is, of course, open to some question. Social conditions and needs vary enormously from one country to another and the role, form, and organization of social planning will vary accordingly. Furthermore, readers should be warned that this book is somewhat biased, particularly in the choice of examples, towards those countries with which the author is most familiar, notably the English-speaking countries of Africa and the South Pacific. However, it is our belief that the general content of the book will be relevant to most parts of the Third World. In fact, it is possible that, although the book is directed specifically towards the Third World, it may also be of some relevance—or at least some interest—to planners in developed nations, particularly when dealing with problems of 'underdevelopment' and the allocation of scarce resources within their own countries.

Guide to further reading

For those interested in pursuing some of the issues touched upon in this chapter, some suggestions for further reading are made in this section.

Further reading on particular aspects of social planning will be recommended at the end of appropriate chapters in Part Two of the book. However, there are a few books on social planning in general which the interested reader may like to examine. The majority relate primarily or entirely to social planning in the developed world; they include:

Eversley, D.E. C., *The Planner in Society* (London, Faber, 1973).

Kahn, A. J., *Theory and Practice of Social Planning* and *Studies in Social Policy and Social Planning* (New York, Russell Sage Foundation, 1969).

Mayer, R. H., *Social Planning and Social Change* (Englewood Cliffs NJ, Prentice-Hall, 1972).

There are very few books on social planning in the Third World. The most comprehensive work available is *People Planning and Development Studies* edited by R. Apthorpe (London, Frank Cass, 1970), which has been referred to in this chapter. It is a collection of essays on various aspects of social planning, including case studies from a number of countries. Also useful is the United Nations *Report on the Symposium on Social Policy and Planning* (New York, 1971), which is the report of a conference held in Copenhagen in 1970.

Another United Nations publication quoted in this chapter, *Social Welfare Planning in the Context of National Development Plans* (New York, 1970), looks at the relationship between social welfare and social planning; and Midgley, J., *Professorial Imperialism: Social Work in the Third World* (London, Heinemann, 1981) examines social work in the Third World.

For those readers requiring further information on development planning in general, one of the older but more useful basic texts is *Development Planning: Lessons of Experience* by A. Waterston (Baltimore, Johns Hopkins Press, 1965). More recently, a number of books and articles have been published on the deficiencies of the more conventional approaches to development planning and the basic components of a 'new' approach. The following are particularly recommended:

Caiden, N., and A.Wildavsky, *Planning and Budgeting in Poor Countries* (New York, Wiley, 1974).

Faber, M., and D. Seers (eds.), *The Crisis in Planning* (London, Chatto & Windus, 1972).

Helleiner, G. K., 'Beyond growth rates and plan volumes—planning for Africa in the 1970s', *Journal of Modern African Studies*, **10** (1972), 333–355.

Mehmet, O., *Economic Planning and Social Justice in the Developing Countries* (London, Croom Helm, 1978).

Some attempt to define the term 'social' is made in most introductory texts on sociology and in the books on social planning referred to above. Particularly useful for the study of social planning in the Third World is Apthorpe's discussion of 'the economic and the social' in the introductory chapter to his book *People Planning and Development Studies* and Chapter 2 of the United Nations *Report on the Symposium on Social Policy and Planning*. Further reading on social policy and social development is given at the end of Chapter 2.

CHAPTER 2

SOCIAL POLICY, SOCIAL PLANNING, AND SOCIAL REFORM

In this chapter we look at some of the more important policy issues involved in social planning in developing countries and the role of the planner in bringing about social change or social reform. This provides an important framework for the more detailed analysis of specific aspects of social planning in Part Two.

In so doing we shall be touching upon a field of study generally known as the sociology of development. We shall not attempt to review the many different theoretical approaches to this subject, although the reader who is interested in pursuing this field of study may refer to the guide to further reading at the end of the chapter for sources of additional information. In this chapter we shall merely focus on a few aspects of the field which are of particular concern and relevance to social planners at the present time. We shall, more specifically, be concerned with issues related to social equality or social justice and their impact on processes of social change or social development. When we use the term 'social' in this chapter, we shall therefore be thinking particularly of the last of its five meanings discussed in Chapter 1, in which it is associated with certain fundamental rights or entitlements of the individual in society.

However, we shall also find that the issues we are discussing are of central concern not only to sociologists but also to economists, political scientists, and any social scientist involved in development studies. This reflects the difficulty of distinguishing clearly between social, economic, and political factors and their complex interaction in the development process. Issues such as equality and social justice, for example, have major economic and political implications and are therefore major topics of discussion in all fields of development studies. In other words, as we indicated in Chapter 1, we are interpreting terms such as social policy and social planning in a rather broad sense, which means that they cannot be confined within the conventional boundaries of any one discipline.

Social policy and social planning

Before looking at specific social policy issues, it is necessary to give some thought to the relationship between policy and planning, in order to see why it is important for social planners to have some understanding of social policy. The relationship between the two is often a matter of some concern among

19

planners and it is something to which we shall refer on several occasions in later chapters.

It was pointed out in Chapter 1 that planning should not be regarded as an isolated activity but as part of a complex process of decision-making, which begins with the formulation of broad policy goals and objectives and then extends through a series of stages in which these goals are translated into detailed plans for specific programmes or projects which are then actually implemented. This suggests that planning and policy-making are closely related and that the planner should therefore have some understanding of the policy decisions which he is trying to implement.

However, is it still possible to distinguish between the 'policy-making' and 'planning' stages of this process, to the extent that they can, for example, be carried out at different times or by different people? In theoretical terms, this may appear to be possible. Very simply, one may say that policy-making means making decisions about the type of change or development which is required, while planning is the process of deciding how best to bring about this change or development. For example, in the field of education the policy may be to give priority to the development of primary rather than secondary schooling with the aim of achieving universal primary education in, say, 10 years' time. Planning will then involve making decisions about how much money must be spent on primary education during this period, how many new schools must be built, how many teachers trained, and so on, in order to implement the policy.

In practice, however, it is often difficult to draw the line between what is policy formulation and what is planning, particularly when one looks at it from the planners' point of view. To pursue the example of giving priority to primary education, those responsible for education planning in the ministry of education or a national planning agency will be very much involved in making the initial decision to concentrate on primary education, as well as in deciding how to implement this policy. In most cases, the actual policy decision will be made by the politicians, or some semi-political body, rather than by the planners. However, this decision will be based on information and alternatives presented by the planning staff.

Furthermore, although the basic policy decision is the decision to give priority to primary education, subsidiary policy decisions have to be made during the subsequent 'planning' stage. For example, should the expansion be achieved by building new schools, increasing the size of existing classes, or increasing the capacity of present schools by having two 'shifts', with one group of children attending school in the morning and another in the afternoon? Similarly, if some new schools are to be built, in which regions should they be located? These are sensitive 'policy' decisions, which often have to be referred back to the political level, and yet they are an integral part of the so-called 'planning' process.

In the rest of the book we shall not attempt to draw a clear distinction between policy-making and planning. We shall tend to focus on activities which are more obviously concerned with planning—such as the type of information which is needed to make and implement policy decisions, the ways in which this information can be analysed and presented, and the organizational structure within which such activities can best be undertaken—and we shall be concerned with the role of civil servants or others employed in a professional 'planning' capacity, rather than the role of the politicians who make the more obvious policy decisions. However, we shall also consider the policy goals and objectives which plans are designed to achieve, because we believe that the interaction between policy-making and planning is such that planners will inevitably become involved in policy-making and must therefore have an understanding of the issues involved.

Inequality, dependency, and social justice

Sociologists have always been interested in inequalities between different social groups because of their concern with the stratification of society. However, until the later 1960s their interest in patterns of inequality within developing countries—or between developed and developing countries—was very limited and confined to a rather static, descriptive account of the existing structure of Third World societies. This reflects the fact that for many years sociologists and anthropologists were interested in the Third World primarily as a source of information about 'small-scale' or 'primitive' societies which could no longer be found in other parts of the world.

However, during the last one and a half decades significant changes have occurred in the study of development by sociologists. The pattern of inequalities now receives much more attention and a much more dynamic and analytical approach is adopted. Particular attention is given to the causes of inequalities and changing patterns of inequality within and between countries, and to the implications of this for future development policies. Furthermore, there is a tacit assumption that the reduction of inequalities should be one of the main aims of development policy. This is reflected in the use of terms such as 'social justice', as in the following statement from a book entitled *Economic Planning and Social Justice in Developing Countries*:

A process of economic growth which worsens social and economic inequalities is elitist and morally indefensible. It is growth without equity. It is against the ideals of social or distributive justice, which are broader in scope than the concepts of legal and political justice. The latter proclaim equality of all before the law and grant equal political rights . . . social justice goes beyond this, proclaiming the idea of a fair distribution of economic and social benefits as well as costs. (Mehmet, 1978, pp. 29–30)

This change in approach reflects the influence of a neo-Marxist school of thought in development studies which has affected other disciplines as well as sociology. Particularly significant is the fact that economists—who, as we saw in Chapter 1, have tended to dominate the fields of development studies and development planning until relatively recently—are now much more concerned with issues related to equality and social justice.

One of the first economists to advocate this new approach to development thinking was Dudley Seers, who wrote in 1969:

The questions to ask about a country's development are therefore: What has been happening to poverty? What has been happening to unemployment? What has been happening to inequality? If all three of these have declined from high levels, then beyond doubt this has been a period of development for the country concerned. If one or two of these central problems have been growing worse, especially if all three have, it would be strange to call the result 'development', even if per capita income doubled. (Seers, 1969, p. 3)

More recently, the work on economic planning and social justice, quoted earlier, was in fact written by an economist, Ozay Mehmet. Later in the book, Mehmet admits that in the past:

The problem of distribution was more the task of sociologists, political scientists and, above all, practical politicians. These, and not the economist, were regarded as experts in coping with the tedious process of bargaining in the political arena between competing . . . groups. (Mehmet, 1978, p. 188)

Let us now look in more detail at the dimensions of inequality and their implications for planning purposes. In terms of the focus of this book it is useful to distinguish three main types of inequality:
  (i) inequalities between different social groups within developing countries;
 (ii) inequalities between geographical regions within developing countries;
(iii) inequalities between developed and developing countries.
We shall examine each of these in turn.

(i) *Inequalities between social groups*

Information on inequalities between different social groups within developing countries is very difficult to obtain, partly because of the problem of deciding what sort of inequalities to measure and partly because there is very little distributional data of any kind available. These problems are discussed in more detail in Chapter 8, when we consider methods of collecting data for social planning purposes.

However, considerable effort is now being made to improve the availability of data, particularly by international agencies such as the World Bank and the International Labour Organization (ILO), and the limited information which is so far available does suggest two important, and related, facts. Firstly, the gap between rich and poor tends to be greater in developing countries than in the developed world. This is indicated in Table 1, which summarizes information on income distribution for 28 countries published by the World Bank. Although the World Bank data is rather unreliable and available for only a limited number of countries, it is supported by the few other studies which have been made. For example, in one of the earliest studies of income inequality in developing countries, Adelman and Morris analyse information obtained from a variety of sources in 43 developing countries, which suggests that in these countries the most affluent 5 per cent of the population received on average 30 per cent of national income while the poorest 60 per cent received only about 26 per cent (Adelman and Morris, 1973, pp. 160–161).

Table 1   Distribution of income in developed and developing countries

		% share of total income by income group					
	No. countries in sample	Top 10%	Top 20%	Second 20%	Third 20%	Fourth 20%	Lowest 20%
Low- and middle-income countries	17	35.9	52.3	22.3	13.5	8.9	4.5
Industrialized countries	11	26.3	41.8	23.3	17.2	11.8	6.0

Source: Extrapolated from data published by the World Bank (World Bank, 1980a, pp. 156–157). The data are reproduced in full as Table 12 in Chapter 8, where the shortcomings of the data are discussed.

Secondly, it appears that in most developing countries inequalities have increased rather than decreased in the last one to two decades. Tables 2 and 3 present some preliminary data published in an ILO Working Paper on rural poverty. Table 2 indicates that in several Asian countries the proportion of the population living below the 'poverty line' (i.e. earning an income considered inadequate to meet basic requirements) appears to have increased. And Table 3 suggests that in 14 out of 24 African countries the proportion of the population estimated to be undernourished increased between 1969/71 and 1972/74. The World Bank suggests that a comparison between average per capita income and income distribution indicates that 'the incomes of the poorest 40 per cent of the population normally grow more slowly than the average until income per person reaches a range of $700 to $900' (World Bank, 1980a, p. 40).

We shall see in Chapter 8 that data on inequalities between social groups in Third World countries, of which the data in Tables 1–3 is a sample, is so poor that even the broad generalizations we have made here have to be treated with extreme caution. Nevertheless, there is little doubt that significant inequalities do exist in many developing countries and there is at least a serious risk that these will increase rather than decrease in the future.

This has important implications for the formulation of development policies and, therefore, for development planning. It is necessary for the policy maker or planner who is concerned with questions of equality and social justice to consider the impact which any particular policy or programme will have on the pattern of inequalities between social groups and, more positively, to formulate policies which are actually designed to reduce such inequalities. This is not easy, since policies designed to reduce inequalities may conflict with other national objectives, such as rapid economic growth. Furthermore, in many countries such policies are likely to encounter serious opposition from the more affluent

Table 2   Percentage of the rural population in poverty

Country or state	Year	Rural population in poverty	
Asia			
Pakistan	1964–4	72	
	1971–2	74	
Punjab, India	1960–1	18.4	
	1970–1	23.3	
Uttar Pradesh, India	1960–1	41.6	
	1970–1	63.6	
Bihar, India	1960–1	41	
	1970–1	59	
Tamil Nadu, India	1957–8	74.1	
	1960–1	69.8	
	1969–70	74.0	
Bangladesh	1963–4	40.2	
	1975	61.8	
Malaysia	1957	30.0	
	1970	36.5	
Philippines	(1) 1956–7	10.4	
	1970–1	12.7	
	(2) 1961	61.0	
	1971	64.0	
Indonesia:			
All Indonesia	1969	47.0	
Java	1969	62.0	
Thailand	1962–3	47.0	
	1968–9	26.0	
Latin America			
		(a)	(b)
Argentina	circa 1970	1.0	19.0
Brazil	,,	42.0	73.0
Colombia	,,	23.0	54.0
Costa Rica	,,	7.0	30.0
Chile	,,	11.0	25.0
Honduras	,,	57.0	75.0
Mexico	,,	18.0	49.0
Peru	,,	39.0	68.0
Venezuela	,,	19.0	36.0
Total Latin America		34.0	62.0

Source: Ghai *et al*. 1979, p. 11. Copyright 1979, ILO, Geneva. The sources of the data are discussed in detail on p. 12 of the report. It should be noted that comparisons between countries are not valid because of different methods of measuring the 'poverty line'. The two sets of data for the Philippines represent the results of two different studies, which used different definitions of the 'poverty line'. Data on Latin America is only included as a copyright requirement.

sectors of the population, including many politicians and senior civil servants. We shall look in more detail at the impact of specific development policies on the pattern of inequalities and the problems which arise in trying to reduce such inequalities in subsequent chapters.

Table 3   Estimates of malnutrition in Africa

Country	Estimate of percentage of population undernourished	
	1969/71	1972/74
Botswana	33	36
Cameroon	14	16
Chad	34	54
Ethiopia	26	38
Ghana	22	20
Guinea	38	41
Ivory Coast	9	8
Kenya	24	30
Liberia	42	37
Madagascar	14	17
Malawi	19	14
Mali	38	49
Mauritania	36	48
Mozambique	34	36
Niger	36	47
Senegal	25	25
Sierra Leone	20	21
Somalia	42	40
Sudan	30	30
Swaziland	35	33
Tanzania	35	35
Togo	24	24
Zaïre	34	44
Zambia	35	34

Source: Ghai *et al.*, 1979, p. 15. Copyright 1979, ILO, Geneva. The original data were obtained from statistics published by the Food and Agriculture Organization (FAO). 'Undernourished' was defined as consuming less than approximately 1,500 calories.

(ii) *Regional inequalities*

Traditionally, sociologists have been less concerned with regional inequalities than with inequalities between social groups. The study of regional inequalities has often been left to geographers and regional economists. However, one cannot consider the attainment of social equality or social justice within developing countries without including the reduction of inequalities between regions.

Information on regional inequalities in developing countries is often as difficult to obtain as information on inequalities between social groups. In many countries national income data is not broken down by region and, in any case, its value as an indicator of regional well-being is limited, particularly in predominantly rural areas. Furthermore, it is very difficult to compare data for different countries. The few attempts that have been made to make international comparisons have been based on rather limited data and have made a number of rather dubious assumptions about the patterns of development in the Third World (compare Slater, 1975, Chapter 1).

Nevertheless, the little information which is available from studies of individual countries and from attempts to make international comparisons, does suggest that significant regional income inequalities do exist in most countries, including those in the developing world. Cole, for example, in a recent study of inequalities within and between nations, concludes that:

It seems reasonable to observe at this stage that even on the limited evidence given in this chapter, great regional disparities in living standards exist *within* countries. Government policy in many countries in recent decades has been to reduce existing regional disparities and to prevent further disparities from emerging. Even so, positive results have been limited. (Cole, 1981, p. 100)

Furthermore, the evidence also suggests that in developing countries these inequalities tend to be greater than in developed countries. As with inequalities between social groups, it appears that regional inequalities—at least in income—tend to be greatest in countries in the middle-income group.

A particular dimension of the pattern of regional inequalities which is a source of major concern in many developing nations is the inequality between rural and urban areas. Once again this inequality is very difficult to measure, especially since many of the criteria which one might use to compare rural and urban areas cannot be easily quantified, or even measured in a more subjective way. This difficulty is reflected in the fact that there is seldom an obvious answer to a question such as: 'Is it better to be poor in the city or poor in the village?'

However, the available information does suggest that, as with other inequalities, the inequality between rural and urban areas is significant in most developing countries and, in most cases, considerably greater than that in the developed world. Michael Lipton, in a major study of what he terms 'urban bias' in development, states that:

Three sources of information are available on rural and urban output and income: surveys of income and consumption; estimates of wages and earnings in different occupations; and output per person and output per worker figures for agriculture and industry. Taken together, these three sources reveal that rural rewards lag far behind urban rewards. All three leave out some component of the welfare gap and overstate others. Yet, while much is made of the concealed benefits of rural life, little is made of its concealed drawbacks. Planners, scholars and governments are thus led to underestimate urban-rural welfare gaps. (Lipton, 1977, p. 146)

Most Third World governments now accept the existence of such inequalities, and this is reflected in the increasing emphasis placed on rural development programmes at national and international levels.

Regional inequalities within developing countries can, of course, be attributed partly to inequalities in the distribution of natural resources which cannot normally be altered by adopting alternative development policies. However, in most cases inequalities due to the distribution of natural resources were exacerbated by colonial development policies, which tended to develop a few areas—particularly those with the greatest potential for the exploitation of natural resources, such as cash cropping or mining, and communication centres such as ports—at the expense of the rest of the country.

In order to counteract the impact of colonial development policies and reduce regional inequalities—including inequalities between rural and urban areas, planners in the Third World today have to give particular attention to the regional implications of development policies and programmes. This means not only considering the location of individual projects or programmes but also looking for ways of restructuring the economy so that some areas are not developing at the expense of others. Development of the rural areas, in particular, requires a major change in many aspects of development policy. Once again we shall look at specific examples of policies and programmes designed to reduce regional inequalities, and the obstacles which are likely to be encountered in doing so, in subsequent chapters.

(iii) *Inequalities between developed and developing countries*

The third dimension of inequalities which has become a major focus of attention in development studies is the inequality which exists between the developed and developing worlds. Table 4 gives some indication of present inequalities, measured in terms of per capita income, adult literacy, life expectancy, and food production. And Table 5 indicates that, at least in terms of income, the gap between rich and poor countries actually increased during the three decades from 1950 to 1980.

It is not possible—or necessary—for this book to analyse the causes of inequalities between developed and developing nations or to examine all the implications for national and international development policy. Our main concern here is with the implications for social planners in Third World countries. In this respect, it should be emphasized that much of the inequality can again be attributed to colonial development policy, which resulted in the development of the metropolitan powers at the expense of the countries of the Third World, thus creating a situation where the majority of developing nations are still to some extent economically, technologically, and culturally dependent on the developed world, although they are now politically independent. In later chapters we shall examine specific examples of such dependence and consider possible action by policy-makers and planners to reduce it. It should, however, be remembered that the problem of inequalities between developed and developing nations cannot be solved by the latter alone.

Table 4   Indicators of inequality between developed and developing countries

	GNP per capita 1978 (US $)	Adult literacy 1975 (%)	Life expectancy at birth 1978 (years)	Ave. index of food prod. per capita 1976–78 (1969–71 = 100)
Low-income countries	200	38	50	97
Middle-income countries	1,250	71	61	106
Industrialized countries	8,070	99	74	108

Source: Extrapolated from data published by the World Bank (World Bank, 1980a, pp. 110–111). The data are reproduced in full as Table 11 in Chapter 8.

The 'basic needs' approach to development

Brief mention should be made here of a particular approach to development which has attracted considerable attention among students of development and international agencies, such as the World Bank and the ILO, in recent years. This is generally known as the 'basic needs' approach.

The basic needs approach states that the aims of development policies, in individual countries and in the world as a whole, should be to meet the 'basic needs' of the entire population. There is a great deal of debate about exactly what constitutes a 'basic need', but it is generally agreed that basic needs can be divided into three main kinds. Firstly, there are certain basic consumption goods—such as food, clothing, and shelter—to which everyone should be entitled. Secondly, there are basic services—such as education, health services, and a clean water supply—to which everyone should have access. And thirdly, there is the right to participate in making and implementing decisions which affect one's own development. It is also assumed that the provision of productive employment is an essential component of a basic needs approach, partly as a means of earning an income which in turn can be used to purchase basic goods and services, but also because of the sense of personal satisfaction which it provides for the individual.

This approach to development is of particular significance to social planners for two reasons. One reason is that it is concerned with questions of equity and

Table 5   Income inequalities between developed and developing countries, 1950–80

	GNP per capita (US $)			Average annual growth rate (%)	
	1950	1960	1980	1950–60	1960–80
Low income countries	164	174	245	0.6	1.7
Middle-income countries	625	802	1,521	2.5	3.3
Industrialized countries	3,841	5,197	9,684	3.1	3.2

Source: World Bank, 1980a, p. 34. Reproduced by permission of Oxford University Press.

social justice. The emphasis on meeting the basic needs of the *entire population* means that development policies and programmes must be directed towards the poorest sectors of the population, if necessary at the expense of more affluent sectors. Furthermore, it is assumed that every individual is entitled to these basic requirements as part of his (or her) rights as a member of society. In other words:

The final goal is an egalitarian society, at both the national and international levels. Its basic principle is the recognition that each human being, simply because of his existence, has inalienable human rights regarding the satisfaction of basic needs . . . that are essential for complete and active incorporation into his culture. (Ghai, 1977, p. 12)

The other reason why the basic needs approach is particularly relevant to the social planner is that the concept of basic needs includes much more than just 'economic' needs. It includes a wide range of 'social' goods and services which contribute to the overall 'quality of life' and it includes the right to participate in one's own development. As we saw in Chapter 1, these are important concerns of the social planner.

Many problems arise when any attempt is made to translate the general principles of a basic needs approach into specific development policies and programmes. Who should determine what is and what is not a basic need? Is it possible to identify a set of basic needs which can be applied to many different countries—or even to all people in any one country? Should the basic needs of the poorest people be met by redistributing existing assets and resources from the rich to the poor, or merely be directing any additional resources to the poor rather than to the rich? What happens if meeting basic needs conflicts with other national goals? And what can be done if the more affluent sectors of the population try to obstruct the implementation of a basic needs policy?

There are no easy answers to these questions; in subsequent chapters we shall find many examples of the way in which these and other related issues affect the work of the social planner. However, this does not mean that the basic needs approach is irrelevant or that all attempts to achieve a more socially appropriate and equitable form of development should be abandoned. Throughout this book we shall emphasize that the social planner's task is not easy—but it is important.

Social policy and social change

The increasing concern with the extent of social inequalities, together with the realization that these inequalities are related to the structure of society, has important implications for the nature of social policy and, in particular, the relationship between social policy and social change. In the introduction to *Ideology and Social Welfare*, George and Wilding emphasize that:

Theories of society, of the State, of social problems and of social policy are inter-related. The view a social scientist holds of societal organization and of the distribution of political and economic power will affect the explanation he gives of the nature of social problems and of the government's responses in the form of social policy measures. (George and Wilding, 1976, p. 1)

It is possible to distinguish two main approaches to the nature of social problems, and therefore the nature of social policies designed to overcome these problems. One approach is based on an acceptance of the existing structure of society, in which inequalities inevitably arise. This acceptance results from a belief that the existing structure is for some reason desirable, or at least that it is inevitable. In this approach social problems are attributed either to deviancy—that is, to people who, because of their own deficiencies, are unable or do not choose to conform to the norms of society—or to some relatively minor disorganization or malfunctioning of society. Policies designed to overcome these problems therefore focus on attempts to make people more able or willing to conform and on efforts to improve the existing organization of society.

The alternative approach does not accept the existing structure of society. It maintains that social problems arise from deficiencies in this structure and that the only effective solution, at least in the long run, is to change this structure. In other words, social policy should be concerned with changing the structure of society, or with what sociologists call *social-structural change*.

These two approaches to the analysis of social problems and social policy have been discussed particularly in relation to social welfare policy in developed countries. For example, if the first approach is adopted, poverty in an industrialized society is attributed either to some sort of disorganization within society—such as unemployment in an area of declining industrial activity—or to personal deficiencies, such as lack of education, illness, or laziness, of the poor themselves (compare George and Wilding, 1976, p. 5). Social welfare policy, therefore, should attempt to solve these problems by such measures as unemployment benefits, education, and retraining, and attempts to 'motivate' the poor to 'help themselves'.

The alternative approach, on the other hand, attributes poverty primarily to inequalities inherent in the existing structure of society. It therefore adovcates measures designed to reduce these inequalities; for example, taxation policies which redistribute income from high- to low-income groups, changes in the structure and ownership of industry in order to distribute profits more equitably, and employment policies designed to provide jobs to those areas and social groups where the need is greatest. Less radical measures, such as unemployment benefits and other forms of income supplements, may still be needed in order to alleviate immediate hardship; but they should not be regarded as long-term solutions.

However, the debate is just as relevant to social policy in the Third World. For example, the problem of urban crime in the Third World can be regarded either as one of social deviance, in which some individuals are breaking the laws made to preserve the balance of society, or as a structural problem, related to problems of rural-urban inequalities, urban unemployment, and the class structure in urban areas. The first approach results in measures to improve the police force, introduce urban curfews, assist or repatriate the unemployed, and so on; while the second approach emphasizes the need for policies designed to improve conditions in the rural areas, encourage labour-intensive industry, and reduce inequalities in urban wages.

Similarly, inequalities in the distribution of education, health, or other social services may be regarded either as problems due to lack of money, manpower, or supplies or as problems primarily resulting from the fact that certain social or regional groups have better access to existing services than others. And the problems of small farmers and landless labourers in many of the countries of Asia and Latin America may be tackled either by trying to improve their methods of production or provide non-farm employment or by the reform of the land tenure system.

Our analysis of the extent and causes of social inequalities in the previous section suggests the need to adopt the second approach to social problems and social policy; in other words, social policy must be concerned with changes in the structure of society. This does not mean that other measures are unnecessary or irrelevant. It may still be necessary to improve the police force, provide assistance to urban unemployed, allocate more money and manpower to social services, and look for ways of increasing the incomes of small farmers. But it must be recognized that such measures will only alleviate the more obvious or immediate effects of the problem; they will not remove the underlying causes which rest within the structure of society. The implications of this for various aspects of social policy will be demonstrated in later chapters, which examine specific aspects of social policy and social planning.

The role of social planning

Social planning is sometimes defined specifically as planning to achieve change in the structure of society. Mayer, for example, in his *Social Planning and Social Change*, rejects more conventional definitions of social planning and declares that 'the concept of social planning which we advocate is called *social-structural change*' (Mayer, 1972, p. 132). Other writers regard planning to achieve social-structural change as one possible concept or type of social planning. Apthorpe, for example, includes it as one of his nine categories of social planning (Apthorpe, 1970, p. 16).

We prefer to view the relationship between social planning and social–structural change slightly differently. In this book we regard the pursuit of social–structural change not as the *definition* of social planning nor as one *type* of social planning, but as a particular *approach* to the formulation of social policies or plans, which can be adopted in any of the aspects of social planning identified in Chapter 1—or in any other form of development planning. As we have already indicated, we consider it a very important approach to social policy and social planning. Throughout this book we assume that social planners are concerned with the achievement of social justice and recognize the relationship between social problems, social policy, and social–structural change, and we analyse the implications of alternative policies and plans in terms of the impact they will have on social justice and social change.

However, at the same time, we acknowledge that many social planners in the Third World, particularly those employed as professional planners in national or local government agencies, may find themselves in a position where they have little chance of achieving—or even advocating—any significant change in the structure of society. In other words, they are working for governments which, for a variety of reasons, are either unable or unwilling to bring about such changes, even though change may be urgently required. Consequently, in subsequent chapters we not only devote considerable attention to the obstacles which planners may encounter when they try to bring about social–structural change, but we also consider other aspects of the work of the social planner which may not be directly related to the achievement of such change. This does not mean that we feel that the social planner should give up the struggle for social justice, merely that it is usually necessary for him to adapt to the social, economic, and political environment in which he is working. The problems which this may create for the more concerned planner are discussed in more detail in Chapter 10.

Guide to further reading

The sociology of development

There are a number of introductory textbooks on the sociology of development. Some of the most widely used are:

De Kadt, E., and G. Williams (eds.), *Sociology and Development* (London, Tavistock Publications, 1974).

Goldthorpe, J. E., *The Sociology of the Third World* (Cambridge University Press, 1975).

Hoogvelt, A. A. M., *The Sociology of Developing Countries* (London, Macmillan, 1976).

Long, N., *An Introduction to the Sociology of Rural Development* (London, Tavistock Publications, 1977).

Sociology and Development is particularly useful as an introduction to neo-Marxist approaches to the sociology of development (see particularly the introductory chapter and the chapter by A. Foster-Carter).

Inequality, dependency, and social justice

For discussion of the extent and causes of social inequalities within the Third World, the following may be useful:

Adelman, I., and C. T. Morris, *Economic Growth and Social Equity in Developing Countries* (Stanford, Stanford Univerisity Press, 1973).

Bairoch, P., and M. Lévy-Leboyer (eds.), *Disparities in Economic Development since the Industrial Revolution* (London, Macmillan, 1981).

Chenery, H., *et al.*, *Redistribution with Growth* (London, Oxford University Press, 1974).

Elliott, C., *Patterns of Poverty in the Third World* (New York, Praeger, 1975).

International Labour Organization, various publications produced as part of the World
Employment Programme Research (Geneva).
For particular coverage of spatial inequalities—including inequalities between rural
and urban areas, see:
Cole, J. P., *The Development Gap* (Wiley, 1981).
Lipton, M., *Why Poor People Stay Poor: Urban Bias in World Development* (London,
Maurice Temple Smith, 1977).
Slater, D. (ed.), *Underdevelopment and Spatial Inequality*, Vol. 4, Part 2 of *Progress in
Planning* (Oxford, Pergamon Press, 1975).
Inequalities between developed and developing countries are discussed in many
different books and articles. Some more recent sources relevant to the discussion in this
chapter are:
Cole, J. P., *The Development Gap* (Wiley, 1981). This book provides a very thorough
analysis of the extent and causes of inequalities within and between nations from a
spatial perspective.
George, S., *How the Other Half Dies: the Real Reasons for World Hunger*
(Harmondsworth, Penguin, 1976).
Heatley, R., *Poverty and Power: the Case for a Political Approach to Development and
its Implications for Action in the West* (London, Zed Press, 1979).
Independent Commission on International Development Issues (Brandt Commission),
North-South: a Programme for Survival (London, Pan Books, 1980).
Thomas, H., *A Picture of Poverty* (Oxford, Oxfam, 1979).
World Bank, *World Development Report* (New York, Oxford University Press, pub-
lished annually).
Finally, perhaps the most useful recent discussion of the relationship between plan-
ning and social justice is *Economic Planning and Social Justice* by O. Mehmet (London,
Croom Helm, 1978).

The basic needs approach

Numerous articles and a smaller number of books on the 'basic needs' approach to development have been published since the mid-1970s. Some of the most useful of these
are:
Ghai, D. P., *et al.* (eds.), *The Basic Needs Approach to Development* (Geneva, ILO,
1977) (especially Chapter 1).
Institute of Development Studies, University of Sussex, 'Down to basics: reflections on
the basic needs debate', *IDS Bulletin*, **9**, No. 4 (June 1978).
Sheehan, G., and M. Hopkins, *Basic Needs Performance: an Analysis of some International Data* (Geneva, ILO, 1979).
Streeton, P., and S. J. Burki, 'Basic needs: some issues', *World Development*, **6** (1978),
411–421 (reproduced by the World Bank as No. 53 in its Reprint Series).
Streeton, P., 'A basic-needs approach to economic development', in Jameson, K. P.,
and C. K. Wilber (eds.), *Directions in Economic Development* (Indiana, University
of Notre Dame Press, 1979), 73–129.
For a very brief account of the basic needs approach, set in the context of general
trends in development thinking, the reader may also like to read Chapter 2 of *The Third
World Tomorrow* by P. Harrison (Harmondsworth, Penguin, 1980).

Social policy, social change and social planning

For further reading on the relationship between social policy, social change, and social
planning, the following are recommended:
George, V., and P. Wilding, *Ideology and Social Welfare* (London, Routledge and
Kegan Paul, 1976), especially Chapter 1.

Gil, D. G., *Unravelling Social Policy* (Cambridge, Mass., Schenkam, 1973).

Mayer, R. H., *Social Planning and Social Change* (Englewood Cliffs, NJ, Prentice-Hall, 1972).

Unfortunately, all these books are concerned with developed rather than developing countries. The gap in literature relevant to the developing world should, however, be partially filled in the near future by the publication of *Social Policy in the Third World* by S. MacPherson (Brighton, Harvester Press, 1982).

PART TWO

FIELDS OF SOCIAL PLANNING

CHAPTER 3

PLANNING SOCIAL SERVICES

One of the three main aspects of social planning identified in Chapter 1 was the planning of social services. Although this is perhaps the most limited interpretation of social planning, it is nevertheless very important and frequently occupies a high proportion of the social planner's time. In this chapter we consider what kinds of services are normally included in this category, the main components of the planning process, some major policy issues which are often involved, and the planning machinery required. Finally, we also look at some common problems which arise when planning social services.

Social services

It was pointed out in Chapter 1 that the term 'social services' can be somewhat confusing because most services have both a social and an economic component. However, the term is generally used to refer to a variety of services provided—entirely or at least in part—by the state with the main aim of improving the general quality of people's lives rather than contributing directly to production or bringing direct financial benefits. Those services most often included in this category are social welfare, education, health, housing, domestic water supply and sanitation, and a variety of recreational services. Some other services—such as power, transport, and telecommunications—have some important social implications but are usually not regarded primarily as social services.

In this chapter we shall attempt to generalize about the process of planning a variety of different social services; but we shall illustrate the discussion with examples from specific services. We shall, in particular, draw upon the experience in education and health planning, partly because these two sectors provide some good examples of issues which arise in most aspects of social service planning, and partly because in most Third World countries education and health absorb more financial and manpower resources than other social services, although still much less than in developed nations. The proportion of government expenditure allocated to education and health services varies considerably from one country to another and accurate data is difficult to obtain. However, statistics published by the World Bank in 1980 indicate that on average developing countries allocate around 15 per cent of total government expenditure to education and about 6 per cent to health (World Bank, 1980b, Table 3; World Bank, 1980c, Annex 3).

It should be noted at this point that, although there is a tendency to assume that each social service covers a clearly defined sphere of activity, there is in practice considerable overlap between different social services and between social services and other aspects of development activity. Social welfare is a particularly nebulous area of activity and, as indicated in Chapter 1, there are several different views about what is and what is not included under the general heading of social welfare services. Education and health are more easily definable, but there is still considerable overlap with other activities. For example, 'non-formal' education—that is, education outside the formal school system—overlaps with a variety of other extension and training activities. Similarly, many aspects of health care—for instance, nutrition, family planning, and environmental sanitation—require close coordination between health workers and those involved in such activities as agricultural extension, education, and the provision of water and sanitation.

Components of the planning process

In most forms of planning three main components of the planning process can be identified: data collection and analysis; policy formulation; and the preparation of specific programmes and projects. This section looks briefly at what each component involves in the case of social service planning.

(i) *Data collection and analysis*

As in any form of planning, the collection and analysis of data is an important component of social service planning. Two main kinds of data are required: firstly, data on the existing provision of services, and secondly, data on the need or demand for future services.

In the case of education, for example, the first type of data includes such information as the number of students, the number of staff, and the amount of money spent on various categories of education, usually broken down by administrative region and often expressed in terms such as the proportion of children in a particular age group attending the appropriate level of school, the proportion progressing from one level of schooling to another, the student/teacher ratio, and so on. Table 6 illustrates this type of data, using an example from Zambia.

The second kind of data—that is, information on the future demand for particular services—is more difficult to obtain, since it involves making projections based on existing data and taking into account the likely demand from the people for particular services and official government policies regarding the provision of these services. Nevertheless, this information is very important since it is the basis on which detailed plans are produced.

Table 6   Zambia: Primary education indicators by province, 1976

Province	Population 1976 ('000)	Enrol- ments per 1,000 people	Enrol- ments as % of children 7–14 yrs.	Grade 1 enrol- ments as % of child- ren aged 7[a]	Pupil: teacher ratio	Pupil: trained teacher ratio
Central	454	174.8	82.7	97.9	47.2	61.9
Copperbelt	1,183	167.0	75.2	82.8	46.7	54.8
Eastern	607	166.1	88.8	111.5	49.6	67.9
Luapula	353	201.3	93.0	115.8	47.2	57.3
Lusaka	590	150.1	72.0	76.3	47.4	51.6
Northern	610	192.7	91.5	116.3	49.9	67.6
North-western	273	168.7	98.4	119.6	45.8	58.3
Southern	571	222.4	103.7[b]	128.3	47.9	59.1
Western	497	160.8	91.7	106.2	45.6	58.8
Total Zambia	5,138	176.7	86.3	103.0	47.6	59.1

[a] Percentage over 100 indicates children under or over 7 years in Grade 1.
[b] Indicates children under 7 or over 14 in primary schools.
Source: Zambia, 1979, p. 72. Reproduced by permission of Government Printer, Zambia.

(ii) *Policy formulation*

Although this book is concerned with planning rather than policy-making, we have already indicated in Chapter 2 that the processes of planning and policy-making are interrelated. Those involved in planning social services have to be familiar with the relevant policy issues, they have to provide information on the basis of which policy decisions are made and, very often, actually make recommendations on policy matters, and they have to devise ways of implementing policy decisions. Consequently, much of their time is spent on matters related to policy, and the next section will examine some of the main policy issues which are likely to arise in many kinds of social service planning.

(iii) *Preparation of programmes*

The third component of the planning process is the preparation of detailed proposals for the future development of the particular service with which one is concerned. In the case of education, for example, these proposals will include estimates of the number of students to be catered for in each type of education, the provision of staff and new capital resources (notably school buildings), and the amount of money required to implement these proposals. They will also include details of the nature of the education to be provided; for example, the design of curricula and the preparation of regulations regarding standards of educational attainment.

It is not possible to draw a clear line between policy formulation and preparation of programmes. Thus, in the above example, curriculum design involves making significant policy decisions (such as the relative importance of 'academic' and 'vocational' subjects) as well as the preparation of detailed programmes (such as writing textbooks), while even an apparently simple decision such as where to locate a new school may become a major policy issue. As we have already emphasized, we prefer to regard planning as a continuous process of decision-making, involving both the formulation of policy and the preparation of detailed programmes, rather than to try to draw a clear line between the two.

The process of social service planning often involves the preparation of a plan document. In Chapter 1 it was suggested that planning involves much more than just producing a plan document and that, in fact, it may not be necessary actually to produce such a document at all. However, many countries do, for a variety of reasons, decide to produce formal plan documents for various social services.

These plans may be divided into two types. The first type are plans which are concerned only with one particular social service; for example, an education plan, a health plan, or a housing plan. These tend to be lengthy documents covering a period of several years (often five years) and their preparation generally involves months—or even years—of discussion, in which attempts are made to involve as many relevant organizations and individuals as possible. They usually include a statistical analysis of the present situation, recommendations on major policy issues, and detailed proposals for the future development of each aspect of the particular service concerned.

The second type of plan are those which are integrated into a comprehensive national development plan. Thus, most national plans have sections on education, health, housing, social welfare, and so on. These plans include less information, but they generally require less time and effort to prepare and, because they are incorporated into a comprehensive national plan, they are more likely to be coordinated with plans for other related sectors. In many cases, they also tend to be more realistic, in the sense that the proposals made are less ambitious and take more account of practical constraints, such as shortages of money or staff and social or political factors. Consequently, there is often a better chance that they will be implemented. We shall examine some of the problems of plan implementation later in the chapter. At this point we would merely remind those involved in planning social services that the implementation of policies and plans is much more important than the prepration of an impressive plan document; the plan document should not be regarded as an end in itself.

Some policy issues

Because of the close relationship between planning and policy-making, it is useful to look briefly at some of the policy issues which are likely to arise in planning social services. It will, of course, not be possible to examine all the issues which the planner may encounter in any social service, but we shall look at some of the more important ones.

(i) *The importance of a social service*

The relative importance of any particular social service—and therefore the proportion of national resources which should be devoted to it rather than to other activities—is a matter of considerable concern to planners in a national planning agency. They are likely to be under considerable pressure from individual ministeries—health, education, housing, and so on—to increase expenditure on their particular service; but these demands have to be weighed up against each other and against the need for expansion in other sectors of the economy. This problem occurs in any aspect of planning, but it is particularly difficult to decide what priority sshould be given to a social service, since the benefits of investing in social services cannot be measured simply in terms of economic criteria, such as increased output or monetary gain, although they may have some indirect effect on economic development.

In the case of education, for example, increased investment may be justified either as a means of achieving economic development, through the provision of skilled manpower, or on the grounds that education is a basic social right to which all citizens are entitled. If the first view is adopted, the amount of resources devoted to education will depend on the demand for specific kinds of skilled manpower and the educational resources required to meet this demand. In this case, education planning becomes very closely linked to manpower planning, which is basically concerned with forecasting the need for various categories of skilled manpower and ensuring that these needs are met. However, if education is seen rather as a social right, it is possible to argue for the provision of almost unlimited resources, at least until the whole population has access to a certain basic level of education. Most countries seek for some compromise between these two viewpoints. This is often achieved by regarding primary education as a basic right and thus aiming to provide universal primary education as quickly as possible, but expanding secondary—and in particular tertiary—education only in line with demands for skilled manpower.

In the case of health, in most developing countries a good case can be made for increasing expenditure on health services on both social and economic grounds. From a social point of view, an increase in health expenditure should (it is claimed) help to alleviate the very considerable human suffering caused by ill-health and in many instances actually save lives; while from an economic point of view, it is argued that an improvement in health will raise the productivity of the labour force. Oscar Gish, in a book on health planning, points out that:

The problem of applying economic and financial criteria to the health sector is particularly difficult because of the special nature of the service being provided; that is one that sometimes touches upon human life and death. (Gish, 1977, p. 8)

Consequently, there is usually considerable pressure from the ministry of health, politicians, and the general public to devote almost unlimited resources to health services; and certainly any attempt to cut expenditure on health is likely to encounter serious opposition. This is, of course, an unrealistic attitude, since resources are inevitably limited and have to be shared between all sectors, and Gish goes on to say that:

It ought not to be necessary to point out that the health sector is attenable to rational planning and control even though human life and illness are involved. (Gish, 1977, p. 8)

In other words, staff in the national planning agency or finance ministry must attempt to weigh up the social and economic benefits of devoting more resources to health against similar increases in other sectors and advise the politicians accordingly.

(ii) Choosing between different kinds of service

In most developing countries the need for improved social services is great, but the resources required to provide them are scarce. This means that a number of fundamental choices have to be made, and one such choice concerns the relative importance attached to various components of any particular service. Thus, in the case of social welfare services, it may be necessary to decide whether to give priority to family and child care services, care of the physically or mentally disabled, services related to crime prevention and the rehabilitation of prisoners, or some other form of welfare service. Similarly, in education choices have to be made between primary, secondary, and tertiary education or between 'academic' and technical or vocational education. In the field of health planning one of the most significant issues is the relative importance which should be attached to curative and preventive health care. A brief examination of this issue will illustrate the complexity of the choices involved.

At one time health services were seen primarily as a means of curing rather than preventing disease. The emphasis was on treating people who were ill in order to prevent death and reduce human suffering. In most countries, this emphasis is reflected in the nature of the health facilities which exist today—which are fundamentally places to which people come when they need treatment—and in the training of medical personnel and the attitudes of the general public. It is also reflected in government expenditure on health services. Gish reckons that in most developing countries between 70 and 80 per cent of the health budget is spent on curative services (Gish, 1977, p. 14).

However, in recent years health policies in most countries have begun to focus more on the prevention of disease. This means more emphasis on health improvement programmes like environmental sanitation, maternal and child health care, family planning, vaccination and immunization, and the elimination of vectors of disease (flies, mosquitoes, etc.). It also means less emphasis on hospitals and other more conventional health facilities and more emphasis on mobile medical teams, health education, and the incorporation of health programmes into integrated programmes for the social and economic development of an area.

The theoretical arguments in favour of an emphasis on preventive health services are relatively straightforward. From an economic and a social point of view it is more desirable to prevent people becoming ill than to try to cure them when they are ill, partly because there is less human suffering and loss of productivity if they do not actually become ill and partly because elimination of the cause of the disease is likely to have a much longer-term effect than treatment of individual cases. Take malaria, for example. Treatment of malaria is a continuing process with no end in sight, since people become reinfected over and over again. Consequently, there is no end to the human suffering, the loss of productivity, and the cost of providing the treatment. However, if malaria can actually be eradicated from an area, there are no further costs to the people or the government. Similar principles apply in the case of another very common ailment in the Third World, diarrhoeal diseases, which can often be almost eliminated by improvements in environmental hygiene.

These arguments are reinforced by the fact that, in most developing countries, medical resources are so scarce that it is only possible to treat a relatively small proportion of those who need treatment. Consequently, even if most of the resources are used for providing curative services, many people still suffer and in many instances die—and more often than not these are the poorest, least privileged sections of the population. This argument is particularly important, since curing disease generally requires individual treatment of patients, while many preventive measures affect a relatively large number of people.

However, in spite of these arguments in favour of preventive services, the change in emphasis from curative to preventive medicine—as measured in terms of the distribution of health resources, notably finance and manpower— is actually occurring very slowly, if at all, in most countries. In Papua New Guinea, for example, one of the main aims of the 1974–78 Health Plan (Papua

Table 7   Papua New Guinea: distribution of health expenditure by function, 1973–78

Function	Percentage of total health expenditure					
	1973/74	1974/75	1975/76	1976/77	July/Dec. 1977	1978
Health care (curative)	68.8	68.0	71.5	71.6	72.7	69.3
Health improvement (preventive)	14.1	13.5	13.6	13.1	11.9	14.9
Medical training	7.7	6.8	7.4	5.8	7.9	7.5
Policy and administration	9.4	11.7	7.6	9.5	7.4	8.3

Source: MacPherson, 1979a, p. 14.

New Guinea, 1974) was to increase the proportion of resources devoted to health improvement. However, as Table 7 indicates, there was virtually no change during the plan period.

The main reason for this is that, because total resources are limited, a significant expansion of preventive services can only be obtained by reducing the existing curative services; and although this may be easy to justify in theory, in practice it is very difficult to do. Measures such as closing hospitals, reducing the number of conventional doctors, or reducing supplies of drugs and medical equipment are seldom socially or politically acceptable and in some cases not economically practicable in the short run either. Part of the problem is the fact that preventive measures do not generally result in an immediate reduction in disease and, in the meantime, can one refuse to treat those who are suffering?

(iii) *Distribution of services*

The fact that needs are great and resources limited means that important decisions also have to be made about the distribution of social services, and one of the most important roles of the planner is to make recommendations about how such decisions can be made. Two aspects of distribution are of particular significance: distribution between different social groups or classes and distribution between different geographical regions, including rural and urban areas.

In Chapter 2 we discussed at some length the extent of inequalities between groups and between regions and the role of the social planner in trying to reduce such inequalities. If we assume that most planners involved in the provision of social services are concerned to reduce inequalities, one of their functions is to gather information on the existing distribution of services and the need for additional services and to recommend that priority be given to those areas or groups where the need is greatest.

In practice, however, the situation is more complicated. In the first place, it is often very difficult to obtain accurate, up-to-date information on the existing distribution of services. Secondly, it is not always possible to compare the needs of one area or group of people with those of another. For example, is the need for clean drinking water greater in a rural or an urban area? Is it more important to eradicate bilharzia in one area or improve nutrition in another?

Thirdly, even if it is possible to make some reasonably reliable and meaningful recommendations, these recommendations may not be practical or politically acceptable. In many countries, it may not be possible to withhold resources from a politically powerful class or region, even though it already has a higher level of social services than other areas. And most planners are familiar with the situation where their plans are upset by individual politicians who demand a school, hospital, water supply, or other facility in their own area.

The reduction of inequalities between rural and urban areas creates particular problems. To take the case of health, for example, in most developing countries per capita expenditure on health services is much higher in urban than rural areas and the range and quality of services provided is consequently much better. Many countries recognize the need to reverse this trend and give priority to rural areas; but this is not easy.

In the first place, the provision of medical care in the rural areas requires a significantly different approach to that of urban medicine, including an emphasis on different health problems, the use of different kinds of medical personnel, and alternative methods of diagnosing and treating diseases. This involves a major transformation of the health service which cannot be achieved overnight.

Furthermore, any significant expansion of rural health services can only be obtained if there is no further increase—and if possible some decrease—in expenditure on urban services. And although this may be theoretically desirable, it is very difficult to achieve, at least in the short run. One reason for this is that it is likely to result in the deterioration or underutilization of existing capital resources; thus, urban hospitals deteriorate because of inadequate maintenance funds or are underutilized because of a shortage of doctors or medical supplies. In Zambia, for example, 'go-slow' action by doctors in June 1980 in protest at the indisputably poor working and living conditions in the three main urban hospitals, forced the government to devote more resources to these hospitals at a time when its official policy (see Zambia, 1980) was to give priority to rural health services.

The other reason is that there are likely to be serious protests from urban residents—including senior civil servants and politicians—if there is a deterioration in urban health services. In Papua New Guinea, for example, charges in urban hospitals were raised unexpectedly in 1978, but the protests were so great that the government was forced to retract its decision and reduce the charges again. It is significant that those countries which have been most successful in redirecting expenditure on health—and other social services—towards the rural areas are those like China and Cuba, where the change has been achieved as part of a complete revolution in the social, economic, and political structure of society.

(iv) *Quantity versus quality*

Because resources are limited, planners also have to make a choice between the quantity and the quality of the services provided. Thus, in the case of education, many countries have decided that the achievement of universal primary education is so important that it is worth making certain sacrifices in terms of the quality of the education. For example, several African nations have expanded primary education by having a double intake of students, one group attending school in the morning and the other in the afternoon. In fact, some urban primary schools in Zambia have three 'shifts' of students in the lower classes, in order to make maximum use of school buildings and teachers. Other ways of expanding rapidly are to increase the size of classes (in other words to increase the pupil/teacher ratio) or to use unqualified teachers' aides to assist the existing qualified teaching staff. And in some countries, such as Tanzania, school buildings and teachers are also used outside normal school hours to provide adult education.

In health care, there is a similar move in many countries to employ paramedical health workers, who can be trained much more quickly and cheaply than fully qualified doctors, in an attempt to provide at least some form of health care to as many people as possible. This approach was pioneered by China, whose 'barefoot doctors' have become a model for the provision of many forms of social service throughout the developing world.

It may be noted that this issue is related to that of the distribution of social services, discussed above. The choice between quantity and quality is not merely a question of saving money but of whether it is better to provide very basic services to a large number of people or a much higher level of service to a small number of relatively privileged people.

(v) Appropriate forms of social service

The search for low-cost methods of providing social services leads on to the broader question of what are the most appropriate forms of social service for the Third World. At one time it was assumed that standards and methods adopted in developed countries should be reproduced as far as possible in the developing world. Consequently, most Third World countries inherited education systems, standards of medical care, housing styles, and approaches to social welfare work modelled on practices in Europe and North America.

More recently, however, most Third World governments have realized the need to modify these practices to meet the particular conditions and needs of their own country. It is not merely a question of searching for cheaper ways of providing social services, but of evolving standards and methods which are appropriate in the physical, social, economic, and political environment of the Third World. The move is, of course, part of a much wider search for 'appropriate technology' in all aspects of development.

The search for more appropriate forms of social service is resulting in significant changes in education systems, methods of health care, approaches to social work, and the standards adopted in the provision of housing, water supplies, sanitation, and other services. The issues and problems which this involves can be illustrated by looking briefly at attempts to make education systems more relevant to the needs of developing countries. Most Third World nations inherited education systems modelled on those of the metropolitan powers and, since independence, they have attempted to adapt these inherited systems to meet local needs.

There are two forms of change which have received particular attention. One is to remove all 'colonial overtones' from the system so that education can contribute to the development of a sense of national identity and pride among its people. The degree and manner in which this is done varies considerably from one country to another. However, action often includes the redesign of the curriculum in areas like social studies (particularly the 'rewriting' of history from a local point of view), the inclusion of new subjects such as local politics and culture, and the introduction of various extra-curricular activities—such as singing, dancing, or paramilitary activities—to encourage a sense of national identity.

China presents one of the best examples of a country which has 're-volutionized' its education system in this way. In Chinese schools some form of political education is incorporated into virtually all parts of the curriculum and into extra-curricular activities, although recently China has begun to place rather more emphasis on academic matters. Few other countries have gone to the extremes of China, but the majority have made some attempt to 'nationalize' the education system.

The other form of change which receives a great deal of attention is designed to reorientate the education system towards the needs of the rural areas. As a result of colonial influence, education was in the past geared towards training people to take up urban or semi-urban employment rather than to return to village life, and this has contributed to problems of urban drift and unemployment among school-leavers. Therefore, one of the aims of many countries today is to reorientate the education system so that it provides a training for rural life as well as for urban employment. Again, there are several ways in which this is attempted. They include the introduction of courses on agriculture and rural life, the establishment of school farms and other practical projects, and the division of students into 'academic' and 'non-academic' streams. Such changes can affect every level and type of education. Even at university level many countries try to introduce some form of rural bias, so that students will not be completely alienated from their home environments.

One of the pioneers of this reorientation of the education system towards rural needs was Tanzania, whose document *Education for Self Reliance* (Nyerere, 1967) has become a model for many countries. However, in most countries, including Tanzania, many problems have been encountered. One common problem is that of reconciling the move towards a rural-based education with the need to maintain certain minimum academic standards and ensure that some students are still prepared for urban employment. The dilemma is often resolved by some form of streaming of students at secondary level (either within the same school or into two types of school); but this creates further problems, particularly a feeling of inferiority among those students allocated to the rural-based or non-academic stream or school. This leads on to the other major problem, which is the fact that many pupils and parents—and consequently also many politicians—resist such changes. They tend still to regard education as a passport to an urban job and resent any attempt to deprive them of this. Consequently, proposals for change are often resisted at the political level and, if they are introduced, they do not necessarily result in a marked decline in the proportion of school-leavers seeking urban employment. This has led to the view among some educationists, such as Philip Foster, that it is not worth trying to reorientate the education system towards rural needs (Foster, 1965 and 1966).

(vi) *The role of the state*

Although it is normally assumed that the state plays a major role in the provision of social services, it is not usually the only organization involved. In most developing countries voluntary agencies, private enterprise, and individual communities or families play a role in the provision of at least some services. For example, voluntary agencies—such as religious organizations—often run schools and hospitals and provide some form of social welfare service; private commercially run schools, health facilities and housing are often available for those willing or able to pay for them; and individual communities or families play a major role in providing their members with the support and care which in many developed countries would be the responsibility of the state.

The most controversial aspect of this issue is the role of private enterprise in the provision of social services. In the case of private medical care, for example, many governments attempt to restrict the activities of private doctors and hospitals which operate on a commercial basis. One reason for this is that, because private doctors charge high fees, it is a service which only the élite can afford. This élite may be individuals who pay directly for the treatment, or senior employees of private companies who either provide their own health facilities or pay for their employees to attend private doctors. The existence of private health facilities thus tends to perpetuate inequalities in access to health services at a time when one of the main aims of many governments is to reduce such inequalities. The other major reason for discouraging their existence is that national doctors tend to take up private practice instead of working for the government, thus increasing the already serious shortage of doctors in the national health service and resulting in the state receiving very little direct return from the large sums of public money spent on training these doctors.

As with several other issues we have discussed here, it is easy to point out the disadvantages of private health services, but much more difficult to actually get rid of them because of the vested interests of those in positions of authority. Politicians, senior civil servants, and others directly or indirectly involved in policy-making are likely to be among the main users of private health facilities and so to resist any attempts to abolish them. A few countries do actually abolish such services; for example, Tanzania did so in June 1980. However, others are more likely to compromise by allowing private services to operate, but introducing some controls to reduce their harmful effects. For example, they may introduce a bonding system whereby doctors have to work for the government for a certain number of years after graduation.

(vii) *Financing social services*

The role of private social services raises the more general question of how social services should be financed. The theoretical options available to governments may be presented in terms of a continuum. At one end of the continuum social services would be provided on an entirely commercial basis, either by private enterprise or by the state on a commercial fee-paying basis. At the other end of the continuum such services would be provided free by the state; in other words, they would be financed entirely by subsidies from other sectors of the economy.

In practice, most countries in both the developed and the developing world adopt some sort of compromise between the two extremes of the continuum. For example, many Third World countries charge small fees in state schools—at least at certain levels in the school system—and charge fees for all or some health services. The problem is to decide how much subsidization there should be, which types of service and which social groups or regions should benefit most from the subsidies, and how the money required for subsidizing social services should be raised. An additional issue in countries with more than one tier of government is the way in which the costs of providing social services should be distributed between the national government and state or local authorities. It is beyond the scope of this book to discuss any of these issues in detail. However, it should be pointed out that whatever solution is adopted should reflect the particular social goals or policies which the government is attempting to implement. For example, if the reduction of inequalities between rural and urban areas is an important goal, social services in rural areas should be more heavily subsidized than those in urban areas.

The planning machinery

So far in this chapter we have discussed the type of work involved in planning social services and some of the more important policy issues which are likely to arise. This section will consider the organizational framework within which social services are planned, and in particular the relationship between the various agencies involved.

In most countries, the main responsibility for providing particular social services is in the hands of individual ministries, departments or divisions of the government machinery. For example, there is usually a ministry of education, a ministry of health, ministries or sections of ministries responsible for social welfare and housing, and so on. Nevertheless, although the main responsibility is thus clearly allocated, there are still a number of other agencies or organizations involved and it is important that their activities are effectively coordinated. In this section we shall examine the role of four main kinds of agency: the functional ministry or section responsible for the particular social service; the national planning agency; local authorities or community groups; and voluntary or private agencies.

(i) The functional ministry

In order to ensure effective planning of any social service, it is important that an adequate planning capacity exists within the functional ministry, so that both policies and programmes are carefully formulated and not merely determined on an ad hoc basis. In most government organizations the majority of staff tend to be preoccupied with day-to-day administrative matters, and so it is usually necessary to establish a special section or unit within the ministry with full-time responsibility for planning. If this is not done, routine matters and unanticipated 'crises' will inevitably take precedence over any longer-term policy formulation or planning.

The optimum size and composition of the planning unit will obviously vary considerably, depending on the type of service, the size of the country, and the role of planning and other factors. In general, however, it is advisable to keep the planning unit relatively small and to rely on staff in the various technical divisions of the ministry to assist in the preparation of plans for their particular area of responsibility. This approach not only makes maximum use of scarce resources of technical manpower but also ensures that plans are relatively realistic and have the support of those responsible for their implementation. The main role of the planning unit in this situation is to encourage the various technical divisions to engage in some sort of planning activities, coordinate their efforts, and ensure that they are in line with general ministerial policies.

The planning unit is frequently staffed by people with professional training in the particular social service. For example, an education planning unit may be staffed by educational administrators (who more often than not started their careers as teachers), a health planning unit by doctors or health administrators, and so on. However, it is often desirable to have a few other staff in order to provide specialized planning skills. Thus Oscar Gish, in a useful book entitled *Guidelines for Health Planners*, suggests that the most important staff needed in a health planning unit are a doctor, an economist (or someone with some training in economics), and a statistician (Gish, 1977, Chapter 2). The doctor will provide the basic medical input—supported by the various technical divisions of the ministry, while the economist will ensure that adequate attention is given to 'the economics of delivering health care' (Gish, 1977, p. 7), and the statistician will assist in the collection and analysis of the basic data which is such an essential requirement for effective planning. Other staff, such as a sociologist or social planner or specialists in particular health fields, may be added in a larger planning unit.

(ii) *National planning agency*

It is not our intention in this chapter to consider the general role of a national planning agency or of social planners within that agency. At this stage we shall merely assume that most developing countries with a genuine commitment to planning have some form of national planning organization and focus our attention on the role which such an organization might play in planning social services. In Chapter 10 we shall attempt to draw together some conclusions about the more general role of a planning agency, particularly in relation to social planning.

The relationship between the national planning agency and a functional ministry—such as education, health, or housing—is not unlike the relationship between the planning unit and the technical divisions within a functional ministry. The most important role of the planning agency is to coordinate the functional ministry's plans with plans for other sectors and ensure that they are in line with general national policies and priorities. Many national planning agencies find that this can best be done by keeping a relatively low profile and relying on the functional ministry to do the detailed planning work. As with the preparation of plans within the ministry, this encourages the production of relevant plans which have the support of the implementing organization. However, in some cases one finds the planning agency playing a more dominant role. This may be due to inadequate planning capacity within the functional ministry, the fact that the ministry refuses to take a serious interest in planning or to comply with national policies, or merely the desire of the national planning agency to dominate the planning process.

The role of the planning agency is not always easy and frequently conflicts occur between it and the other organizations involved in social service planning, particularly the functional ministry concerned. The most obvious source of conflict is the total amount of resources to be devoted to a particular social service, since the national planning agency has to balance the needs of that service with those of all other sectors, while the ministry is concerned only to obtain as large a share as possible of national resources. However, conflicts also occur over less obvious issues. For example, in the case of education, the planning agency is likely to be concerned about the relationship between education and employment and therefore to favour the expansion of education only in line with manpower requirements and the reorientation of the curriculum towards the needs of the rural areas. The education ministry, on the other hand, may have a more realistic (or more conservative?) approach to the feasibility of such measures in the light of popular demand for education and the practical difficulties of introducing curricular changes.

Who should be responsible for social service planning in the national planning agency? The answer to this question will depend on the size of the planning agency and the role it decides to play in the planning process. In some cases there may be a small unit within the agency responsible solely for one particular social service, such as education or health; but more often such a unit—or sometimes just one person—is responsible for planning all social services. The most important consideration is probably to ensure that there is some continuity, in the sense that the same person (or group of people) always deals with matters related to a particular service. And there should then be close coordination between this person and the planning unit of the relevant functional ministry. Those responsible for social service planning in the planning agency may be either people with a professional training in a particular social service, such as education, health, social welfare, or housing, or more generalist social planners. We shall consider this issue in more detail in Chapter 10.

(iii) *Local authorities or community groups*

It is difficult to generalize about the role of local authorities or local communities in social service planning because it depends on the role which they play in the provision of particular services, and this in turn depends on a country's political structure. In some countries there is a significant decentralization of powers and functions and local authorities (such as local government councils or, in a federal system, state governments) play an important role in the provision of many social services and may also have considerable autonomy in relation to the determination of policy. In such cases, there is usually a need for some sort of planning capacity at this level, located either in the local offices of appropriate functional ministries or within a multipurpose regional or local planning office.

In other countries, administration—and therefore planning—is much more centralized and there is no need to develop a special planning capacity at the local level. However, it is still necessary to have some local involvement in the planning process in order to ensure that plans are relevant to local conditions and needs. For example, local involvement is essential when planning the location of new facilities—such as schools, health centres, or community facilities—or when planning programmes which require particular support, understanding, or cooperation from the local people. A study of alternative approaches to health care, sponsored by the World Health Organization, concluded that: 'Participation makes communities more readily mobilized, increases their health awareness, and provides health authorities with the information they need for a better and more sensitive administration' (Djukanovich and Mach, 1975, p. 101). We shall be examining the role of popular participation in planning in much more detail in Chapters 6 and 7.

Whenever there is some form of decentralization or local involvement in planning, conflicts between national and local interests are bound to occur. The most likely sources of conflict are the distribution of resources between regions and policy issues where local interests differ from national ones. For example, in the case of education, a region where the proportion of children going on to secondary school is already above the national average may press for the further expansion of secondary education without fully appreciating the impact which this could have, either on inequalities between regions or on manpower planning at the national level. In Papua New Guinea, a recent decentralization of education (and other) powers to provincial level governments has already caused confrontations between national and provincial governments and raised many issues concerning the degree of control the national government should have over education (Papua New Guinea, 1979).

(iv) *Voluntary or private agencies*

The role of voluntary agencies or other private organizations also varies from one country to another. However, as we have already indicated, in many developing countries voluntary agencies—particularly church organizations—play a major role in the provision of social services, and where this is the case they must be involved in the planning process. This is often achieved through their representation on planning committees at national, and often also at local, level. The type of issues in which such organizations are likely to be involved—and where differences of opinion often occur—include both administrative matters, such as the administration of private services and the extent to which they are subsidized by the state, and more fundamental issues about the type of service provided. Thus, in the case of education, sensitive issues may include curriculum content (particularly, but not only, the amount of time devoted to religious instruction), procedures for the allocation of grants to government-aided schools, policies about school fees, and procedures for the recruitment and training of teachers. Sometimes, competition between different organizations (for example, different religious denominations) may also create problems for the planners, who may find themselves having to act as arbitrators between rival agencies or organizations.

Problems in planning social services

This section is concerned with the problems encountered in social service planning. Many problems have already been mentioned in passing earlier in the chapter; but in this section we shall examine them rather more systematically, dividing them into four main categories: disagreement over policies; lack of coordination between different sectors; failure to achieve plan targets; and problems related to the politics of social service planning.

(i) *Disagreement over policies*

One of the more fundamental problems in any form of planning is lack of agreement over one or more basic policy issues. It should be apparent from the earlier analysis of key policy issues that in planning any social service there is plenty of room for disagreement over the best approach to any particular issue or problem. Such disagreement can occur either within the functional ministry responsible for a particular social service or between this ministry and any of the other agencies involved.

Disagreement over basic policy issues may make it impossible to plan effectively or at least delay the process of plan preparation. In Papua New Guinea, for example, the 1976–80 Education Plan (Papua New Guinea, 1976) took nearly three years to prepare and, during this time, three preliminary versions were rejected before final agreement was reached. The points of disagreement in this case included the number of years of basic primary education, the language of instruction in the first years of primary school, and the extent to which the curriculum should be adapted to make it more relevant to the needs of rural areas.

(ii) *Lack of coordination between different sectors*

Another common problem is lack of coordination between the plans for one social service and plans for other services or other forms of development activity. This problem is particularly likely to occur in relation to those aspects of a particular social service which overlap with other sectors and have to be planned as part of an integrated development programme. In the case of health planning, for example, the provision of primary health care—especially preventive health services—at the village or community level must be planned as part of an integrated programme involving not only the ministry of health but also those ministries responsible for agriculture, education, water supply and sanitation, and community development.

Lack of coordination between different sectors can often be attributed simply to inadequate communication between the different agencies involved, rather than a deliberate desire for conflict on the part of any one ministry. In this case, much of the blame may rest with the national planning agency, whose job it is to coordinate the planning activities of the various sectors of government. However, on some occasions there may be a fundamental disagreement between the planning agency and a functional ministry, or between different functional ministries, resulting in a deliberate lack of cooperation. In the worst cases political intervention at a fairly high level may be necessary to solve the problem.

(iii) *Failure to meet plan targets*

One of the main criticisms of any form of planning is that the targets set in the plan are not achieved, and this is a common occurrence in social service planning. We have already mentioned some of the difficulties involved in implementing particular policies—such as a change in emphasis from curative to preventive health services or from urban to rural health care and the redirection of the school curriculum towards the needs of rural development—and similar examples occur in other social services.

Sometimes the failure to meet plan targets can be blamed on the planners. As we have already indicated, planners do not always take full account of the availability of financial and manpower resources or other factors which might limit the rate at which goals can be achieved. For instance, plans for the expansion of primary education may be made without giving adequate attention to the implications for the training of additional primary school teachers, or new schools may be planned without consultation with the ministry of works which will be responsible for their construction. The failure of Papua New Guinea's 1974–78 Health Plan, to which we referred earlier, can be attributed—at least in part—to over-ambitious assumptions about the amount of resources available (MacPherson, 1979a). Alternatively, the planners may not prepare their plans in a manner which will facilitate their implementation or take steps to ensure that the implementation process is set in motion—in which case the plan targets, and perhaps even the existence of a plan, are soon forgotten.

However, it is not always fair to blame the planners. Even the best planners cannot foresee all the obstacles which will occur during the implementation period. The national financial situation may deteriorate, resulting in budgetary cuts in all sectors; unexpected events may necessitate the diversion of resources from one project to another, or from one sector to another; overseas aid—in the form of money or personnel—may not materialize; construction problems may delay the building of new schools, health centres, or houses; and so on. Furthermore, even if plans are prepared carefully, one cannot always anticipate people's reaction to them. For example, targets for increasing the number of girls attending secondary school or university may not be met because of parents' resistance to the education of girls; and family planning programmes may fail because of unforeseen opposition to limiting family size.

As with other forms of planning, the most important thing is to ensure that the implementation process is monitored so that plans can be revised when unforeseen circumstances do occur. As emphasized in Chapter 1, planning thus becomes a continuous process, in which plans are continually being revised and the planning and implementation stages arc not clearly separable.

(iv) *The politics of social service planning*

Planners often maintain that their biggest problem is politics. They complain that they cannot plan 'properly' because of political interference or that their plan targets were not achieved because of political factors. And it can perhaps be argued that social service planning is particularly susceptible to this so-called political interference because of the generally high level of popular demand for social services in general, and education and health services in particular. Thus, individual politicians exert pressure for the construction of new schools or hospitals in their electorates, since this is one of the most tangible ways in which they can demonstrate their concern for the development of the area and thus improve their chances of re-election. Similarly, powerful regional groups influence the allocation of resources so that it is impossible to move towards an equitable regional distribution of social services; and members of cabinet or parliament reject plans to restrict private education or health services because they are the people who use such services.

These obstacles can make the planner's work very difficult. If he ignores the political realities of the situation, his plans are unlikely to be implemented and so planning becomes a futile exercise. This was a large part of the problem in the case of the Papua New Guinea Health Plan to which we have already referred. But if he tries to take full account of such factors and ensure political support for his plans, the planning process is likely to take much longer and plans may end up full of compromises and contradictions. For example, a plan may state the need for the more equal distribution of services but, in fact, include very few measures which will do anything to achieve this.

However, the relationship between politics and planning is not so simple that one can simply regard politics as a problem. For convenience we have included it under the general heading of problems in social service planning, but the situation is rather more complex. All forms of planning must be regarded as political exercises, in the sense that planning involves making decisions about the distribution of scarce resources and such decisions inevitably involve conflict— or potential conflict—between political groups. The relationship between politics and planning varies considerably, depending on the political structure of individual countries; but in all cases politicians play a crucial role and 'political' decisions tend to override any others. In other words, politics must be seen as an integral part of the planning process, not merely as an annoying problem.

The process of planning social services, therefore, cannot be separated from the much wider issues related to the distribution of social and economic resources and the distribution of political power which plays such a large part in determining the allocation of these resources. In other words, it cannot be separated from the processes of social and political change. This is reflected in the fact that those countries which have had most success in bringing about radical changes in the provision of basic social services, such as China and Cuba, have achieved these changes only as part of a much wider social, economic, and political revolution.

Let us conclude this chapter with two quotations which emphasize the relevance of this in both education and health planning. In the case of education, Williamson, in a book on the relationship between education, social structure, and development, maintains that:

Planning in education is . . . never neutral, never a matter reducible to criteria of technical efficiency. In an increasingly bureaucratised world . . . the power of the expert is enhanced and arguments about technical expediency conceal the essential political character of planning and decision-making. (Williamson, 1979, p. 209)

And in the case of health planning, Gish emphasizes the relationship between ill-health and poverty and concludes that:

The road to the reduction of morbidity and mortality is more likely to be paved with social and political advances, which are reflected in an improved system for the distribution of health services, than with further advances in medical science as such. (Gish, 1970, p. 75)

Guide to further reading

General

There is very little literature on planning social services in general, since most material is concerned with specific services. A fairly recent book entitled *Planning the Social Services* by N. Falk and J. Lee (Farnborough, Saxon House, 1978) provides a useful introduction, but is concerned only with developed countries. Raymond Apthorpe discusses social service planning briefly in his introduction to *People Planning and Development Studies* (London, Frank Cass, 1970).

A number of existing books and forthcoming books include chapters on a variety of specific social services, although the majority are concerned with social policy issues rather than with planning. They include:

Livingstone, A., *Social Policy in Developing Countries* (London, Routledge and Kegan Paul, 1969).

MacPherson, S., *Social Policy in the Third World* (Brighton, Harvester Press, 1982).

Midgley, J., and M. Hardiman, *Policy Issues in Social Planning in the Third World* (London, Wiley, forthcoming).

World Bank (International Bank for Reconstruction and Development), *The Assault on World Poverty: Problems of Rural Development, Education and Health* (Baltimore, Johns Hopkins Press, 1975).

It is impossible to list here all the relevant literature on individual social services. However, since this chapter has included a number of examples from education and health planning, we give a few useful references on these two topics.

Education planning

There are a large number of books and articles on education policy and planning in developing countries. However, it is possible to select a few which are likely to be particularly useful. They are:

Adams. A. (ed.), *Education in National Development* (London, Routledge and Keegan Paul, 1971).

Altbach, P. G., and G. P. Kelly, *Education and Colonialism* (London, Longmans, 1978).

Coombs, P. H., with A. Manzoor, *Attacking Rural Poverty: How Nonformal Education can Help* (Baltimore, Johns Hopkins Press, 1974).

Dore, R., *The Diploma Disease* (London, George Allen and Unwin, 1976).

International Institute for Educational Planning, *Education Development in Africa* (Paris, UNESCO, 1969) (three volumes; includes case studies of Tanzania, Uganda, and Nigeria).

International Institute for Educational Planning, series of pamphlets entitled *Fundamentals of Education Planning* (Paris, UNESCO).

Mazrui, A., *Political Values and the Educated Class in Africa* (London, Heinemann, 1978).

Simmons, J. (ed.), *The Education Dilemma: Policy issues for Developing Countries in the 1980s* (Oxford, Pergamon, 1980).

Tuqan, M. I., *Education, Society and Development in Underdeveloped Countries* (The Hague, Centre for Study of Education in Changing Societies, 1975).

Williamson, W., *Education, Social Structure and Development* (London, Macmillan, 1979).

World Bank, *Education: Sector Policy Paper* (Washington DC, 3rd edition, 1980).

Health planning

There is also a large volume of material on health policy and planning. The most useful sources of information specifically on health planning in developing countries are those by Oscar Gish, including:

'Health planning in developing countries' in Apthorpe, R. (ed.), *People Planning and Development Studies* (London, Frank Cass, 1970), Chapter 5.

Planning the Health Sector (London, Croom Helm, 1976).

Guidelines for Health Planners (London, Tri-Med, 1977).

For useful summaries of the main issues and problems involved in the provision of health services, the following are recommended:

Djukanovich, V., and E. P. Mach (eds.), *Alternative Approaches to Meeting Basic Health Needs in Developing Countries* (Geneva, World Health Organization, 1975).

Heller, T., and C. Elliott (eds.), *Health Care and Society: Readings in Health Care Delivery and Development* (University of East Anglia, School of Development Studies, Monograph in Development Studies No. 2, 1977) (includes extensive bibliography).

World Bank, *Health: Sector Policy Paper* (Washington DC, 2nd edition, 1980).

CHAPTER 4

SOCIAL PLANNING ROLE IN NATIONAL DEVELOPMENT PLANNING

In Chapter 1 we explained how the social aspects of development have grad-ually received more attention and how this has affected the nature of develop-ment planning and contributed to the rise of social planning in its various forms. This chapter examines the impact which this change in emphasis has had on the nature of development planning at the national level. It considers what sort of social factors are of importance in national development planning, how such factors are actually taken into account and the organization required for doing so, and finally the problems which arise in this form of social planning.

The importance of social factors

The importance now attached to so-called social factors in national develop-ment planning can best be illustrated by quoting from a number of national development strategies. As examples, we shall look at those of Tanzania, Papua New Guinea, Zambia, and India.

President Nyerere of Tanzania, discussing the implications of his country's most significant policy declaration—the Arusha Declaration announced in 1967—explains that:

The Arusha Declaration is . . . a commitment to a particular quality of life. It is based on the assumption of human equality, on the belief that it is wrong for one man to dominate or exploit another, and on the knowledge that every individual hopes to live in society as a free man able to lead a decent life in conditions of peace with his neighbours. The document is, in other words, Man-centred.

Inherent in the Arusha Declaration, therefore, is a rejection of the concept of nat-ional grandeur as distinct from the well-being of its citizens, and a rejection too of material wealth for its own sake. It is a commitment to the belief that there are more things in life than the amassing of riches, and that if the pursuit of wealth clashes with things like human dignity and social inequality, then the latter will be given priority. (Nyerere, 1968, p. 316)

In Papua New Guinea the national constitution includes five national goals which are used as the basis of policy-making and quoted in most planning docu-ments. The constitution describes the first two of these goals as follows:

We declare our first goal to be for every person to be dynamically involved in the process of freeing himself or herself from every form of domination or oppression so that each man or woman will have the opportunity to develop as a whole person in relationship with others.

We declare our second goal to be for all citizens to have an equal opportunity to participate in, and benefit from, the development of our society. (Papua New Guinea, 1975, p. 2)

The ideology of 'Humanism' in Zambia places a similar emphasis on the importance of man in development. One writer says that Zambian Humanism:

has been vigorously prompted to reverse the situation from Property-centredness to man-centredness. Property is to serve man and not Man to be controlled by property, after all, property is only an attribute of man as a creative being. (Kandeke, 1977, p. 45)

And he later goes on to explain that, because of this humanist philosophy, planning in Zambia:

is considered necessary not for its own sake but as a function of the demands of social evolution, which is adapted to a political line. In other words, planning is not only a method of economic mobilisation but also a general instrument for comprehensive socio-economic transformation within a definite political and ideological framework. (Kandeke, 1977, p. 93)

As a final example, India's Third National Plan pointed out that:

ever since Independence, two main aims have guided India's planned development—to build up by democratic means a rapidly expanding and technologically progressive economy and a social order based on justice and offering equal opportunity to every citizen. (India, Planning Commission, 1961, p. 4)

But what does all this really mean? What are the social factors or social aspects that one must take into account in a 'man-centred' approach to development planning and why is it so important to do so? The various meanings of the word 'social' were discussed at some length in Chapter 1. From that discussion it is possible to identify four main kinds of 'social factor' or 'social aspects' which may be taken into consideration in development planning and which are reflected in the above quotations from various national development strategies. Let us look briefly at each of these.

(i) The human factor

One kind of social factor is what Apthorpe (1970) and others have called the 'human' factor in development planning. This includes a variety of aspects of people's social and cultural environment which influence the way they perceive their needs and react to development programmes. The examples quoted in Chapter 1 of family planning programmes which are ineffective because of the importance attached to large families, the commercialization of livestock production which fails because of the traditional attitude to cattle and new food crops which are not acceptable to the farmers, demonstrate the impact of the human factor.

The concept of the human factor is important in discussions of human rationality. Before the importance of social factors was fully recognized, people in developing countries were often criticized—especiallly by economists—for acting 'irrationally'. However, when their behaviour was studied carefully, it was realized that, although in economic terms they were not being rational because they were not choosing an option which would maximize income or output, their behaviour was perfectly rational when social factors were also taken into account.

(ii) *Provision of social needs*

A rather different interpretation of the social aspects of development planning is the provision of social needs, including basic social services (for example, health, education, housing, or welfare services) and less easily defined needs, such as the preservation of traditional culture or what Nyerere referred to in the quotation above as 'human dignity'. In the past, many development programmes concentrated on achieving economic goals and ignored the need to meet these various social needs as well.

(iii) *Social equity or justice*

Taking account of social factors when planning development programmes also means considering what impact they will have on inequalities between individuals and groups. For example, will an agricultural extension programme benefit all farmers or only the wealthier ones? What impact will a change in school curriculum have on the development of an élite in society? In other words, development planning must be concerned with the questions of social equality and justice which we discussed in some depth in Chapter 2.

(iv) *Integral human development*

Finally, the social aspects of development include consideration of what in Papua New Guinea is called 'integral human development'. The first of Papua New Guinea's national goals, quoted above, calls for the development of 'each man or woman . . . as a whole person', and this means meeting his (or her) economic, social, political, and other needs through a programme of integrated development. This is closely related to the Zambian ideology, in which man is seen as the focus of all development efforts, and it calls for 'man-centred' rather than 'property-centred' development planning.

Why is it so important to consider these various social factors in national development planning? As we indicated in Chapter 1, there are two main reasons. One is the fact that plans often fail if social considerations are not taken into account. A family planning programme will not be effective if the planners do not consider people's attitudes to family size, alternative methods of contraception, and so on; a new industrial project will not be successful unless provision is made to meet the social needs of the employees; and the agricultural extension programme which reaches only the wealthy farmers will not, in the long run, solve a country's rural development problems.

The other major reason is that the achievement of social goals or objectives is now recognized in most countries as an important end in itself, not merely as a means of ensuring that economic objectives are achieved without hindrance. This is reflected very clearly in the earlier quotation from Nyerere, in which he not only emphasizes the need to consider social factors but goes so far as to say that 'if the pursuit of wealth clashes with things like human dignity and social inequality, then the latter will be given priority' (Nyerere, 1968, p. 316). Later in the chapter we shall examine some of the problems which can arise when such a clash of interests does occur.

Incorporating social factors into development planning

The above discussion of what is actually meant by the social aspects of development should give some indication of the role of the social planner in ensuring that social factors are taken into account in national development planning. It should by now be apparent that his (or her) role is very broad and, at times, rather vague or ill-defined. In this section we shall look at some of the activities in which he is likely to become involved, in order to give a clearer picture of this kind of social planning.

(i) *Monitoring social change*

The most straightforward activity of the social planner in the context of national development planning is monitoring and analysing processes of social change. These processes may include changes in social structure (for example, family size, the importance of the extended family, the existence of social classes, and so on); changes in the availability of social services (such as education and health) and in people's access to—or use of—these services; and changes in customs (for example, the importance of certain traditional customs or ceremonies) and attitudes.

Information about these changes may be needed in order to provide data on existing social conditions in the country, to indicate general trends in social conditions over time, or to examine the social impact of particular phenomena—such as increases in income or migration from rural to urban areas. The general monitoring of social change in this way provides the basis for some of the more specific social planning activities described below.

The information required may be obtained from a variety of sources. Some information may be available from regular statistical series, collected and published by a central statistics office or appropriate ministries, and the social planner may have to give advice on the type of *social statistics* which are needed for planning purposes. Other information may be obtainable only by carrying out special surveys. For example, in order to examine the changes in social structure which occur when people move from rural to urban areas, published statistics may be of some use, but it will also be necessary to organize special surveys of sample populations in both rural and urban areas. We shall return to the problems of data collection later in this chapter and in Chapter 8.

(ii) *Formulating social policies and programmes*

The social planner is likely to be involved in the formulation of social policies at the national level and the translation of these into concrete development programmes. Such policies may range in scope from very broad general principles regarding the nature of social goals or the relative importance of social and economic factors, to much more specific policies related to particular social issues or problems. In Papua New Guinea, for example, social planners have been involved in the formulation and implementation of the national goals of 'integral human development' and 'equality and participation' quoted above, and also in the design of policies to deal with issues such as a rapid increase in urban crime, the use of appropriate technology, and the role of women in national development.

The role of the planner in these activities raises once again the question of where policy-making ends and planning begins. As we have emphasized in previous chapters, we prefer not to draw a clear distinction between the two, but to look upon planning as a continuing process which involves the formulation of policies at varying levels of detail and the translation of these policies into programmes of action. Thus, although the final decision to adopt a particular national policy will probably be made by the politicians rather than by professional planners, the planners will be involved in the preparation of alternative policies and the implementation of the one which is chosen by the politicians.

Tanzania provides an interesting example of the interaction of policy-making and planning in a situation where the achievement of social goals receives very high priority. As the earlier quotation from President Nyerere suggests, Tanzania's philosophy of development emphasizes social objectives, particularly the elimination of the basic problems of 'poverty, ignorance, and disease' and the building of a socialist society:

in which all members have equal rights and opportunities; in which all can live at peace with their neighbours without suffering or imposing injustice, being exploited or exploiting; and in which all have a gradually increasing basic level of material welfare before any individual lives in luxury. (Nyerere, 1968, p. 340)

One of the main tasks which Tanzanian planners thus face is the translation of these broad national goals into more detailed policies and programmes which can actually be implemented on the ground. This can be illustrated by looking at efforts to achieve these goals in the rural areas through the formation of *ujamaa* villages. *Ujamma* villages are nucleated villages organized on a cooperative or socialist basis and they are intended to perform two functions: to bring the previously scattered population together into nucleated settlements, where they can more easily be provided with basic services, such as education, health, and water; and to spread the benefits of rural development more equitably and discourage the emergence of a pronounced class structure in the rural areas.

Policy regarding the methods which should be used to implement the *ujamaa* village policy, the speed with which it should be implemented, and the exact form which *ujamaa* villages should take, has changed significantly since the policy was first introduced in 1967 (see Hyden, 1980; Mwansasu and Pratt, 1979). However, throughout this period the *ujamaa* policy has influenced most other aspects of rural development planning, including the operation of agricultural and other extension services, the provision of basic services (education, health, water, roads, and so on) and detailed land-use planning of individual village sites. During the 1970s the rate at which people were moved into nucleated settlements—a process which became known as 'villagization'—was rapidly accelerated. The policy at that time was to give priority to the formation of nucleated settlements so that rural services could be provided more easily; it was hoped that the transformation of these settlements into true *ujamaa* villages, organized on a cooperative basis, would then follow more slowly—although so far this transformation does not seem to have been occurring very successfully. The rapid acceleration of villagization which occurred at that time placed an enormous strain on all those sections of government involved in planning the layout of the new villages and ensuring that they were provided with the basic services which had been promised as an incentive to encourage people to move.

The emphasis on social goals—particularly that of social equality—has had a similar impact on other aspects of national development planning in Tanzania, from prices and incomes policy and industrial development planning to the formulation of policies in education, health, and other social services. In other words, planners are obliged to take social factors into account in all aspects of policy-making and planning. In fact, Tanzania has recently received considerable criticism for devoting too much attention to the achievement of social goals at the expense of economic development. The justification for this criticism is open to some question and ultimately any conclusions which one may draw regarding Tanzania's progress over the last one and a half decades depend very much on one's own priorities and point of view. On the one hand, Tanzania has undoubtedly encountered enormous economic problems and these have not always been helped by policies such as villagization and state ownership of industrial enterprises. But on the other hand, a very large part of the blame for the economic problems can be attributed to the international economic situation and, on the positive side, Tanzania has made very real gains in terms of the provision of social services and the reduction in income inequalities (Lappé and Beccar-Varela, 1980; Honey, 1980).

(iii) *Examining the social impact of national development programmes*

Another important role of the social planner is to examine the social impact of specific national development policies and programmes. His role in this respect is twofold. Firstly, when new policies or programmes are being formulated, he should attempt to predict the effect which they will have on social conditions, including the social structure, the availability of social services, and the attitudes and general social well-being of the people concerned. He must then ensure that these effects are taken into account when deciding whether or not to go ahead with the programme and designing the final form which it will take. Secondly, he also has a role to play in monitoring the impact of policies and programmes which have already been implemented, in order to learn lessons which can be applied in similar cases in the future and—if it is not too late—to introduce measures to alleviate any social problems which have occurred.

The social planners's role is particularly important in the case of development programmes which are primarily economic in nature. Such programmes are likely to be designed with the main aim of achieving economic objectives, such as an increase in output, cost reductions, or the generation of foreign exchange, and there is a danger that social considerations will be overlooked.

A good example of a development programme where social implications were not adequately considered during the planning stages is the intensification of agricultural production in India which began in the late 1960s. This programme, widely known in India and elsewhere as the *green revolution*, involved the introduction of new high-yielding varieties of seeds, together with improved cultivation methods, in selected areas of the country. The programme was successful in the sense that it resulted in a marked increase in crop yields and so helped to transform India from a country with an acute food shortage to one with a food surplus. However, from a social point of view its achievements were much more dubious because the direct benefits accrued only to a few areas of the country and, within those areas, only to a small minority of more affluent farmers who, because of their superior economic and social status, had better access to the land, capital, and extension services required to grow the improved crops. Thus, the programme did little or nothing to alleviate what is perhaps India's most fundamental problem—that of social inequality (compare Pearse, 1980).

Similarly, in many countries one may find cases of programmes designed to increase the production of agricultural produce for sale which have had a negative effect on the nutritional status of the population because effort has been concentrated on production for sale instead of for domestic consumption. To take another example from India, a more recent programme designed to promote development in drought-prone areas included the introduction of a system of daily milk collection, to encourage commercial milk production. The programme was successful in that farmers sold their milk, but there was an immediate decline in the standards of nutrition in the area because milk was being sold instead of drunk (Watson, 1980).

What can the social planner do if he is involved in the planning of such prog-rammes and foresees that they will have a negative social impact? In some cases he may be able to suggest minor changes in the programmes which will avoid or reduce the social problems without upsetting their basic aims. In other cases a major reorientation of a programme may be necessary, but it may be possible to do this and still achieve the basic economic objectives. For example, the search for more appropriate forms of technology for developing countries can be explained in both social and economic terms. The use of small-scale, labour-intensive technology, utilizing wherever possible local materials and skills, is both socially desirable—hence the adoption of the expression 'tech-nology with a human face' (Dunn, 1978)—and economically practical in most developing nations.

However, sometimes consideration of the likely social effects of a proposed programme may have more serious implications, involving a major conflict be-tween economic and social objectives. In the case of India's green revolution, for example, a proper evaluation of the social impact of the programme in the planning stages might have resulted in significant changes in its design and im-plementation. Thus, particular efforts could have been made to spread the benefits of the programme more widely and give priority to poorer farmers when providing inputs, extension services, and so on. However, given the existing social structure in India, it is doubtful whether such efforts would have had a significant social impact, at least without greatly reducing the economic achievements in terms of increased agricultural output. Thus, in cases like this, it is necessary to make a choice between the maximization of economic object-ives and the maximization of social objectives (or minimization of social costs)—and this is not an easy choice for planners or politicians to have to make.

How does the social planner obtain the information needed to evaluate the social impact of national policies and programmes? The information collected as part of the routine monitoring of social change (see section (i) above) will usually be of some assistance to him. However, it is generally necessary to carry out special surveys designed to provide information on the specific policy or programme concerned. The form of such a survey will depend on whether the planner is evaluating the likely impact of a proposed programme or the impact of one already in operation and also on the nature of the programme.

We shall return to some of the problems involved in this form of social plan-ning, including the conflict between economic and social objectives and data collection, later in the chapter.

(iv) *Incorporating social considerations into routine planning procedures*

The social planner has a related but more general role to play in ensuring that social factors are taken into account in all routine planning procedures, not only when considering specific development policies or programmes. There are various ways in which this can be done, but two main approaches can be identified.

One approach involves the use of formal controls to ensure that social factors are taken into consideration, often as part of a system of budgetary control. For example, when ministries or other government agencies submit requests for funding particular activities, they may be required to produce evidence that they have considered the likely social implications of the activities they wish to undertake. We shall be examining alternative budgeting systems in more detail in Chapter 9; however, at this point it is useful to look briefly at some forms of budgetary control which can assist the social planner in this way.

One of the most common forms of control is to introduce a system of project budgeting, in which government agencies subdivide their budgets into particular projects or programmes (for example, livestock development, farmer training, research into new varieties of rice) instead of into general categories of expenditure (such as salaries, travel, or equipment). Project budgeting makes it much easier to evaluate a project or programme as a whole, weighing up its costs and benefits—including the social costs and benefits.

Papua New Guinea, for example, has introduced a system of 'national public expenditure planning' in which all new or expanded activities have to be justified on a project basis, not merely included in the normal recurrent budget. All requests for such activities have to be submitted to the National Planning Office, and the Planning Office then examines all the requests, taking into account a variety of factors, including the social costs and benefits of each proposed activity, and recommends to the cabinet which ones should be approved for funding (see Allen and Hinchliffe, in press; Papua New Guinea, 1977).

However, even in a budgeting system such as that used in Papua New Guinea, it is not easy to ensure that social factors are really given adequate consideration. It is difficult for the planning agency, or other controlling body, to determine how social factors should be defined and measured and to ensure that the information submitted by the various government agencies is based on thorough analysis of the proposed project, not merely hasty 'guestimates' dreamed up to satisfy the criteria laid down by the planning agency.

Instead of—or in addition to—the introduction of formal controls, social planners can attempt to influence decision-making in more subtle ways. They can encourage staff in government agencies to pay more attention to social factors by issuing guidelines explaining why they should be taken into account and how this can be done, discussing plan proposals with those involved in their preparation, attending appropriate meetings and providing relevant information on social conditions. Moreover, they can also try to educate the politicians and the general public about the importance of social factors. Hopefully, in this way people will gradually become more aware of the social aspects of development and so begin to take social factors into account more or less automatically, as they do economic or political factors. As we have suggested elsewhere, there is evidence that this is already happening in many countries and it is reflected in the increasing demand for social planning in some form or other.

(v) *Allocating resources for social development*

Finally, a rather different but related role of the social planner concerns the allocation of national resources—particularly finance and, to a somewhat lesser extent, manpower—to social development programmes. His (or her) main concern in this context is to ensure that social development receives adequate priority in the allocation of resources and to advise on the distribution of resources between different aspects of social development.

What is meant in this case by social development? Theoretically, the term must be interpreted broadly to include any aspect of development which is primarily 'social' rather than 'economic' in nature, bearing in mind the alternative interpretations discussed at the beginning of this chapter. In practice, however, social planners often find themselves preoccupied mainly with the allocation of resources for the provision of social services, such as education, health, housing, and welfare services. They play a central role in discussions about how much of the annual budget—and of other resources—should be devoted to such services and how this amount should be subdivided between individual services.

There is, of course, no one answer to the questions of how much of the national cake should be allocated to social services or to social development in general, or how this amount should be divided between such activities as education, health, and so on. These decisions can only be made after taking into account existing social and economic conditions, national goals and policies, the total volume of resources available, the capacity to utilize resources within individual sectors (for example, the ministry of education's ability to spend the money allocated to it effectively), and numerous other factors.

The social planner can contribute to this decision-making process in three main ways. Firstly, he can ensure that people are aware of the existing proportion of resources devoted to social development. In some cases, this can best be done not merely by showing the allocation of resources to particular ministries or government departments but by attempting to relate the allocation of resources to the achievement of specific social (and other) goals. For example, Table 8 shows the proposed expenditure in Papua New Guinea's national public expenditure plan for the year 1979, broken down not by government agency or individual project but by the specific objectives which the projects are designed to achieve. Secondly, he can emphasize the importance of social development and press for the allocation of more rather than less resources to it. He need not be afraid that his efforts will result in overexpenditure on social development because he can be sure that his views will be counterbalanced by those of the economists, who will call for more emphasis on economic development! And thirdly, he can attempt to weigh up the relative needs of different forms of social development and advise that resources be allocated accordingly.

The planning machinery

In the previous sections we have referred to 'the social planner' and described his various roles in relation to national development planning. However, we have not really considered who he (or she) is, where he is located, and how he fits into the overall planning and administrative structure of the country. To put it another way, we have not considered the administrative machinery required in order to incorporate social factors into the national planning process in the various ways described above.

Table 8   Papua New Guinea: 1979 National Public Expenditure Plan project allocations by strategic objective

	Project expenditures	
Objective	Kina '000[a]	% of total
Rural welfare	14,067	23.1
Helping less developed areas	5,921	10.1
General welfare	4,145	7.0
Economic production	14,738[b]	25.0
Food and nutrition	1,420	2.6
Training and participation	3,901	6.6
Urban management	1,955	3.3
Effective administration	7,065	12.0
Environmental management	621	1.1
Fiscal Commission[c]	5,000	8.5
Total	58,835	100.0

[a] One Kina is equivalent to approximately £0.65.
[b] Excluding commercial projects worth Kina 6.438 million.
[c] The Fiscal Commission is a body which allocates additional grants to provincial level governments on an unconditional basis.
Source: Papua New Guinea, 1978, p. 11.

The use of the term 'social planner' in earlier sections is somewhat misleading in that it implies that there are in various organizations people officially classified or designated as 'social planners' who have duty statements clearly stating that they are responsible for one or more of the activities which we have described. In practice, this is seldom the case. It is much more likely for these activities to be carried out by people with a variety of titles and backgrounds who are responsible for doing all sorts of other things as well. One reason for this is that the type of social planning which we are discussing in this chapter has only recently begun to gain recognition as an important activity in its own right, and so there are very few positions created specifically for this purpose. Another reason is that this kind of social planning is very closely related to many other planning activities, and it is thus difficult to create a specific position with a clearly defined duty statement. In many cases it is even difficult to decide which section of government it should be located in because this type of planning cannot easily be confined to conventional ministerial boundaries. In this respect, it is very different from the planning of specific social services, such as education or health, which can clearly be allocated to specific ministries.

Nevertheless, in view of the increasing importance of this type of social planning, it is useful to consider the type of administrative machinery which could be most effective. The most important location for this kind of planning activity is within a national planning agency—a ministry of development planning, national planning office, or whatever is the appropriate organization in any particular country. Within this agency there should be some staff specifically responsible for the social aspects of planning, including all those activities described in the previous section.

The number of staff involved in social planning and their relationship with other staff in the planning agency will depend on the size and organizational structure of the agency. For example, in a relatively large planning body organized along disciplinary lines, it may be feasible to have a separate division or section responsible solely for social planning. But elsewhere, particularly when the planning agency is organized along project rather than disciplinary lines, it may be better to distribute the social planning staff between the various divisions or sections. Thus, if there was a division responsible for agricultural or rural development planning, it could include a social planner whose job it would be to ensure that social needs and implications were taken into account in any agricultural or rural development programmes. Similarly, a section responsible for budgetary control could include a social planner who would take steps to ensure that social considerations were incorporated in all requests for funding and taken into account when allocating funds.

These people do not need to be officially designated as social planners or necessarily to have a formal qualification in social planning—although it may help if they do. It is more important that they have both a general understanding of the country's planning and administrative structure and, more particularly, an awareness of the importance of considering social factors and the various ways in which this can be done. Such an awareness may be gained in a number of ways; for example, through formal training in a subject like sociology or social planning, by work experience in a particular social service, or involvement in interdisciplinary projects where social factors played an important role. Equally important, there must be a recognition of the need for social planning within the planning agency, so that they are allowed to spend sufficient time on social planning activities, their services are fully utilized by other staff, and their views are heard and taken into account.

In ministeries or government bodies other than the national planning agency, there is less likely to be a need for staff officially classified or qualified as social planners. However, there is a need for people with what might be called a social planning 'bias'. For example, in a ministry of agriculture or industry there should be at least one person who is particularly concerned to see that social factors are taken into account when planning policies, programmes, or projects within the ministry and to monitor their social impact when they are in operation. Such people may be agriculturalists or industrialists by experience or training and they may also have a variety of other responsibilities; but they should be sensitive to social needs and problems and they should be given specific responsibility for the social side of planning in the ministry.

A similar need exists in regional planning offices or planning offices attached to local government bodies. At this level it is unlikely that the employment of a full-time social planner will be justifiable—except perhaps in some larger countries or those where local authorities have substantial planning responsibilities—but it is necessary to have someone who will realize the importance of social factors and ensure that they are incorporated in local plans.

There is a more specialized requirement for staff within the national statistical unit or bureau (which in some countries is located within the national planning ministry) who are able to collect social statistics. Such people would be trained statisticians, but they would be particularly equipped to deal with statistics used to measure social conditions and social change. They should appreciate the importance of such statistics and be aware of the particular problems involved in their collection.

The development of social planning in the various parts of government—national and local—outside the national planning agency is as much a question of education, orientation, and informal communication as it is one of formal structures. Planners and decision-makers within these organizations must become aware of the importance of social factors and the ways in which they can be taken into account in their particular sphere of activity. Once this is achieved, they will be prepared to take steps to ensure that the necessary staff and administrative machinery are provided; and in most cases this will be a relatively simple task, perhaps involving a redesignation of the duties of one or two members of staff, some minor changes in administrative procedures, and so on.

The responsibility for this educational process must rest to a considerable extent with the social planners in the national planning agency. As we have indicated earlier, one of their tasks is to educate other government staff, politicians, and the general public about the social aspects of development and, since social considerations impinge on the activities of most sections of government, this means that they must maintain very close contact with a wide range of ministries and agencies.

Problems and pitfalls

The increasing efforts to incorporate social considerations into national development planning have not by any means always been successful. It is relatively easy to find statements of intent regarding the importance of social goals—like those we quoted earlier from Tanzania, Zambia, India, and Papua New Guinea—but it is much more difficult to find examples of countries which have followed up such statements with concrete action.

For example, Myrdal, in a discussion of the relationship between planning and social equity in South Asian countries, points out that:

although greater equality has been proclaimed as an immediate practical goal for planning and policy, marked inequality exists everywhere. The disparity is the more striking because, despite more or less successful attempts at planning, economic inequalities have generally not decreased since independence; if anything they have increased. (Myrdal, 1968, p. 756).

In the case of Zambia, Molteno comments that:

more needs to be done—and soon—if the active enthusiasm of the urban workers and rural villagers is to be mobilized behind the social principles and values of the ideology. (Molteno, 1977, p. 235)

And similarly, MacPherson states that:

In Papua New Guinea, the values and principles comprising social policy have been clearly established. The important task is not then the formulation of social policy goals but the translation of these goals into specific social programmes. (MacPherson, 1979b, p. 3)

Tanzania has perhaps made more progress than most countries in translating social goals into practice. As we saw earlier in the chapter, a significant attempt has been made to develop policies and programmes which will implement the country's basic social objectives and considerable progress has been made, particularly in the provision of social services to the majority of the population and the reduction of at least some aspects of inequality. However, even in Tanzania many problems have occurred, and these have not been only economic problems. For example, there are still very few true *ujamaa* villages in the country, the emergence of a bureaucratic élite has not been entirely prevented, and the majority of the population still play only a very limited role in planning and development. President Nyerere, in a review of progress made during the first 10 years after the announcement of the Arusha Declaration, frankly admitted that progress had been slower than anticipated and the country was still a long way from becoming a truly socialist state (Nyerere, 1977).

Why has it proved to be so difficult to give adequate priority to social factors and, therefore, so difficult to put into action the broad social goals which already exist in so many countries of the Third World? There are many reasons but they can perhaps be grouped together into four main categories. Let us look briefly at each of these.

(i) *Difficulty of isolating social factors*

We have already mentioned on several occasions that it is easy to talk vaguely about 'social' factors, 'social' development, and 'social' planning, but very difficult to define what we actually mean by the word 'social' in these contexts and to distinguish the 'social' from the 'economic', the 'political', and so on.

Consequently, although it is easy for a country to identify broad social goals, it is much more difficult to define these goals more precisely and translate them into programmes of action. In Papua New Guinea, for example, it was readily agreed that social factors must be taken into consideration when evaluating any request for new funds through the national public expenditure plan, but social planning staff in the National Planning Office had difficulty in deciding exactly what social factors should be taken into account and how this should be done.

For the same reason, it is seldom easy to define exactly what a social planner should do. Those staff technically responsible for social planning are, as we have already seen, frequently also responsible for a variety of other planning activities, and one reason for this is the difficulty of defining what is meant by social planning and separating the 'social' from the other aspects of planning. Because of this confusion they tend to spend much of their time either engaged in other, more tangible activities or holding meetings and writing papers to try to decide what they should be doing!

(ii) *Difficulty of measuring social factors*

A more serious problem concerns the measurement of social aspects of development. In most of the planning activities which we have described in this chapter, it is necessary to identify criteria which reflect the social aspects of development policies or programmes and to find ways of measuring changes in these criteria. And in some cases it is also necessary to compare these with changes in the economic aspects of development, in order to weigh up the economic and social costs and benefits of the policy or programme. Let us look more closely at what this involves.

In order to monitor either the process of social change in general or the social impact of particular policies or programmes, the planner has to first define the criteria he is going to use to measure the change. For example, if he is concerned with the impact of urbanization on social conditions, he may decide to measure such things as family size, income distribution, health, evidence of mental strain, access to social services, breakdown of traditional customs, and so on.

He then has to decide how he is going to measure these criteria. Should health be measured in terms of crude death rates, infant mortality, or incidence of certain diseases? How can he obtain some realistic indication of mental strain or the breakdown of traditional customs? Should access to social services be measured in terms of the population for which a particular service has to cater (for example, population per doctor), the number of people who utilize particular services (such as attendance at primary schools or health clinics), or the distance people have to travel to reach the service—and which services should be monitored? In making such decisions he has to consider not only the best way of indicating what he is trying to measure but also the ease with which the information may actually be obtained. For example, it may be desirable to know how far people have to travel to reach the nearest health clinic, but such information may not be available, and carrying out special surveys to obtain it could be both expensive and time-consuming.

Wherever possible the planner will be expected to measure the criteria in quantitative terms, and in some cases he may also be under pressure to attach some monetary value to them. For instance, if he is trying to show that urbanization can cause serious social problems, he may be expected to provide quantitative 'proof' of the extent of these problems and to estimate the financial costs incurred either by individuals or by the state as a result. This is often very difficult to do. For example, how do you attach a monetary value to the fact that people have to travel a long distance to reach essential services, or to the effects of mental stress or the disintegration of traditional customs?

Similar problems occur in other forms of social planning, particularly in the evaluation of individual projects, which is discussed in Chapter 5, and we shall return to the general problems of measuring social development in Part Three. In this chapter, it is only necessary to demonstrate that measuring the social aspects of national development does create particular data collection problems. Because of the difficulty of defining social development in concrete terms, it is hard to identify criteria which reflect exactly what one is trying to measure and, even when criteria have been identified, it is often difficult to actually measure changes in them, particularly in quantitative terms. And more specifically, it is seldom possible to attach a direct monetary value to social factors and so to calculate the social costs and benefits of a policy or programme in a way that enables them to be compared with the economic costs and benefits.

Any form of data collection presents problems, particularly in developing countries, but the problems mentioned here apply much more to social data than they do to economic data. Consequently, there is a tendency for social factors either to be completely ignored or to be underrated, simply because they cannot be easily measured or expressed in quantitative or monetary terms. For example, if it can be shown that an agricultural improvement programme— such as India's green revolution—will produce economic benefits which can be measured in concrete terms (such as increased output of grain, higher farm incomes, or a reduction in food imports) while the possible negative social effects, such as an increase in social inequality, can only be vaguely indicated, the economic benefits are likely to be considered more significant than the social costs and so the programme will go ahead.

(iii) *Conflict between social and economic goals*

A more fundamental problem is the conflict between social and economic priorities. Even if social costs and benefits could be adequately measured and so compared with economic factors, it would still be necessary in many cases to make a choice between economic and social goals and priorities. Governments often announce that they will give priority to the achievement of social objectives without giving adequate consideration to the implications of such a statement. Waterston points out that:

Political authorities often hesitate to come to grips with the basic issues which must be decided if development objectives are clearly stated and appropriate measures are adopted to implement them. . . . [They] prefer to list objectives which, although mutually inconsistent, will include something for everybody. (Waterston, 1965, p. 149)

And he goes on to explain how this leads to the production of plans with conflicting objectives—including conflicting economic and social objectives, such as 'rapid rate of increase in national income and a high level of investment in social welfare' (Waterston, 1965, p. 149).

The conflict between these objectives becomes apparent when efforts are made to implement them and, when this happens, there is a tendency to give precedence to the achievement of economic goals, even if the government has earlier expressed an intention to give priority to social considerations. One of the most significant aspects of the changes which have been occurring in China since the death of Mao Tse-tung is the increasing emphasis now placed on economic objectives—such as more efficient agricultural and industrial production—at the expense of achieving social, and political, goals. This is reflected in such things as the adoption of modern western industrial technology, a relaxation of the restrictions on the cultivation of private plots, and changes in the education system.

Why is there this tendency to give priority to economic factors when a choice actually has to be made? The problems of identifying and measuring the social aspects of development, the fact that it is only recently that planners have begun to acknowledge their importance, and consequently the tendency for economists still to dominate the development planning process, are all partly responsible. However, there are other more fundamental reasons.

One reason is that many forms of social development are dependent on the achievement of a basic level of economic development. For example, if the incomes of individuals increase they have money to spend on improving their social well-being, while at the national level an increase in national income may be used by the government to provide social services such as education, health, housing, water supplies, and welfare assistance. This is perhaps the most common argument used for giving priority to economic development, at least in the 'early stages' of a country's development. Even Nyerere admits that:

we need [economic development] because only when we increase the amount of wealth we produce in Tanzania will there be any chance of our people living decent lives, free from the threat of hunger, or want of clothing, and free from ignorance, or disease. (Nyerere, 1968, p. 199)

However, although this argument is basically sound, it does have to be qualified. Firstly, it assumes that economic development generates income which will be spent either by individuals or by the state to improve the social well-being of the majority of the population. In fact, this is often not the case, either because a large part of this income accrues not to the state or to the majority of the population but to a small minority, or because the social services provided by the state are not available to the majority of the population. The most obvious examples are some of the oil-rich states in the Middle East, where the revenue from oil benefits only a small minority; but the problem occurs on a smaller scale in many countries—developed as well as less developed.

Secondly, the argument ignores the existence of other forms of social development, such as social justice, preservation of culture, freedom from anxiety and stress, and so on. Nyerere recognizes this and qualifies the statement about economic development quoted above by adding:

> But we also need other things too. We need to live harmoniously among ourselves; we need to safeguard our society, we need to respect ourselves and deserve the respect of others. These things are equally important. 'Man does not live by bread alone.' (Nyerere, 1968, p. 199)

And these things are much less dependent on economic development. In fact, economic growth frequently has a negative impact on this sort of social development. For example, it tends to result in the breakdown of traditional culture, an increase in crime, greater mental stress, and—as we saw in Chapter 2—in many cases an increase in social inequalities. We indicated earlier in this chapter that Tanzania's efforts to achieve social goals—and in particular to develop an egalitarian society, have in some cases contributed to its economic problems.

In other words, although economic development is a prerequisite for some forms of social development, the relationship between the two is not as simple as that. Consequently, it is not enough for a government to say: 'We shall concentrate on economic development for the time being and social development will then follow.'

Another reason why economic objectives tend to receive priority over social objectives is that economic problems tend to be more obvious and it is difficult for both planners and politicians to ignore them. If there is a slump in export production, a worsening of the balance of payments, a very high rate of inflation, or a large number of unemployed in the urban areas, they are immediately aware of the fact and there is a great deal of pressure to at least try to improve the situation. But except in the case of a major social disaster—such as a famine, flood, or epidemic—social problems are less obvious to the decision-makers. It is much easier for them to forget (or never know) how many children suffer from malnutrition, how far people in the rural areas have to walk to fetch water, what life is like for the inhabitants of a squatter settlement on the outskirts of a city, or how much the social gap between themselves and these people is widening each year. Consequently, in spite of intentions to the contrary, the attainment of social goals tends to be ignored—or at least postponed—while efforts are concentrated on trying to solve the country's economic problems.

Furthermore, many developing countries are under considerable pressure from overseas creditors and aid donors to improve their economic performance. They have to generate a reasonable amount of national income in order to repay the interest on previous loans and to convince prospective donors that they are creditworthy. Many aid donors, including international aid agencies, do not seem to have yet come to grips with this basic conflict between economic and social objectives. For example, although the World Bank has fully accepted the need to give more attention to social factors—as reflected in the emphasis it now places on programmes directed towards rural development, the provision of social services and the reduction of inequalities (see World Bank, 1980d)—it still insists that any country to which it lends has a planned programme for the improvement of its economy. The International Monetary Fund makes similar demands and this has recently created problems for several Third World countries seeking financial assistance, including Tanzania. Such demands are understandable in that the aid donors are concerned that the countries which receive assistance are not only able to repay the loans but also able gradually to reduce their dependence on foreign aid. But they do reflect the existence of a basic dilemma between economic growth and the achievement of certain social goals, and they do contribute to the tendency for priority to be given to economic considerations if a choice has to be made.

(iv) *Conflict between social ideals and political reality*

The last problem which we shall consider in this chapter is the existence of a somewhat similar conflict between social objectives and political reality. In this case, the problem is that, although political leaders and others in positions of authority are generally quite happy to incorporate social goals into national policy statements and declarations of intent, they are much less willing to support their implementation, particularly if they may suffer personally in the process. This form of conflict may occur in relation to the implementation of a variety of goals. For example, in Papua New Guinea one of the national goals which was strongly supported in principle by national politicians and senior civil servants was decentralization. But when plans for a comprehensive decentralization of the political and administrative system were prepared, there was much more opposition from these people because, as national leaders, they would lose some of their power and status to the new tier of leaders to be established at the provincial level. It was only after a great deal of conflict and debate that the system was eventually introduced and in the end the determining factor was the threat of secession from the province of Bougainville (later renamed North Solomons), which has a copper mine which is the country's most important single source of foreign exchange (Conyers, 1976). Thus, it was economic and political rather than social considerations which finally determined the outcome of the debate.

However, such conflict is most likely to occur in relation to the goal of social equality or justice. Oscar Mehmet maintains that the main reason for the failure of many countries to implement goals aimed at reducing inequalities is 'the élite management of planning and economic policy' in these countries. He explains that these élites have succeeded in 'influencing the allocation of planned investment expenditures and channelling them into projects calculated to augment their own wealth, status and power' (Mehmet, 1978, p. 31). Although Mehmet has in mind particularly countries where social inequalities are greater than average, the statement can be applied at least to some degree in many countries. Any attempts to distribute social services more equitably, reduce income differentials, or generally improve the relative well-being of the less affluent sectors of the population are likely to be resisted by those in positions of authority if, as is almost inevitable, they will suffer as a result. Even in a country like Tanzania, which has made more effort than most to implement a policy of social equality, the gap between what is socially desirable and what is politically feasible has created major problems. In Tanzania *social* planning is also *socialist* planning; but in a book on Tanzania entitled *Towards Socialist Planning*, John Saul reminds us that 'the problem of planning for socialist development remains first and foremost an ideological and a political problem, whatever other important dimensions it may have' (Saul, 1974, pp. 25–26).

Guide to further reading

There is relatively little published material directly related to this aspect of social planning. In particular, there is very little on the way in which social factors can actually be incorporated into the planning process and the machinery required for doing this. Most of the relevant literature is concerned with the role of social factors in development and the failure of many countries to give adequate attention to them.

The various works actually quoted in the chapter give some indication of the range of material which bears some relation to this aspect of social planning, and the following are recommended for those wishing to pursue some issues in more depth:

Apthorpe, R. (ed.), *People Planning and Development Studies* (London, Frank Cass, 1970), especially chapters 10 and 11 which are case studies illustrating the role of the 'human' factor.

Cochrane, G., *The Cultural Appraisal of Development Projects* (New York, Praeger, 1979). This book is more concerned with the planning of specific projects, which is the subject of our next chapter; however, it also considers the general arguments for incorporating social factors into development planning.

Grindle, M. S. (ed.), *Politics and Policy Implementation in the Third World* (Princeton University Press, 1980). This book provides a useful analysis, based on a series of case studies, of the relationship between politics and the implementation of policies and plans.

Mehmet, O., *Economic Planning and Social Justice in Developing Countries* (London, Croom Helm, 1978).

Myrdal, G., *Asian Drama* (Harmondsworth, Penguin Books, 1968; originally published by Twentieth Century Fund).

We have devoted considerable attention in this chapter to Tanzania because it provides a particularly good example of a country which has attempted to incorporate social factors into development planning. The Tanzanian philosophy is spelled out in the writings of President Nyerere, from which we have quoted extensively. For further discussion of the country's actual aims and achievements, including the many problems it has encountered, the following are particularly recommended:

Coulson, A. (ed.), *African Socialism in Practice* (Nottingham, Spokesman Books, 1979).

Hyden, G., *Beyond Ujamaa in Tanzania: Underdevelopment and an Uncaptured Peasantry* (London, Heinemann, 1980).

Lappé, F. M., and A. Beccar-Varela, *Mozambique and Tanzania: Asking the Big Questions* (San Francisco, Institute for Food and Development Policy, 1980).

Mwansasu, B. U., and C. Pratt (eds.), *Towards Socialism in Tanzania* (Tanzania Publishing House and University of Toronto Press, 1979).

Rweyemamu, J. F. *et al.* (eds.), *Towards Socialist Planning* (Tanzania Publishing House, 1974).

CHAPTER 5

SOCIAL PLANNING'S ROLE IN PROJECT PLANNING

Introduction

The previous chapter looked at the importance of taking social factors into consideration in national development planning and the various ways in which this can be done. The type of planning examined in this chapter is similar, but it focuses more specifically on the planning of particular projects.

The word 'project' can be used to mean many different things. So far in this book we have used it very generally; but at this stage it is necessary to try to define it more precisely. There are two important characteristics of a project, in the sense in which it is used in this chapter. Firstly, a project is normally planned and implemented as a single identifiable activity, or set of related activities. It may have many component parts or involve many different agencies or individuals; but these components are interrelated and it is therefore important that the project is planned and implemented as a whole. Consequently, a project often has its own plan document, a special project manager or management committee, its own budget allocation, and so on.

The other important characteristic of a project is that it is normally located in a specific geographic area. This area may vary in size from a project such as a factory which occupies a very limited area to a regional development project covering the whole of an administrative region; but in each case the area covered by the project can be specifically defined. This characteristic is often used to distinguish a 'project' from a 'programme'. The term 'programme', which we have also used very vaguely until now, generally implies a much broader and less easily defined geographic coverage. For example, a nutrition *programme* suggests a general attempt to improve nutrition throughout the country (or in all areas where it is particularly needed) by a variety of means, such as cultivation of food crops, nutrition education, child health care, and so on. A nutrition *project*, on the other hand, suggests a more specific activity, such as a nutrition campaign in a particular area or community or the construction of a special clinic for treating cases of malnutrition. It should, however, be emphasized that these distinctions are made here in order to assist the reader to distinguish between different kinds of planning activity, and in particular to understand what is meant by 'project planning' in the context of this chapter. We are not attempting to provide universally accepted definitions of terms such as 'project' and 'programme', which are used in very many different ways.

In this chapter we are concerned with the social implications of specific development projects, the importance of taking social factors into consideration when planning such projects, and the various ways in which this can be done. In other words, we are examining the role of the social planner in planning, monitoring, and evaluating development projects. This work is often referred to by terms such as 'social impact analysis' or 'social impact studies'. It is an essential component of all project planning, but it becomes particularly important—and often also particularly sensitive or controversial—in the case of projects which are designed primarily to achieve economic objectives. In such cases, there is a danger that the social aspects of the project will be ignored and the social planner has to guard against this.

We shall study this kind of social planning by taking three case studies of different types of project and looking at the planning process involved in each. The first case study, which is of copper mining projects in Papua New Guinea, demonstrates the problems of large-scale natural resource exploitation in developing countries. This is followed by a study of the planning of water resource development, using the Mwamapuli Dam in Tanzania as an example. And the third case study describes the planning of two tobacco schemes in Zambia, providing an example of small-scale agricultural project planning. In the last section of the chapter we attempt to draw a few general conclusions about the role of the social planner in project planning, based on the three case studies.

Copper in Papua New Guinea

(i) *Introduction*

Large-scale mining ventures provide one of the most obvious examples of economic development projects which have serious social implications. The establishment of a large mine in a previously rural area of a developing country can cause enormous social disruption, particularly in the immediate area of the mine but sometimes also in the country as a whole. Consequently, the planning of such projects presents a major challenge for the social planner.

However, it should be pointed out that the social problems associated with a mining project are by no means the only problems which those planning the project may have to face. There may also be engineering problems related to the construction of the mine and associated infrastructure, there is often the danger of environmental damage, and there are sure to be numerous economic and political problems, particularly in relation to the ownership of the mine and the sale of the produce on the world market.

On the other hand, the potential economic value of such projects can be very high. The development of one or two large mines can make an enormous difference to a country's economic situation, particularly by providing much-needed foreign exchange. Therefore, there is usually tremendous pressure to go ahead with the project, in spite of all the problems which are likely to occur.

The process of planning a major project such as a mine is thus a formidable task, in which many different disciplines have to be involved and some very difficult decisions have to be made. In this section we look at the planning process associated with the exploitation of copper in Papua New Guinea, a country which has only recently become involved in large-scale mining, and we look at it particularly from the point of view of the social planner.

(ii) Copper in Papua New Guinea

Although Papua New Guinea only began to produce copper in 1972, it already ranks twelfth among the world's main producing countries (Intergovernmental Council of Copper Exporting Countries (CIPEC), 1980). Copper is the country's most important export commodity. Table 9 shows the value of copper as a percentage of total exports between 1971 and 1978. The table also shows the proportion of the country's budget funded from overseas (mainly untied grants from Australia) during this period. The size of this aid indicates the pressure on the Papua New Guinea government to develop internal sources of revenue, such as copper.

At present all the copper comes from one mine on the island of Bougainville in the eastern part of the country. However, there are several other large deposits of copper which are currently being investigated; a second mine at Ok Tedi, on the country's western borders, is at present under construction and production is expected to begin in 1984 (see Figure 1). Here we examine the social problems which have arisen from the establishment of the Bougainville mine and the implications of these for planning Ok Tedi and any other future mining developments.

Table 9   The role of copper in Papua New Guinea's economy, 1971–78

Year	1971	1972	1973	1974	1975	1976	1977	1978
Copper production ('000 tonnes copper content)	—	124	183	184	173	177	182	199
Value of copper as percentage of total exports	—	18	60	56	58	46	35	41
Percentage of national revenue from external sources	58	56	57	53	43	39	45	41

Sources: Data on copper production and copper exports obtained from Intergovernmental Council of Copper Exporting Countries (CIPEC), 1980. Data on percentage of national revenue from external sources made available to author while in Papua New Guinea.

(iii) The Bougainville mine[1]

The Bougainville mine is located on the island of Bougainville, within the North Solomons Province (Figure 1).[2] It is the largest opencast copper mine in the world, covering an area of 150 square kilometres, employing over 3,000

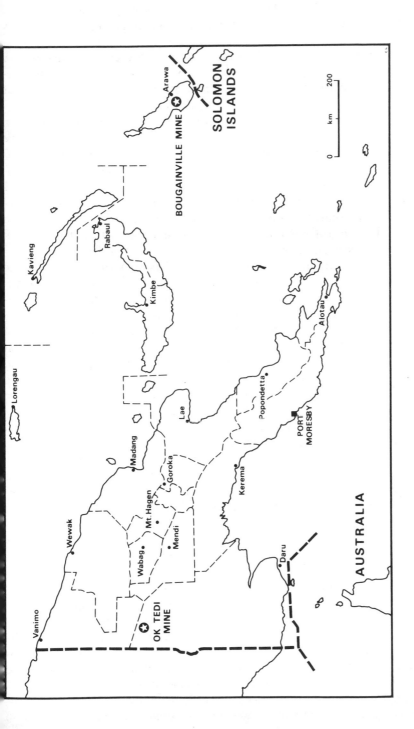

Figure 1   Papua New Guinea: location of Bougainville and Ok Tedi mines

people, and producing 700,000 tonnes of copper at the height of its production. It thus has a very big impact on the province, which has a population of only 129,000.

The mine, which came into full production in 1972, was established before Papua New Guinea became independent. It was therefore planned and developed by the Australian colonial administration. Bougainville Copper Limited, the company operating the mine, is a subsidiary of the giant international mining company Rio Tinto Zinc, which is engaged in mining activities in many parts of the world (see West, 1972). However, the Papua New Guinea government owns 20 per cent of the shares, and a year after attaining self-government in 1973, the government renegotiated the agreement with the company in order to obtain a much larger share of the profits. The government's success in this renegotiation was an important landmark in the history of relations between international mining companies and the governments of Third World countries and it put the Papua New Guinea government in a much stronger economic position when it became independent in 1975.

Relatively little attention was given to social factors when planning the Bougainville mine. It was necessary to conduct negotiations with the inhabitants of the area in relation to the acquisition of land for the mine and related infrastructure and some attempt was also made to explain to the people what the mine would involve and how it would benefit themselves and the country as a whole. The field officers of the colonial government's district administration were used as liaison officers for this purpose. However, the acquisition of land was, as we shall see, one of the major causes of social tension resulting from the mine and there was no comprehensive survey of social conditions or of the likely social impact of the project.

The social problems which developed as a result of the Bougainville mine can be divided into four categories: problems related to the acquisition of land; problems caused by environmental pollution; problems resulting from the development of a large urban complex associated with the mine; and social and political problems which emerged at the national level due to relationships between the North Solomons and other parts of the country. These problems are discussed briefly below.

The problems related to the acquisition of land were the first to occur. It was necessary to acquire large areas of land for the mine itself, for a new urban area to house mine-workers and government staff, and for the construction of port facilities for the import of raw materials and export of copper. Although compensation was paid to those who lost land, there was enormous opposition from the people. The Bougainvilleans, like other Papua New Guineans, have a very strong attachment to their land, and in this case most of the area involved was productive agricultural land. Opposition was so great that eventually the administration was forced to take over an expatriate-owned plantation for the development of the main urban area, known as Arawa.

Fortunately, it was not necessary to resettle many people since the appropriated land did not include many actual village sites. However, one village in the mine area itself did have to be relocated and the story of this resettlement provides a perfect example of misconceived planning. The people were re-housed in prefabricated houses—like those built in urban areas—in an exposed compound on a hillside overlooking the mine site. Those responsible for the re-settlement genuinely thought they were doing the best thing for the people by providing them with 'modern' housing, including facilities such as electricity and water. On the contrary, however, the unfamiliar accommodation merely added to the social trauma caused by having to leave their traditional land and watch it being transformed into a giant industrial enclave.

The payment of compensation for the land which was acquired also created problems. Large sums of money were involved and a new class of relatively wealthy villagers was thus created overnight. The administration tried to help those who received the money to invest it in small business enterprises or in a savings bank. But again its efforts were misguided because its assistance was directed at individuals rather than groups and so merely contributed to the emergence of a new élite of rural businessmen, rather than the well-being of the people as a whole.

The second group of problems was related to the environmental pollution re-sulting from the mine. During the planning stages inadequate consideration was given to the possible environmental damage which would occur, par-ticularly from the disposal of waste material. During the first few years of the mine's operation it became obvious that serious damage was being done, and one of the terms of the 1974 renegotiation of the agreement between the com-pany and the government was that a thorough environmental impact study should be undertaken. From a social point of view, the most serious environ-mental damage was the pollution of a river running from the mine area to the west coast of the island, which had previously been used by the people as a source of water and for fishing. When the mine came into operation, the water soon became undrinkable and the fish died.

The third group of problems were those caused by the sudden emergence of a large industrial and urban community in a previously quiet rural area. Any form of urban development in the Third World tends to bring with it a series of social problems. These include marked inequalities between those with well-paid jobs and those who are unemployed or in menial positions, thus leading to deprivation and crime; lack of basic social services, especially housing, result-ing in overcrowding and the growth of squatter settlements and shanty towns; and a variety of social and psychological problems caused by the strain of urban living upon people who are accustomed to the relatively slow and peaceful mode of life in the rural areas.

All these problems occurred in the new urban areas of the island of Bougain-ville and were, in fact, accentuated by the nature of the urban development. The suddenness of the change from rural to urban environment was one factor which distinguished it from other towns in the country which had grown up much more gradually. Related to this was the fact that Arawa was an entirely new town, with all the problems of new towns anywhere in the world. Many basic facilities were lacking in the early days of its establishment, it had a cold impersonal atmosphere and there was no sense of community identity or spirit. The design of the town also caused problems because, like many new towns in the Third World, it had been designed according to western standards of architecture and town planning. Consequently, the feeling of alienation among most of the inhabitants was intensified.

Another factor which made the situation worse was the enormous influx of people from other parts of Papua New Guinea and from other countries to work at the mine or in related industries. Socially and culturally Papua New Guinea is an excessively fragmented nation and most social groups are wary of, if not openly hostile towards, people from other parts of the country. The Bougainvilleans—who differ significantly from other Papua New Guineans in appearance, culture, and history—are well known for their mistrust of 'outsiders' and so particularly resented the intrusion into their privacy. The government and the mining company made some attempts to minimize possible conflict. For example, Bougainvilleans were given priority in obtaining certain jobs in the mine, particularly senior managerial positions, and non-Papua New Guinean employees were not allowed to visit local villages. However, these measures were not enough to reduce tension and conflict and the mine has undoubtedly increased rather than reduced the resentment of 'outsiders' harboured by most Bougainvilleans.

The conflict between Bougainvilleans and other Papua New Guineans has been evident not only in the mine area. It has also had repercussions at the national level, which have had a major impact on the country's political organization. The existence of the mine led to political tension between the North Solomons and the other 18 provinces in the country. The other provinces felt that the North Solomons, which was already relatively well off according to conventional indicators of social and economic development, was even more advantaged as a result of the mine. Political leaders in the North Solomons, on the other hand, believed that the mine had made them worse off because they had to suffer all the social problems already described, while the rest of the country reaped the benefits in terms of increased national revenue.

This is not the place to describe in detail the political conflicts which resulted from this situation, since we are concerned with the social rather than the political implications of the mine. However, it may be mentioned that in 1975 the tension became so great that the North Solomons Province attempted to break away from the rest of the country and establish itself as an independent nation. The situation was eventually resolved but, in order to retain the North Solomons and its valuable copper resources, the Papua New Guinea government had to agree to a political, administrative, and financial decentralization which would not only give all provinces more control over their own development but would also give the wealthier provinces, like North Solomons, a larger share of national revenue (Conyers, 1976). This agreement appeased the Bougainvilleans, although it did not eliminate all suspicion of the national government in the province; but it increased the resentment of the North

Solomons felt in many other provinces—and it has made the national government's task of reducing inequalities between provinces rather more difficult.

(iv) *Lessons from Bougainville*

The independent government of Papua New Guinea is very much aware of the many problems—environmental, economic, social, and political—which have arisen as a result of the Bougainville mine and it is attempting to minimize these problems in future mining projects. The efforts to do this can be illustrated by looking briefly at the planning which is being done in connection with the next large-scale mine at Ok Tedi and in relation to the possibility of establishing another mine in the North Solomons.

The Ok Tedi mine site is located in one of the most isolated and least developed parts of the country. The mine is currently under construction and production is planned to commence in 1984. The original exploration was undertaken by another international mining company, the American-based Kennecott Copper Corporation, but the Papua New Guinea government, encouraged by its success in the renegotiation of the Bougainville agreement, took over the project when Kennecott refused to develop it on Papua New Guinea's terms. The government has since gone into partnership with the Australian-based mining company, Broken Hill Proprietary Limited, on terms acceptable to both parties.

Social factors have received considerably more attention in planning the Ok Tedi mine. Detailed studies of the social conditions in the area have been undertaken, and considerable attention has been given to the type of social facilities and services which will be required when the mine is developed and to the social problems which are likely to occur. Furthermore, several years prior to the construction of the mine, a form of community development programme was begun in the area, in an attempt to prepare the people for the transformation which would eventually occur. This programme was initiated by the Kennecott Company, but continued by the government when it took over the project. It included the expansion of education facilities in the area so that there will be more local people qualified to work in the mine, the formation of a cooperatively owned development company through which any income which the people earn directly or indirectly from the project can be used for the overall development of the area, and a general information and education programme designed to explain to people what the project will involve.

It is too soon to judge whether these efforts will have any marked effect in reducing social problems when the mine comes into existence and, of course, it will never be possible to measure their effects exactly because no one will know what would have happened if nothing had been done. Anyone with any knowledge of the Ok Tedi area is rather pessimistic about the social impact of the project. The area has been so isolated and neglected in the past that, whatever precautions are taken, it seems inevitable that the effect on the people will be much more traumatic than in the Bougainville case. However, the government realizes that this should not be used as an excuse for giving up and doing nothing; we can hope that those efforts which are being made will at least partially alleviate the problems which are bound to occur.

Meanwhile, the Papua New Guinea government is also beginning to consider whether another mine should be developed in the North Solomons Province when the output from the present mine is exhausted in perhaps 20 years' time. In 1981 the government, at the request of the North Solomons provincial government, employed consultants to examine the possible impact of a second mine. It is not yet known what decision will result from this study; but it is at least encouraging that the matter is being considered well in advance and that social factors are receiving particular attention in weighing up the advantages and disadvantages of developing another mine in the area.

(v) *Conclusions*

The conclusions which may be drawn from this brief analysis of copper projects in Papua New Guinea are not particularly encouraging from the social planner's point of view; however, they are relatively easy to identify. Firstly, it is obvious from the Bougainville case study and from experience in other parts of the world that large-scale mining projects can and usually do create very serious social problems, particularly for the people in the immediate area.

Secondly, evidence does suggest that these problems can be at least partially alleviated by careful planning before the mine is actually developed. There should be a thorough study of existing social conditions in the area and an evaluation of the likely social impact of the project; and steps should be taken to ensure the provision of adequate—and appropriate—social facilities and services and to prepare and protect the interests of the local people and preserve as much as possible of their traditional culture and life style. There is, therefore, a major role for the social planner in the planning of any such project.

However, it seems that the social planner—and any other socially concerned person—has to accept that, however much effort is made to anticipate and avoid problems, there will be a significant amount of social disruption. Projects of this nature provide some of the most obvious examples of the situation where a choice has to be made between economic and social objectives. In many cases—including the Ok Tedi project in Papua New Guinea—the anticipated social problems are so formidable that many people question whether the project should go ahead at all. However, in Papua New Guinea, as in many developing countries, the pressure to increase national revenue, and in particular foreign exchange, is still so great that the economic objectives take precedence and the project does go ahead.

The Mwamapuli Dam in Tanzania

(i) *Introduction*

This section of the chapter examines a planning project undertaken in the Tabora Region of Tanzania between 1969 and 1971, in association with the construction of a dam in the area. The main purpose of the project was to ensure that the dam did not merely provide economic benefits but also led to the integrated development of the area as a whole, for the benefit of the people living there.

(ii) *Dams in Africa*

The decision to plan for the integrated development of the area in this way was based on previous experience with the planning of dams in Tanzania, and in Africa as a whole. During the 1950s and 1960s the use of dams as a means of providing both hydroelectric power and water for irrigation and human and animal consumption became very important in Africa. The result was the construction of a number of very large multipurpose dams—such as those at Aswan, Volta, Kariba, Owen Falls, and Kainji—and innumerable small dams serving more limited functions.

However, by the end of the 1960s it was becoming apparent that there were a number of problems associated with these projects (compare Warren and Rubin, 1968). These included physical problems, particularly rapid siltation and excessive loss of water due to evaporation, and economic problems, such as the failure to achieve projected increases in agricultural output. However, some of the most serious problems may be broadly described as social in nature. For example, enormous social disruption was caused among people who had to be resettled because they were living in areas which would be flooded (Brokensha and Scudder, 1968; Colson, 1971); there was often an increase in water-borne diseases such as bilharzia; and inadequate measures were taken to provide social infrastructure in the areas affected by the dams.

Many of these problems could be attributed to the lack of integrated development planning prior to the construction of the dams. The dams were seen primarily as engineering feats designed to provide economic benefits; for although it is impossible to separate the economic benefits (such as increased agricultural or industrial output) of such projects from the various social benefits associated with the provision of an improved water supply, it was the economic benefits which were generally used to justify the projects and determine the form which they would take. Consequently, the planning process typically consisted of the preparation of detailed engineering designs, supported by some sort of economic evaluation to justify the cost of the project. Very little attempt was made to consider the social implications of the project or to make plans for the overall development of the area to be affected by it.

As awareness of these problems and their causes increased, it became evident that 'decision-making based solely on technical and economic considerations is wholly unsatisfactory and that the social and political implications . . . need to be clearly presented' (Joy, 1968, p. 19). Consequently, in Africa—and in other parts of the world—there was a move towards an integrated approach in planning dams and other similar water resource development projects.

This attitude was prevalent in Tanzania at the time the project was conceived. Although there was only one large dam in the country at the time—the Nyumba Ya Mungu Dam, which was built in the northern part of the country primarily to supply hydroelectric power—there were many small dams, intended mainly to provide water for domestic or animal consumption, but sometimes also for irrigation. There was a general feeling that these dams had not been properly planned or utilized and so, when a decision was made to construct another larger dam at Mwamapuli, in Tabora Region, it was decided that proper planning was needed.

(iii) The Mwamapuli Dam[3]

The Mwamapuli Dam is located in the north-eastern part of Tabora Region, in what is now Igunga District, but was, at the time the dam was constructed, part of Nzega District (Figure 2). Before the 1960s the Igunga area was sparsely populated. It was estimated that in 1959 there were about 7,000 inhabitants, mostly Nyamwezi farmers in the south-west and nomadic Taturu pastoralists in the east. However, the area was potentially very suitable for cotton-growing and, as a result of increasing population pressure in the cotton-growing areas of Sukumaland to the north and the construction of a main road through Igunga in 1962, Sukuma farmers began to move into the area. The population increased rapidly and in 1969 it was estimated that there were about 50,000 people in the area. By this time the rate of in-migration was beginning to slow down since the best land was already occupied and in some parts of the area the population density was as high as 35 persons per square kilometre.

The main problem faced by the people moving into the area was water supply. The area has a low rainfall and there is very little surface water available. A small dam had been constructed in the western part of the area, but this only served a small proportion of the population. The possibility of constructing another, much larger dam at Mwamapuli had been considered for many years, but it was difficult to justify the project when there were very few people in the area. However, when the population began to increase, its construction became both necessary on social grounds and economically justifiable in terms of the anticipated increase in cotton production from the area. The decision to construct the dam, with Swedish financial aid, was made in 1968 and it was eventually completed in 1971. Pipelines were laid to take water from the dam to the main settlements in the area.

Meanwhile, in 1968 it was agreed that an integrated plan for the development of the area should be prepared and that this should be done by staff of the Bureau of Resource Assessment and Land Use Planning at the University of Dar es Salaam. An integrated plan was considered necessary in order to ensure that the people of the area, and the nation as a whole, received maximum benefit from the project which, it was estimated, would cost approximately £1.5 million. It was, in particular, necessary to study the changes that were likely to occur in the area—including the number and type of people who would move in and the possible increase in agricultural production—and to recom-

Figure 2   Location of Mwamapuli Dam, Tanzania

mend where water taps should be provided and what other infrastructure (including roads, marketing facilities, schools, health services, and administrative services) would be required. Although the main purpose of the dam was to provide water supply for humans—and also cattle, the planners were also asked to consider the possibility of irrigation in some parts of the area. Furthermore, in view of the national policy of socialist rural development through *ujamaa* villages, their terms of reference also included making recommendations on how *ujamaa* villages should be encouraged and organized.

The project was carried out by an interdisciplinary team, which included an agricultural economist a sociologist, a political scientist, and several geographers. The work began with a review of relevant existing data, including anthropological material about the three main groups in the area (the Nyamwezi, Sukuma, and Taturu). This was followed by detailed physical, social, and economic surveys in the area itself, supported by meetings with regional, district, and local politicians and administrative staff. Preliminary recommendations were discussed with national and local officials in 1969 and a final report was published in 1970 (Bureau of Resource Assessment and Land Use Planning, 1970).

Some of the benefits of carrying out such an exercise were immediately felt. To start with, it was found that existing data on the area were very inadequate and in some cases also inaccurate. For example, the number of people already living there had been grossly underestimated and the existing maps of the area were found to be inaccurate. Consequently, the few plans that had been made for such things as the layout of water pipes were based on incorrect information. Furthermore, those plans had been prepared by engineers with little or no consideration of the social conditions or needs. For example, no study had been made of existing patterns of water use and the ways in which these might change when water became more easily available, the possible conflicts between the three different social groups had not been considered, and the social and economic importance of the large number of cattle in the area had also been ignored. Fortunately, on the basis of the information collected by the planning team, most of these deficiencies were rectified before the dam was constructed and the pipelines laid.

The longer-term benefits of the project are rather more difficult to judge. The dam was constructed and the pipelines laid and so the area now has a reasonable supply of good-quality water. The population has continued to increase and so has the production of cotton and there has been a general improvement in social, economic, and administrative infrastructure. Moreover, the growth of the area as a whole is reflected in the fact that it has become a district in its own right. How much of this growth can be attributed to the planning study, how much merely to the provision of water—and how much would have been achieved if the dam had never been constructed at all, is difficult to assess, especially since there has been no proper evaluation of the impact of the project. However, one can be reasonably confident that the adoption of an integrated planning approach did at least help to maximize the benefits achieved from the dam and thus improve the general well-being of the inhabitants of the area.

(iv) *Conclusion*

The Mwamapuli Dam is small in comparison with the giant dams like the Aswan, Volta, or Kariba, and the planning process was relatively simple because it was designed for only one major purpose and there was no large-scale resettlement programme involved. Nevertheless, it illustrates many of the general problems which occur in planning such projects.

The main lesson which emerges from the case study is not the need for a social survey or plan carried out in isolation but for integrated planning which takes into account technical, economic, social, and political factors and produces not merely a design for a dam but an integrated plan for the development of an area. The social planner has a vital role to play in such planning, but he must work as a member of a team. We may conclude with a quotation from the introduction to a collection of essays entitled *Dams in Africa*, to which we have already referred. The editors state that:

Two conclusions emerge. The first is that it is apparent that, in future, all major decisions concerning African dams should be taken in the light of information provided through employing the skills of considerably more disciplines than have hitherto been involved in any single project. And the second is that the practitioners of the various disciplines should themselves become increasingly aware of the relevance and findings of others working in different fields, but who are equally involved in a total human situation. (Warren and Rubin, 1968, p. xi)

Tobacco schemes in Zambia

(i) *Introduction*

The third—and last—case study which we shall look at in this chapter illustrates the need to take social factors into consideration when planning agricultural schemes. Such schemes have played an important role in many developing countries since independence. They vary greatly in nature and purpose, but in most cases they involve the concentration of resources (particularly capital inputs and extension effort) into a relatively small geographic area, in an attempt to bring about a significant increase in agricultural production and an improvement in the standard of living in the area. Usually, it is hoped that the schemes will have a demonstration effect on the people in the surrounding areas, thereby encouraging similar improvements in these areas. Sometimes existing settlements are chosen as the location for such schemes; but frequently they involve the movement of people into an area which was previously sparsely populated or even completely uninhabited.

Many problems have arisen in the planning and implementation of such schemes. These include technical and managerial problems, difficulties in providing infrastructure and services, the reluctance of people to join the scheme, and the absence of any spread effects in the surrounding areas (compare Chambers, 1969, and Long, 1977, Chapter 6). A general survey of these problems is beyond the scope of this book. We shall merely examine some of the social factors which have to be considered in planning such schemes, using the example of two tobacco schemes in Zambia.

(ii) *Tobacco production in Zambia*

Tobacco is the most important export crop in Zambia. It was first grown in the 1950s, mainly on large European-owned farms. In the first few years after independence in 1964, there was a decline in production due to the departure of many Europeans (Table 10), but the Zambian government began a major effort to encourage production by Zambians.

Responsibility for the development of tobacco cultivation rests with the Tobacco Board of Zambia, which was established in 1967. The Board provides services for both large- and small-scale farmers, but its main efforts are devoted to the latter. At the beginning of the 1979-83 Third National Development Plan

Table 10 Tobacco production in Zambia, 1964–1976

Year	1964	1965	1968	1971	1974	1976
Production in metric tonnes	12,970	9,119	6,690	6,302	6,631	6,477

Sources: Zambia, 1971, p. 14, and Zambia, 1979, p. 140

period there were about 3,000 smallholder tobacco farmers in the country, and it is hoped to increase this number to 9,500 by the end of the period (Zambia, 1979, p. 149). These farmers are grouped into schemes, where they are provided with assistance in cultivation, curing, and marketing of the crop. Each farmer in a scheme has to grow at least 0.4 hectare (1 acre) of tobacco and some food crops. Some of these schemes are set up in existing villages where conditions are suitable for tobacco growing, while others are new settlements to which farmers in neighbouring areas are encouraged to move.

We shall look briefly at the way in which two of the early smallholder tobacco schemes, Kabile and Mulilima, were established. Both schemes are located in Central Province (Figure 3). The Kabile scheme encountered many problems which can be attributed to a large extent to the lack of attention given to social factors in the planning stage, while the Mulilima scheme was widely regarded as an example of successful social mobilization.[4]

(iii) The Kabile tobacco scheme

The Kabile scheme is located in the south-western part of the province, in the district known as Kabwe Rural. It was established in 1970 in an existing village which already had some basic infrastructure, including a school and some access roads.

One of the main problems in the planning of the scheme was that the Tobacco Board pushed ahead with the plans without sufficient consultation with local authorities. The Board was anxious to get the project under way because money was available and so it attempted to bypass the district development committee and the local government council, where such matters were supposed to be thoroughly discussed. The plans were prepared independently and authority for the scheme to go ahead was obtained at a higher level, and then the local authorities were merely asked to 'rubber stamp' the proposals. Consequently, the scheme had very little support from local politicians or administrators.

A related problem was that no attempt was made to study the local social and political situation and to consider what effect this might have on the scheme. In particular, the existence of a considerable number of 'outsiders' (including some people from Zimbabwe) in the area and the fact that the local chief had lost much of his traditional authority were ignored.

The effects of these omissions were felt when the scheme was established and

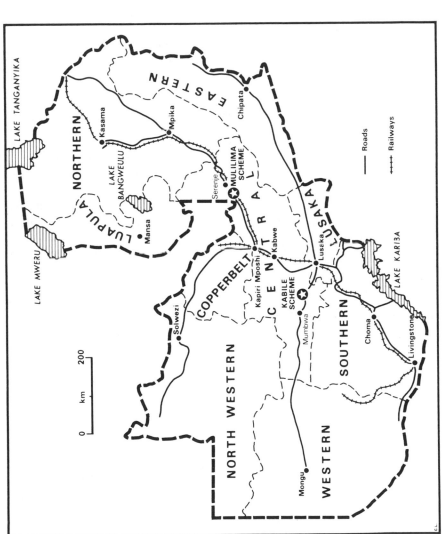

Figure 3 Zambia: location of Mulilima and Kabile tobacco schemes

attempts were made to recruit local farmers to grow tobacco. The scheme manager, who was appointed by the Board, received very little assistance from the local authorities or from extension staff working in the area, and a political conflict arose as to whether or not 'outsiders' should be allowed to join the scheme. The situation was aggravated by the fact that the scheme manager tried to take sole responsibility for the recruitment of farmers, rather than set up some sort of committee to consider applications. Moreover, the scheme itself was organized on an authoritarian basis and relationships between management staff and farmers were rather poor.

The scheme did eventually get off its feet and was still producing tobacco in 1980. However, poor relations between the scheme management and local authorities, the people in the neighbouring area, and the farmers themselves continued to cause problems for some time. And these problems could have been avoided if the project had been planned more carefully.

(iv) The Mulilima tobacco scheme

The Mulilima scheme is located in Serenje District, which is in the north-eastern part of Central Province (Figure 3). It was started on a small scale in 1968 and taken over by the Tobacco Board in 1970. It was a new settlement, located in an area which had previously been under protected forest, and so its establishment included clearing the land, providing all necessary infrastructure, and moving people into the area.

The planning process took much longer than in the case of the Mulilima scheme. The Serenje rural council and the district development committee were fully involved in the discussions and gave their unanimous support. The scheme was started on a pilot basis and plans later modified as a result of the experience gained.

The scheme was not entirely free from problems in the early stages. Farmers were at first somewhat reluctant to join, there were difficulties in providing basic infrastructure (such as a water supply and health facilities) and in maintaining farm machinery, and because of a change in the world market situation it was necessary to turn from Turkish tobacco to Virginia tobacco in the 1970/71 season. However, these problems were tackled in a practical manner, with due regard for their social implications. For example, in the effort to recruit settlers, the scheme manager enlisted the support of the leading political and administrative officials in the district, who in turn worked together with the local chiefs to encourage people to join the scheme. Open days were also held to maintain good public relations and encourage further settlers. And within the scheme itself a system of internal government based on a series of committees was introduced to maintain social control, encourage local self-help activities, and act as a channel of communication between settlers and management staff.

In the early years of its existence, therefore, the scheme was generally regarded as a success, particularly in social and political terms. The turnover of settlers was very low, relations between the scheme management and district officials, the local community, and the settlers were good, and the scheme was generally regarded by politicians and administrative staff as a model of how such projects should be established. Unfortunately, more recently the scheme has encountered some problems. A visit by the author in 1980 revealed considerable disillusionment among the settlers, resulting in a higher turnover than in the past. However, these problems appeared to be due mainly to external factors—such as the state of the international tobacco market and problems in obtaining spare parts for machinery because of import controls imposed by the Zambian government—together with a rapid turnover of scheme managers and over-centralization within the management of the Tobacco Board. Within the scheme itself, relations between settlers, extension workers, and the local community appeared still to be good, and there was a relatively high level of political and self-help activity.

(v) *Conclusion*

Compared with the other projects we have looked at in this chapter, the Kabile and Mulilima tobacco schemes are small projects, which did not involve enormous capital expenditure or complex planning procedures. Nevertheless, they do provide another example of projects which are initiated primarily for economic reasons—in this case, the production of an export crop, tobacco—but can be failures if insufficient attention is given to social factors.

There are three main lessons which can be learned from the case study: firstly, local political and administrative bodies must be fully involved in planning this type of agricultural scheme; secondly, social considerations in the area—such as the homogeneity of the population and local leadership patterns—must be taken into account; and thirdly, the farmers should be fully involved in the management of the scheme. These may seem to be such obvious requirements that they are hardly worth mentioning. However, as the case study demonstrated, they are all too easily forgotten, especially if there is very little time and economic considerations are uppermost in the minds of the planners.

In conclusion, it should perhaps be pointed out that the whole concept of agricultural schemes, like those described here, is open to some serious criticism on social grounds. The main point at issue is that a relatively large proportion of national resources (including capital investment, recurrent costs, and manpower) is being devoted to a relatively small number of people, who more often than not live in an area of higher than average economic potential. This is contrary to any 'basic needs' approach to development which emphasizes reduction in social and economic inequalities and concentration on the poorest sectors of the population who are in greatest need of assistance.

For this reason, many developing countries now place less emphasis on individual agricultural schemes—particularly those with large financial and manpower requirements—than they did in the first few years of independence.

In many cases, this move has been encouraged by the discovery that relatively few such schemes have a significant demonstration effect on the people in the surrounding area, and so the benefits are limited to those people in the scheme itself. Instead more emphasis is placed on general agricultural development programmes, which will benefit many more people, or on projects in areas of special need, rather than areas of economic potential.

Tanzania is one country which made a dramatic change in its rural development policy when it decided in 1967 to abandon its previous emphasis on a small number of capital-intensive settlement schemes and concentrate instead on the development of *ujamaa* villages throughout the country. Zambia also places less emphasis on special agricultural schemes than it did in the past. In the case of crops like tobacco, which require specialist extension services, it is considered that some such organization is still needed; but new schemes are wherever possible established in existing villages in order to minimize overhead costs.

Conclusion: the role of the social planner in project planning

The case studies presented in this chapter represent a wide range of projects, each with its own particular characteristics and problems. Because the range is so great it is not possible to design a model planning process which can be used in planning any project. However, it is possible to draw some broad conclusions about project planning in general, and the role of the social planner in particular. We shall return to some of the methodological implications of this in Part Three.

The social planner's role in project planning can be divided into two parts. He (or she) should first be involved in the initial planning of the project, in order to ensure that social factors are taken into account. And later he has a role to play in monitoring and evaluating the project when it is in operation so that any social problems can be identified, and if possible rectified. In many cases the social planner is not involved in both the 'before' and 'after' stages of the process. Sometimes there is some form of social impact study during the planning stage, but there is no attempt to follow this up later to see what problems have actually occurred. In other cases, social factors are more or less ignored in the initial planning of the project, but when problems arise the social planner is called in to find out what has gone wrong. And of course, in some projects there is no proper attempt to consider the social aspects at all. Let us now look in more detail at what is involved in both the 'before' and 'after' stages.

A social impact study carried out as part of the initial planning of a project should be designed to achieve three main objectives. Firstly, it should attempt to predict the likely social effects—both good and bad—of the project and to take account of these in the planning process. It is particularly important that if the project could have negative social effects—as in the case of the Bougainville copper mine—these are properly evaluated and every effort made to minimize their occurrence.

Secondly, it should examine the social and cultural conditions in the project area and consider what factors have to be taken into account in the planning process, in order to ensure the success of the project and to maximize the social benefits arising from it. Our case study of the two tobacco schemes illustrated what happens when social factors are not taken into account at this stage.

Thirdly, the study should identify what kind of social services and facilities should be included in the project design in order to meet the basic social requirements of the people and minimize the social disruption which often occurs in such projects. It is important that this part of the study should not only consider the type of services required (for example, schools, health services, housing, recreational facilities) but should also make sure that they are designed to suit the particular needs of the area. We have seen that many of the social services provided in association with the Bougainville mine—such as the layout of Arawa town and the housing for villagers moved out of the mine area—might have been suitable for a mining community in a country like Australia, but were not appropriate in Papua New Guinea.

The second stage of the planning process, which is carried out when the project is in operation, is designed to study the actual social impact of the project. It should examine the positive and negative effects which the project is having on the lives of the people, the adequacy of social services and other facilities, and any particular social problems which may have arisen. If a systematic social study was carried out during the initial planning of the project, it will be possible to compare the two studies and to see whether the problems have occurred because the social aspects of the plan were not implemented properly or because they were not anticipated in the initial study.

This form of social impact evaluation serves two main purposes. Firstly, it may be possible to rectify some of the social problems which have occurred, particularly if they are identified fairly early. Thus, it may be possible to improve social services, establish some sort of community organization which will enable the people's views to be made known more easily, and so on. Secondly, even if it is too late to make any major changes in the present project, the results of the study can be used to assist in planning future projects of a similar nature. For example, by the time that the full social impact of the Bougainville mine was appreciated it was too late to rectify many of the problems which had occurred but, as we have seen, it was not too late to use this information in planning the Ok Tedi mine and in considering whether to establish a second mine in Bougainville.

Who should be responsible for undertaking social impact studies either before or after a project is established? We have indicated that this work should be done by a 'social planner' but, as in Chapter 4, this does not necessarily mean that there must be someone officially designated as a social planner. It means that there should be someone who has an appreciation of the social aspects of development and is primarily concerned with the social rather than the economic implications of the project. This person should if possible have some knowledge of social conditions in the project area and of the type of information required in order to assess the social impact of a project; but, more important, he should have a commitment to the social development of the area and its people. It is no good merely asking an economist engaged in an evaluation of the financial costs and benefits of the project to also 'have a look at the social side', because his main objective will be economic development and he is unlikely to give adequate attention to social factors.

However, while emphasizing the importance of having someone with a full-time commitment to the social aspects of the project, it should also be pointed out that the social planner must not work in isolation. He should work as a member of an interdisciplinary team and should be fully involved throughout the planning stages of the project. The case study of the Mwamapuli Dam in Tanzania demonstrated the need, not for social planning as such, but for an integrated approach to the development of the area, incorporating technical, economic, social, and political factors. If the social planner works in isolation, there is not only a danger that his proposals will be unrelated to the plans for other aspects of the project but also that they will be totally ignored or rejected, particularly if the project is designed primarily to achieve economic objectives. In many projects social impact studies are commissioned during the planning stages in order to satisfy the requirement that social factors be taken into consideration; but little or no notice is taken of the results.

Equally important is the social planner's need to work closely with the local community who will be affected by the project. One of the main lessons which can be learned from the case study of the two tobacco schemes in Zambia is that the people in the area—including local politicians and administrators—must be fully involved in the planning process and, as far as possible, in the actual management of the project, even if this prolongs the planning process and delays the start of the project. We shall look at this aspect of social planning in more depth in Chapters 6 and 7.

Finally, it is necessary to warn that in project planning the social planner may find his work at times difficult and frustrating, especially if he is involved in a large-scale development project which is of major importance to the country's economy. He will find that the economic importance of the project is such that, however hard he tries to convey its social implications and requirements, economic considerations are likely to receive priority. We saw how in Papua New Guinea the social implications of projects like the Bougainville and Ok Tedi mines are so formidable that the social planner may wish to recommend that they should not go ahead at all; and yet they will go ahead and the most that he can hope for is that everything possible will be done to minimize the social problems which will inevitably occur.

However, the social planner should not be too discouraged if he finds himself in such a situation. Whatever the nature of the project there is an important role for social planning, even if it is not always recognized. To quote from a book on the 'cultural appraisal' of development projects, he should remember that:

Development projects are intended to create opportunities for poor people to make a better life for themselves. . . . What is important is not the fact that there may be need for a project, as appreciated by national or international civil servants, but that, through appropriate project design and implementation, people can and will take advantage of the project opportunities offered to permanently change their lives. (Cochrane, 1979, p. 9)

Notes

1. The information in this section is based to a large extent on the author's personal experience in the area. However, some of this information is documented in Conyers (1976), Mamak and Bedford (1974), and West (1972, pp. 109–140).
2. The province was originally known as Bougainville but, at the request of the local people, its name was changed to the North Solomons in 1976, following its attempted secession from the rest of Papua New Guinea.
3. This case study is based on research in which the author was personally involved; for further details, see Bureau of Resource Assessment and Land Use Planning (1970).
4. These two case studies are based mainly on information obtained as part of a research project on administration for rural development, undertaken jointly by the Zambian National Institute of Public Administration, the Free University of Amsterdam, and the University of Zambia in 1971-72 (Kapteyn and Emery, 1972, Annexure on the Tobacco Board). The author also visited the Mulilima scheme briefly in 1980.

Guide to further reading

Most of the literature referred to in this chapter relates to specific projects, rather than to the role of social planning in general. The references given in the case studies indicate the range and form of this type of literature.

For more general material, the reader is referred to the books recommended at the end of Chapter 4, especially *The Cultural Appraisal of Development Projects* by G. Cochrane (New York, Praeger, 1979), which is concerned particularly with project planning. The reader may also like to refer to the reading list at the end of Chapter 9 for material on project evaluation and to an article by M. Hardiman and J. Midgley on 'Foreign consultants and development planning' (*Journal of Administration Overseas*, **17** (1978), 232–244) for discussion of the role of consultants in project planning.

CHAPTER 6

PARTICIPATORY PLANNING: AIMS AND METHODS

In previous chapters many references have been made to the need for popular participation or community involvement in the planning process—in other words, the need for *participatory planning*. In Chapter 3 it was emphasized that local people must be involved in decisions about the type of social services to be provided in their area, and in Chapters 4 and 5 we saw how important it is to take local conditions and attitudes into account when formulating development policies and planning programmes and projects, even if the programmes and projects are primarily economic in nature.

Responsibility for ensuring that local people are adequately involved in the planning process is often placed in the hands of the social planner, because of his concern for the 'human' aspects of development and his interest in people—as individuals and, in particular, as communities or groups. Consequently, in this chapter and in Chapter 7, we look in more detail at the concept and methods of participatory planning. In this chapter we consider why popular participation is important and the various ways in which it can be encouraged, and in Chapter 7 we look in more general terms at the problems which are likely to be encountered in any form of participatory planning.

Why is popular participation so important?

There are very few countries who do not publicly declare the need for popular participation in planning. This is reflected in the common use of terms such as 'bottom-up planning', involvement at the 'grass roots', 'democratic planning', and 'participatory planning'. Myrdal, in a review of 'democratic planning' in southern Asia, points out that:

Even the ruling élites of those South Asian countries that have moved toward a more authoritarian regime are aware that there is little hope of effective planning for development without popular support. . . . The quest for mass involvement is the central tenet of 'democratic planning'. (Myrdal, 1968, p. 851)

This statement is supported by the fact that even in China one of the most popular slogans is 'planning from the top down and the bottom up'. We shall examine the Chinese approach to planning later in this chapter.

It is possible to identify three main reasons why popular participation is considered to be so important. Firstly, it is a means of obtaining information about local conditions, needs, and attitudes, without which development programmes and projects are likely to fail. In the previous chapters we have quoted many examples of such failures: family planning programmes which do not take account of local attitudes towards contraception, the tobacco scheme in Zambia which was planned without any knowledge of the local social and political organization, and so on. The only way in which this sort of information can be obtained is to involve the local people directly in the planning process.

The second reason is that people are more likely to be committed to a development project or programme if they are involved in its planning and preparation, because they are more likely to identify with it and see it as *their* project. It is necessary to have such a commitment in order to ensure that a project will be accepted or adopted, particularly if—as Myrdal says—'it requires a change in the way a great number of people think, feel and act' (Myrdal, 1968, p. 851). And it is also important if one is dependent on local assistance in the construction or maintenance of the project. The many attempts to encourage 'self-help' projects in developing countries have shown that local contributions (in cash or kind) are seldom forthcoming unless the people are really committed to the project and see it as something which they have helped to initiate.

The third reason for encouraging popular participation is that in most countries it is considered to be a basic democratic 'right' that people should be involved in their own development. It is felt that people have a right to some say in determining the sort of development which should take place in their country, and particularly in their own local area. This is in line with the concept of 'man-centred' development—in which development is for the benefit of man rather than man being merely an agent of development—which we have discussed elsewhere.

The notion that development is a basic human right is common in all countries, rich and poor; but it is particularly emphasized in the recently independent nations of the Third World, for whom colonialism was seen as a time in which democratic rights were severely repressed. For example, President Kaunda of Zambia states that: 'Having attained political independence, the people, through their Party, have proclaimed participatory democracy as the only political system that could safeguard it.' And he goes on to describe 'participatory democracy' as 'the type of democracy in which citizens participate not only through their freely elected representatives but also by their own direct involvement in the decision-making process (Kaunda, 1974, pp. 9–10). Having thus accepted the importance of participatory planning, how can such planning be encouraged? In the rest of this chapter we examine five possible ways of obtaining participation in the planning process:

  (i) local consultation and surveys;
 (ii) use of extension staff;
(iii) decentralized planning;
 (iv) local government; and
  (v) community development.

Each method is examined in some depth in the following sections. Then in the final section of the chapter, we draw some tentative conclusions about the relative merits of the various methods.

Local consultation and surveys

One method of obtaining participation in planning is for those involved in designing a particular programme or project to visit the area where it will be located and obtain first-hand information about social conditions in that area by conducting surveys, interviewing the people, holding meetings, and so on.

This method is particularly common when planning specific projects, like those described in Chapter 5. For example, in the case study on copper mining in Papua New Guinea, we saw how there was no proper social survey prior to the construction of the Bougainville mine, but surveys were carried out in the Ok Tedi mine area. It is more difficult to undertake a survey in preparation for a nationwide development programme because the survey would have to cover the whole country, although in some cases adequate information could be obtained by conducting sample surveys in a number of selected areas. Before introducing a family planning programme, for example, it might be worth carrying out surveys in several different parts of the country to ascertain people's attitudes to family planning in general and to specific forms of contraception, unless such information was already available from other sources. Surveys of this nature were conducted in Papua New Guinea during 1981 in connection with a population planning research programme.

In many cases a professional social scientist—such as a sociologist, social anthropologist, social psychologist, or someone with a general social science training—is recruited to undertake such surveys, particularly in the case of larger projects planned by interdisciplinary teams. This is because some training in social survey methods is usually an asset in this type of work. However, on other occasions the survey is done by an administrator or planner with no special social survey training. In Chapter 8, which considers the information required by social planners, we shall look in more detail at the methods which may be employed in such surveys, whether they are carried out by professional social scientists or by general administrators or planners.

This approach has some limitations. In the first place, it usually requires a considerable amount of time and money to carry out thorough surveys, and so this method is often only used in the case of large projects which are planned well in advance and involve a major financial investment. However, this problem can be partially overcome by employing certain 'short-cut' survey methods, which are also discussed in more detail in Chapter 8. For example, it is often possible to obtain adequate information by group interviews or by interviewing community leaders, instead of interviewing individual households.

Another problem is that the type of information obtained from such surveys is not always easily used by those actually planning the project. When the surveys are carried out by professional social scientists, there is a tendency for the information to be too 'academic' in nature or biased towards the research interests of the particular surveyor. For example, it is often very difficult to utilize the information collected by social anthropologists for practical planning purposes because they tend to study the present organization of societies rather than the type of change which is likely to occur as a result of some proposed development activity in the area. On the other hand, surveys carried out by people with no specific social science training tend to be more practical, but the information is sometimes less accurate. For example, information may be based on a few random interviews rather than a systematic sample survey, questionnaires may be badly designed so that information is unreliable or ambiguous, and so on. The need is for some sort of compromise which combines the professional training of the social scientist with the pragmatic approach of the general planner or administrator. We shall return to this issue, too, in Chapter 8.

A third limitation is that because such surveys are conducted by 'outsiders', the information obtained is not always entirely accurate, particularly in the case of information about people's feelings and attitudes towards proposed new developments. This is because there is a 'communication gap' between those conducting the surveys and those being surveyed, due often to language or cultural differences, the limited time spent in the area, or a tendency for those being interviewed to give the sort of information which the interviewers would like to hear rather than the true information. In an interesting study of the reasons for the failure of a family planning programme in India, Mamdani describes how the people expressed support for the programme and even willingly accepted supplies of contraceptives in order not to upset the organizers—but had no intention of ever using them (Mamdani, 1972). Even an anthropologist, who usually spends long periods of time in an area and tries to assimilate himself into the community, does not always obtain accurate information, although this may not be discovered until some time later when his findings are disputed by another anthropologist or by someone from the area.

The last, and in some respects most serious, limitation is that the people are still not fully involved in the planning process. They are given the opportunity to provide information and to express their opinions, but in most cases they do not feel as if they are being directly involved. Consequently, this method of survey and consultation does not necessarily result in a real commitment to the project from the local people nor does it represent genuine 'participatory democracy' in the sense intended by President Kaunda. Obviously a great deal depends on the way in which the survey is conducted. A carefully planned survey—in which plenty of time is spent explaining the purpose of the project, discussing its advantages and disadvantages with community leaders, attending group meetings to ascertain people's opinions, and so on—can result in a considerable degree of involvement and commitment; while a poorly conducted survey can actually encourage local antagonism and resistance. On the whole, however, this method—although important as a means of obtaining information required in planning—is not usually very successful as a means of obtaining effective community involvement.

Using extension staff as a means of participation

In most developing countries many government departments or ministries have field staff whose primary role is to provide a link between those making decisions about government policies, programmes, and projects and the local people who are actually affected by these activities. Some of these extension staff are technical officers attached to a specialist department, such as agriculture, health, or education. Others, such as community development officers or (where they have continued to exist after independence) general district administration staff, are intended to perform a more general-purpose role. In either case, they are supposed to channel information both 'up' and 'down'. In other words, they are supposed to communicate information about local needs and conditions to regional or national authorities and to communicate information about national development policies and programmes to the people.

Because of their role as a link between local communities and regional or national authorities, extension staff can be used as a means of achieving popular participation in planning. They can provide information about the type of development projects needed in the area, they can help to assess the likely impact of particular projects or the problems which may occur, and they can explain to the people why a project is being introduced, what form it will take, and how they can benefit from it. They are particularly useful in the case of projects which are planned and implemented by a single department or ministry. For example, it is obviously sensible for an agricultural ministry to involve its extension officers in the planning of a new agricultural project or for the ministry of health to consult local medical staff about the health needs of a particular area.

The main advantage of involving extension staff in the planning process is that they are already in the area and so they have already established links with the local community and gathered a considerable amount of information about local conditions and needs. Consequently, it is a much more economical—and in some respects also more efficient—method of communication than conducting special surveys. However, it also has its drawbacks.

In the first place, most government agencies are not organized in a way which facilitates this sort of communication between field staff and their superiors at regional or national level. In spite of intentions to the contrary, communication is often seriously inadequate, confined to the issuing of orders or instructions from headquarters to the field and the submission of regular reports on routine matters in the opposite direction. This sort of formal hierarchical communication does not encourage the type of information flow which is needed to ensure effective local participation in planning. Extension staff frequently complain that new programmes or projects are imposed upon them with little or no warning, let alone consultation, and if they try to initiate projects in their area at the request of the people, they receive very little support from their superiors and their efforts are often bogged down by bureaucratic 'red tape'.

Furthermore, as already indicated, the problem of communication is increased when more than one government agency is involved in the planning process. In such cases it is difficult enough to get the different agencies to coordinate their plans at national or regional level, let alone involve the various extension staff of each agency. Some countries have attempted to overcome this problem by having multipurpose extension staff—such as India's village level workers—who act as agents for all government departments at the village level. We shall return to this later in the chapter, since it is closely related to concepts of community development.

Another series of problems can be attributed to the nature of the extension workers themselves. Many extension staff are not trained either to communicate effectively with local communities or to collect the sort of information which is needed for planning purposes. For example, a typical agricultural extension officer will know how to grow maize or coffee, or whatever other agricultural skills are relevant in the area, but he will have no idea how to carry out a social survey and in many cases little knowledge of how to communicate with the people among whom he is working. This situation is often exacerbated by the fact that the extension officer comes from another part of the country and is frequently transferred from one place to another so that he does not get to know any area very well. In many cases, he may not even be able to speak the local language. As a result he tends to look upon himself as an outsider and to be regarded as such by the local community.

For all these reasons the information provided by extension workers may not be much more relevant or accurate than that obtained from special surveys. Fortunately, however, these deficiencies are now recognized in many countries and efforts are being made to improve the quality of extension staff. More consideration is being given to the qualities required in an extension worker and to the importance of him being posted to an area for a reasonable length of time and living in a manner which will encourage his acceptance into the community. Similarly, training programmes now aim to equip the staff with skills as extension workers as well as technical expertise.

The final drawback associated with the use of extension staff is that, as in the case of specialized surveys, the people tend not to be directly involved in the planning process. The degree of involvement again depends very much on the quality of the extension staff. An extension officer who is properly trained in extension methods and lives and works in a way that enables him to be fully accepted by the community, may be able to encourage genuine involvement, in the sense that people identify with the development activities in the area and feel that they are fully involved in their planning and implementation. But too often the extension officer does no more than collect information from the people and pass information to them, thereby involving them no more than if he were an 'outsider' come to do a brief survey of the area.

Decentralized planning

So far we have been looking at ways in which planners at the national level can involve the local people in the preparation of their plans. In this section we go one step further and consider attempts to actually prepare plans at the local level.

For the time being we shall use the expression 'local level' rather generally to refer to any level below the national level—region, province, district, ward, community, or whatever; however, at the end of the section we shall make some comments about the effectiveness of different levels of subnational planning. We have also chosen to use the terms 'decentralized planning' or 'local level planning' rather than, for example, 'regional planning' or 'district planning'. This is partly to avoid any confusion due to the fact that words such as 'region' and 'district' mean different things in different countries, and partly because the term 'regional planning', in particular, tends to imply more than just local participation in planning; it suggests a particular planning methodology with which we do not need to concern ourselves here.

There are two main ways in which planning may be carried out at the local level. One way is to have representatives of a national planning agency based at this level to do the planning. The other way is to establish local planning bodies, composed of local officials and/or elected representatives, which are responsible for the preparation of plans for their area. In either case, the preparation of local plans may form an integral part of a national planning exercise or may be carried out more or less independently. If local planning is done by representatives of the national planning agency, it is more likely to be integrated into the national planning process and to adopt a more 'professional' approach. However, plans prepared by local planning bodies tend to be more relevant to local needs and implementable with the resources available in the area. In many countries a combination of both approaches is adopted, with planning carried out by both local bodies and representatives of the national planning agency.

Local level planning is more likely to be effective if there is also some decentralization of plan implementation. If plans are merely prepared at the local level and then forwarded to the national level, where they are incorporated into a national plan and implemented through ministerial or departmental headquarters, those involved in planning at the local level are unlikely to feel a great deal of genuine involvement in, or commitment to, the plans. In fact, they may regard the process of plan preparation as a pointless, time-consuming exercise which has to be done merely to satisfy the demands of the national government.

However, if people at the local level are fully involved in the implementation of the plans—and particularly if they have some direct control over the allocation of financial and other resources within the area—they are much more likely to be committed to the plans and so to ensure that they are relevant and implementable. A significant number of countries have begun to realize the importance of decentralized planning and administration as a means of encouraging local participation and improving the quality of plan preparation and implementation; and some—including Tanzania, Zambia, Papua New Guinea, and the Solomon Islands—have recently undergone major administrative decentralization programmes with these ends in mind (Conyers, 1981a).

As with other ways of obtaining local participation, the decentralization of planning has some limitations. The most obvious one is probably the lack of adequate planning capacity at the local level. In many countries the national planning agency does not have enough staff to have representatives permanently based at the local level, while government staff already working at this level seldom have the necessary training, experience, or—most important—time to devote much attention to planning. Consequently, many countries find that although they would like to decentralize planning, they do not have the capacity to do so. Zambia, for example, announced in the Second National Development Plan, which covered the period from 1972 to 1976, its intention to establish provincial planning offices. The intention was reiterated in the Third Plan, which began in 1979, but by the end of 1980 there were still no provincial planning offices because of the difficulty of finding suitable staff (Zambia, 1971, 1979).*

Another problem is that of integrating local planning into the national planning process. There is a tendency for local plans either to be submerged within a national plan and so be ineffective as instruments of local development, or to be more or less autonomous and so run the risk of being in conflict with national aims and objectives.

The third problem—and from our point of view perhaps the most serious—is that, even when planning is decentralized, the ordinary people at community or village level are more often than not still not directly involved in the planning process. Planning is done by local officials, or in some cases locally elected representatives, and although these people are more likely to be familiar with local conditions and to consult the people than their counterparts at the national level, the ordinary villager—or urban resident—is not usually directly involved.

It is at this point that we need to distinguish between different levels of decentralized planning because the degree of effective participation obviously depends on the level to which planning is actually decentralized. Thus, if planning is only decentralized to provinces or regions with populations of—perhaps—a million or more, it will obviously be much less effective as a means of popular participation than if it is decentralized to local communities of a few thousand people. However, the further planning is decentralized, the more difficult it becomes to find adequate planning staff and to integrate local and national planning efforts.

Before leaving this topic let us look briefly at the Chinese approach to planning, since China is one of the few countries which seems to have evolved a system of decentralized planning which extends right down to the 'grass roots' level and yet is fully integrated into a national planning framework (Conyers, 1977; Robinson, 1975). As we have already indicated, this approach is aptly described by the Chinese as planning 'from the top down and from the bottom up'.

Planning in China is a formidable task since China is a vast country with over 800 million people. The country is divided into 29 main administrative units

---

* The first provincial planning offices were eventually established during 1981.

(provinces, municipalities, and autonomous regions) and each of these is subdivided into a series of smaller units which extend right down to the level of the *production team* in rural areas and the *street* in urban areas (Figure 4). Communication between these levels is maintained by a hierarchy of *revolutionary committees*, under the close supervision of the Chinese Communist Party and the planning process utilizes these communication channels.

The way in which planning takes place can best be explained by describing the process of agricultural planning, which takes place every year. The first stage in the process is for every level in the hierarchy, from production team upwards, to submit to the level above an estimate of the amount of produce it expects to produce in the forthcoming year and the proportion of this which will be available for sale to the state. These estimates eventually reach the provincial level and then the national level, where they are reconciled with those for other provinces and with estimates of national demand. The revised estimates then become production targets, which are passed down again through the hierarchy, each level setting targets for the level immediately below. Thus, a province will set targets for all the administrative areas within its boundaries, an area will set targets for all its component counties, a county for all its communes, and so on. Having received its production target from the level above, it is up to each administrative unit to decide the best way of achieving this target. Other activities are planned in a similar way, the basic principle being that broad goals or targets are set at the upper levels in the hierarchy, but the details of implementation are worked out by the production units themselves.

Although the Chinese approach provides an interesting case study, there are of course limits to the extent to which it can be used as a model elsewhere. The most obvious limitation is the fact that its success is dependent on a highly coordinated and politicized organizational structure, which few other countries can hope to attain. The other major reservation is that, although there is a remarkably high degree of genuine 'grass roots' participation in the Chinese planning system, there are at the same time restrictions on individual liberties which would not be acceptable in many Third World nations, where so much importance is attached to 'democracy'. The changes which have been occurring in China since the death of Mao Tse-tung and the overthrow of the 'Gang of Four', suggest that the present Chinese administration is relaxing some of these restrictions, and it will be interesting to see what effect this has on the planning system.

Nevertheless, there are two very important lessons that can be learned from the Chinese experience and applied elsewhere. One is the need to establish an effective organizational structure which enables communication to take place between the village (or 'street') level and the national level through a hierarchy of intermediate planning levels. The other is the art of decentralizing some decision-making powers right down to the village level, so that people feel that they are really involved, while at the same time retaining central control over matters of national importance and regional control over matters of regional importance.

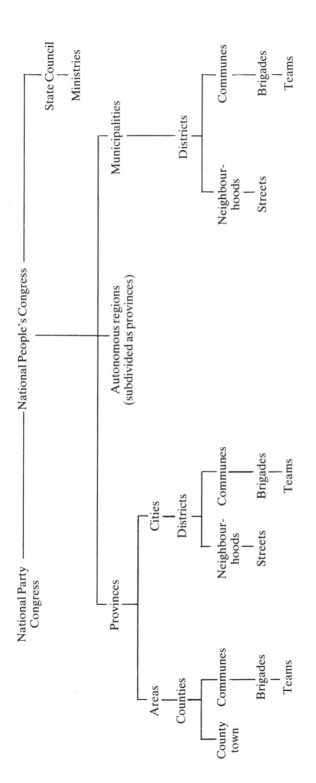

Figure 4 China's organizational structure. *Source:* Conyers, 1977, p. 100. Reproduced by permission of the Controller of HMSO

Local government

It is not possible to draw a clear distinction between decentralized planning and local government. In fact, it would be more accurate to describe the planning carried out by local governments as a form of decentralized planning. However, local government involves much more than just decentralized planning and is thus an important topic in its own right.

Some form of local government was introduced in most former colonial territories of the Third World by the colonial administration. The motives for its introduction were varied and the desire for local participation was only one of these, and often not the most important. The two most important motives were probably the need to remove some of the burden of providing—and financing—local services from the national government and the desire to 'educate' the people in the basic principles of western-style democracy. Ursula Hicks, in a study of local government in the British colonies, explains that:

It had long been recognised that local government has a value as an 'education' for democracy. It is educative for the electors, who are called upon to do their voting in relation to issues that are really comprehensible to them; and for the councillors, who can gain experience in the art of responsible leadership, without being confronted (before they have gained experience) with issues that at that stage may be beyond their grasp. (Hicks, 1961, p. 4)

The importance of local government as a means of encouraging local participation in development was recognized by the colonial authorities, but only within limited terms. This was partly because the concept of development—as opposed to merely administration—was hardly in existence at that time, and partly because local participation was only acceptable if it did not conflict with the policy of the colonial administration. In other words, local participation was desirable to the extent that it encouraged acceptance of, and conformity with, the colonial regime, but not as a means of developing initiative and independent thought at the local level.

The form which local government actually took varied from country to country; but there was a general tendency for the colonial authorities to try to reproduce as far as possible the type of local government already established in their own countries. This created a number of problems because of the very different conditions in the developing countries. Two main problems may be identified. One was the difficulty of establishing an economically viable system of local government in predominantly rural areas with a scattered population and very low income. Consequently, most rural local government bodies remained highly dependent on the national government for both finance and expertise. The other problem was the difference between western concepts of democracy, on which the local government systems were based, and traditional systems of decision-making. In many areas local government tended to be regarded by the people as yet another alien imposition of the colonial administration rather than as a means by which they could participate meaningfully in their own development.

There have been considerable changes in local government in most former colonies since independence. These changes have been introduced partly in order to overcome the problems of the colonial system identified above, and partly in an effort to adapt local government to the very different objectives of an independent government. It is difficult to generalize about the nature of these changes since each country has attempted to develop a system to meet its particular needs and circumstances. Consequently, there is more variety than there was during the colonial period. A brief look at three different models will illustrate the range of local government forms which now exist and the way in which they have been evolved to suit the local political and social environment.

In several countries of the South Pacific, including Papua New Guinea, the Solomon Islands, and Vanuatu (formerly the New Hebrides), political independence has been accompanied by the strengthening of conventional local government bodies. In Papua New Guinea, for example, a new tier of provincial level governments was established in 1976 and the powers decentralized to these new governments were so great that the present system of government in Papua New Guinea bears considerable resemblance to a federal system (Conyers, 1981b). These moves can be attributed partly to the absence of a very strong national government (Papua New Guinea, for example, has had two rather loose coalition governments since independence) and partly to a strong sense of identity among local community groups. The latter has resulted not only in demands for greater autonomy from such groups but also a remarkable acceptance on the part of the national governments that some degree of autonomy—although not complete secession—is not only politically necessary but also socially desirable. In this respect, the South Pacific nations tend to differ from many other Third World countries which have tended to combat tribalism or regionalism by increasing central control.

In contrast to the countries of the South Pacific, many independent nations, particularly those which have adopted a one-party system of government, have tended to centralize political control and this has resulted in a reduction in the powers of local governments. In some cases, such as Kenya (Mulasa, 1970), elected local government bodies have been maintained, but their powers have been gradually reduced. But in others, such as Tanzania and more recently Zambia (Conyers, 1981a), elected local governments have been replaced by local committees or councils composed mainly of national government or party officials. These moves can be explained in terms of the need to strengthen national unity and implement national development policies, and to make the most efficient use of scarce resources such as finance and manpower. Whether or not the new local level organizations can strictly be called 'local governments' is somewhat dubious; but since they have been given an important role as local planning bodies, we may regard them as such for the purpose of this discussion.

The third model of local government which we shall consider briefly here is that found in socialist states, where a local government body is not only a local political and administrative unit but also a unit of economic production. In China, for example, the commune—which is recognized as the basic local government unit—not only controls the government and administration of the area and provides basic services but also owns all resources (natural and man-made) and controls all economic activity. Thus, in some respects the Chinese commune may be regarded as one of the most effective forms of local government, particularly in terms of the way in which it facilitates community participation in the planning process. However, because it is—as we saw in the previous section—only one link in a complex political and administrative hierarchy under tight national control, it is hardly a local government body in the conventional western sense. We have included it as a form of local government here because the Chinese themselves make a point of distinguishing between the commune, which belongs to 'the people', and other units higher up the political and administrative hierarchy, which are regarded as organs of 'the state'. In other words, the commune is the Chinese equivalent of a local government body and its role in the planning process is that of a local government organization.

Although the changes which have taken place in local government vary so much from one country to another, it is probably true to say that in most countries there has been an attempt to make local government more effective as a means of encouraging popular participation in local development. This has resulted in more emphasis on community or village level government, sometimes (as we shall see in the next section) as part of an integrated community development programme, and in efforts to merge local government with traditional decision-making institutions, so that it is more meaningful to the people. Thus, even in countries like Tanzania and Zambia, where elected local governments have been replaced by less representative bodies, a great deal of emphasis is placed on the development of effective political institutions at the village level.

Because of the many different forms of local government which now exist, it is very difficult to generalize about its value as a means of obtaining popular participation in planning. In many respects local governments should, at least in theory, be more effective than the other forms of participation which we have considered in this chapter because local people are more directly involved. However, in practice this is not always the case.

In the first place, local governments are not always very effective planning bodies. They frequently suffer from inadequate staff and financial resources and so do not have the capacity to either plan or implement effective development programmes. Moreover, there is a tendency for their members to become bogged down in very parochial matters rather than consider broader issues related to the future development of their area. Consequently, many local governments do little more than provide very basic services and act as a forum for the discussion of local political issues.

Secondly, there is the question of whether local government bodies do, in fact, really involve the local people very effectively. A great deal depends on the size of the local government. As a general rule, the smaller the area and population it covers, the more likely it is to provide an effective means of participation and this explains why many countries have put more emphasis on village or community level government since independence. However, this often creates a dilemma for the planners, since smaller local governments are less likely to be economically viable and so to have the resources needed to become effective planning bodies.

Equally important is the quality and status of the local government members. Many are not adequate representatives of the people in their electorates, either because of the way in which they were selected or because of their conduct while in office. The question of whether members of local governments should be selected directly by the people or, as is now the practice in many countries, by some system of indirect elections or selection through a national party organization is obviously a major issue in the reform of local government. However, it is probably much less important than many people—especially critical observers in the western world—suggest, at least in terms of its effect on popular participation. What is much more important is that the people who are elected are accepted and trusted by the people in their electorates and that, once they are in office, they make every effort to represent the interests of their electorates honestly and unselfishly.

The other problem associated with local governments is that, even if they do succeed in becoming effective planning bodies and in really involving the people of their own area, there is the question of how local government planning will be integrated with national government policy and planning. In fact, the more effective they are as planning bodies, the more risk there is that local interests will conflict with national interests and thus hamper national development efforts. This is a very real danger in countries like Papua New Guinea and it explains why many countries have tended to reduce the powers of local governments or alter their membership by including national government or party representatives who will ensure that national policies are followed.

Community development

There are numerous different interpretations and definitions of the term 'community development'. One writer has pointed out that if the term was used in its most literal and general sense to refer to any effort to improve the quality of life of a community, 'there would probably be as many different ideas on community development as there are communities' (Jones, 1980, p. 1).

However, the term is normally used in a somewhat narrower sense to imply the input of an external stimulus into a community in order to encourage and assist in the use of local resources to improve the standard of life. In 1955 the United Nations adopted a definition of community development which has been widely quoted and used as a basis for planning and evaluating many community development programmes. According to the United Nations:

The term community development has come into international usage to connote the processes by which the efforts of the people themselves are united with those of governmental authorities to improve the economic, social and cultural conditions of communities, to integrate these communities into the life of the nation, and to enable them to contribute fully to national progress.

This complex of processes is then made up of two essential elements: the participation by the people themselves in efforts to improve their level of living with as much reliance as possible on their own initiative; and the provision of technical and other services in ways which encourage initiative, self-help and mutual help and make these more effective. (Reported in United Nations, 1971, p. 2)

There has been considerable criticism of the United Nations definition of community development. Much of this criticism arises from the fact that it was adopted many years ago, when most community development programmes were organized by colonial governments. The definition thus reflects the rather patronizing relationship between the local community and the outside agency providing support and assistance which was typical of many community development programmes at that time. Since achieving political independence, most countries have modified the colonial approach to community development or established entirely new programmes designed to meet their particular needs. This has resulted not only in some deviation from the United Nations concept but also in the existence of a much wider range of approaches to community development.

Nevertheless, the United Nations definition is still useful as an indication of the concept and scope of community development. From this definition it is apparent that community development is much more than just a method of obtaining popular participation in planning. The United Nations regards it primarily as a *process of development*, but points out that:

It is also a *method* or approach that emphasises popular participation and the direct involvement of a population in the process of development. . . . [And] when community development activity is formally organized with a separate administration and staff it can be considered a *programme*. Finally, to the extent that it represents a philosophy of development, sometimes with an almost religious fervour it can be called a *movement*. (United Nations, 1971, p. 9)

Since our main concern in this chapter is with participatory planning, it is not possible or necessary to discuss all aspects of community development. Consequently, we shall merely indicate the main characteristics of this approach to development and look briefly at different types of community development programme, considering in particular their value as a means of increasing participation in planning. The social planner who finds himself responsible for encouraging, organizing, or evaluating any form of community development activity is referred to the guide to further reading on this topic, which will be found at the end of Chapter 7.

Community development involves a wide variety of activities designed to raise the standard of living and improve the quality of life in the community. The range of activities which may be included is almost unlimited. However, activities which feature in many community development programmes include literacy and adult education programmes, the provision of basic services such as housing, water supply, and health care in the community, the encouragement of sport and other recreational activities, the formation of local organizations—such as clubs and committees, and the promotion of small-scale industries, crafts, or commercial activities. Many programmes also have components directed specifically towards the less privileged or most vulnerable sectors of the community, such as women, young children, school-leavers, or the urban poor; and some programmes tend to concentrate on communities where the potential for more conventional economic development is somewhat limited or where particular development problems exist.

The choice of activities and the way in which they are carried out reflect the particular method or approach to development which is implicit in the concept of community development. One component of this approach is the emphasis placed on the use of self-help, including local resources and labour and local organizational or managerial ability. For example, in the provision of basic services there is usually a significant input of local materials and labour and in the promotion of commercial enterprises effort is concentrated on activities which utilize local resources and require a minimum of outside assistance in the form of finance and technical or managerial skills. And in all activities it is intended that the community itself should play a major role in initiating, planning, and organizing them.

Another component of a community development approach is the emphasis on strengthening the community as an entity. This is reflected in the establishment of local organizations—including committees or councils responsible for the administration or government of the community and organizations such as clubs, which perform a social function— and in the encouragement of sport and other recreational activities on a community basis. It is also related to the concept of self-help, in the sense that the use of local resources and in particular the fact that activities are initiated and organized by the community itself, help to strengthen the community as a viable entity.

A third component is the general concern with the nature and direction of social change and the problems which arise from it. For instance, community development activities in urban areas are preoccupied with the problems created by rapid urbanization; while in both rural and urban areas considerable effort is devoted to the problems of unemployed school-leavers.

A specific aspect of social change which is of particular concern in many community development programmes is that of inequality within and between communities. This is reflected in the fact that community development tends to be more active in less priviliged communities, such as rural areas with few obvious opportunities for economic development and the low-income settlements or townships in urban areas. It is also reflected in the concern for disadvantaged groups within the community, such as women, landless labourers in rural areas, or the unemployed in the cities.

The relationship between community development and social change raises some questions about the United Nations' assumption that one of the aims of community development should be 'to integrate these communities into the life of the nation' (United Nations, 1971, p. 2). This assumption is feasible in a nation without major inequalities, or one which is attempting to reduce inequalities; but in societies which are fraught with socio-economic inequality and injustice, community development may have to adopt a more radical approach, especially if the inequality and injustice is condoned by the government in power. We shall see below that in some countries community development is regarded—at least by some—as a tool for achieving, or consolidating, major socio-economic and political reforms.

So far we have focused on the type of activities undertaken as part of community development programmes and the role of the community itself in planning and implementing these activities. However, as the United Nations definition quoted earlier suggests, community development normally also involves some form of outside input into the community. This may be provided by a government organization or by a voluntary agency or other private body. In either case the input is generally provided through some sort of cadre of *community development workers*. Community development workers are extension staff who, unlike most other extension workers, are not trained in any specific technical skills but in general extension techniques, including an ability to relate to the community in which they are working and to stimulate local initiative. In fact, they are trained in those skills which we noted earlier in the chapter are lacking in most extension workers.

In theory, the outside input in community development programmes is designed to encourage and stimulate local initiative and enterprise and to assist in obtaining any technical, financial, or other help which the community may require. As indicated earlier, the main initiative and effort is supposed to come from the community itself. It is in this respect that community development work differs significantly—at least in theory—from the work of most other government and non-government agencies at the local level.

In practice, however, this is not always the case. The degree and form of outside input varies greatly from one community development programme to another; but there is often a tendency for the community development worker to play too dominant a role, taking the initiative himself rather than waiting for the community to do so, imposing his own ideas—and ideology—on the people and dictating to them instead of merely encouraging and assisting.

This problem results, at least in part, from a basic dilemma which faces all community development workers and is, in fact, inherent in the concept of community development. An essential component of the concept is that the main initiative and effort should come from the community itself; but at the same time it is usually assumed that there will be some sort of external input. These two components of the concept are in a sense contradictory. The aim, of course, is to strike a balance so that outside assistance complements local initiative; but in practice this is not easy to achieve.

There have been many attempts to classify community development programmes into different types according to such criteria as their areal coverage, organization, and scope. Such classifications tend to become very complex— and therefore of limited value—because of the many varieties of community development activity. However, it is perhaps useful for our purposes in this chapter to distinguish between three main types of community development programme.

One type of programme is that administered by a national ministry or department responsible specifically for community development. The department employs professional community development workers who are responsible for encouraging and assisting local community activities throughout the country. This approach is common in many countries, except in Latin America—where it is more common to encourage all extension agencies to adopt a community development approach than to create a special department.

In most countries this form of community development appears to encounter two main problems. One problem is lack of resources, particularly staff. To be effective it is necessary to employ large numbers of extension staff—at least one for each area which is regarded as a community—and in most countries community development is not considered sufficiently important to warrant such a large allocation of resources. The other problem is confusion about what community development work should actually involve and, in particular, the division of responsibility between the community development department and other government agencies. Because community development involves such a wide range of activities, there is often considerable overlap between community development workers and other more technical extension staff. Moreover, in many countries there is also some confusion between community development and social welfare work, due to a great extent to the fact that community development has often emerged out of more conventional social welfare activities; the two activities are frequently found within the same ministerial portfolio.

Nevertheless, this form of community development activity can be utilized by the planner as a means of encouraging participation in planning. Community development workers are often more useful than other extension staff as sources of information about local needs and attitudes because of their particular professional training, and they can also help to mobilize communities to play a more active role in planning and implementing their own development programmes.

The second type of community development activity involves special projects which cover limited geographic areas. These projects tend to be broader in scope than the normal work of a community development department, and sometimes they provide a focus for integrating all aspects of development in the area. They may be initiated to meet a particular need or problem in the area, in response to a demand from the local community or merely because of the initiative of a particularly enterprising individual or organization in the area.

The outside input may be provided by private or voluntary agencies or by national or local government bodies. The amount of outside assistance is often greater than in other forms of community development activity, and such projects often attract foreign aid. However, there are a few projects which are initiated entirely within the community and receive little or no outside assistance.

In some cases, these may be semi-political movements, set up to try to bring about social and political change at the local or national level.

There are so many different types of project in this general category that it is very difficult to draw any significant conclusions about this approach to community development. However, in terms of participatory planning, where such projects are established and operating fairly successfully they may provide a useful base for planning and implementing local development programmes, particularly those which require an integrated approach rather than merely the involvement of one sector. Their main limitation is the fact that they are confined to a few areas and so cannot provide a basis for participatory planning on a nationwide scale. In most cases such projects could not easily be reproduced throughout the country, either because of the amount of resources involved or because they are dependent on the initiative of particular individuals or organizations which exist only in that area.

A few countries have, however, tried to establish this approach to community development on a nationwide basis, and these attempts constitute our third category of community development activity. The best-known example of this approach is the Indian community development programme, which was launched in the 1950s. The basic aim of the programme is to unite the efforts of all government agencies with those of the people to bring about development at the village level. This is attempted by establishing local councils (known as *panchayat*), supported by teams of technical officers and multipurpose community development officers known as *village level workers*. In other words, the community development programme is really a combination of decentralized administration, local government, and the use of trained community development workers.

Many criticisms have been levelled against the Indian community development programme, including its failure to increase production at village level and—more important in terms of social planning—the limited amount of genuine involvement by the majority of the population and the fact that it has done little or nothing to reduce the gross social and economic inequalities in India's villages. The last is perhaps the most serious criticism, since it means that community development has not succeeded in mobilizing the mass of the population to improve their economic and social well-being. However, does this mean that the whole approach to community development adopted in India is inappropriate—or that community development by itself is not enough to overcome the fundamental problems of Indian society?

The Chinese experience provides an interesting contrast to that of India. Although China does not have any programme officially known as 'community development', its whole approach to development—in which local communities (officially demarcated as communes, brigades, and teams in the rural areas and their equivalents in the towns) mobilize themselves, with outside assistance when necessary, to improve their own standard of living and to contribute to the development of the nation as a whole—might well be regarded as community development. Moreover, as in India, it also involves decentralized administration and planning and a form of local government.

However, in China—unlike India—a community development approach has been introduced following a political, social, and economic revolution and has, in fact, been used as a means of consolidating the impact of the revolution. Consequently, although reports issued by the Chinese authorities since the overthrow of the 'Gang of Four' suggest that achievements may not have been as great as we were previously led to believe, there appears to be little doubt that this approach to local level development has helped to improve the standard of living of the majority of the population. In this respect, the Chinese example is probably one of the more encouraging examples of a community development programme, particularly from a planner's point of view. However, its value as a model for other countries is of course limited by the fact that it is dependent on the existence of a political system which is unlikely to be reproduced in many other Third World nations, including India—either because it is impossible to achieve or because it is considered undesirable by those people with any influence over the political system.

Conclusion

This chapter began by explaining the importance of participatory planning and pointing out that the social planner is often specifically responsible for finding ways of increasing participation in the planning process. What conclusions can we now draw about the alternative ways in which he (or she) might try to do this?

There is no easy answer to this question, since a great deal will depend on the political and administrative structure in which the planner is operating and the resources available. Thus, the various methods of encouraging participation which we have examined in this chapter cannot really be regarded as alternatives. Each method has its advantages and disadvantages, and no one method is likely to be appropriate in all countries or in all situations within any one country.

Nevertheless, our brief review of these methods of achieving participation does suggest that community development offers a number of advantages over the other methods, particularly if a comprehensive nationwide approach to community development—such as that attempted in India and China—can be successfully established. This type of community development programme includes many elements of the other methods, including the use of extension workers, the decentralization of administration and planning, and the formation of local level governments, so that it might more aptly be described as a combination of the others rather than as an alternative. And it provides a much greater opportunity for people to be really involved in both the planning and implementation of local development programmes, rather than merely being consulted about them.

However, establishing an effective nationwide community development programme is an extremely complex and dificult task, which very few—if any—countries have so far succeeded in doing. Consequently, many social planners may have to look for other methods of achieving participation, at least in the short run. Nevertheless, our survey of alternative methods suggests that any form of participatory planning is fraught with problems. These problems are so great that it is necessary to examine them more systematically and consider their implications for the nature of planning and the role of the social planner. This is the subject of Chapter 7.

Guide to further reading

A guide to further reading on all aspects of participatory planning is given at the end of Chapter 7.

CHAPTER 7

PROBLEMS IN PARTICIPATORY PLANNING

In Chapter 6 we looked at the reasons why so many countries are concerned about participatory planning and at the various ways in which popular participation can be encouraged and we concluded that, although participation is highly desirable for a variety of reasons, there is no easy way of achieving it This chapter examines in more general terms the problems of achieving such participation by any method and considers their implications for the social planner in his role as an advocate of participatory planning.

Do the people really want to be involved?

In Chapter 6 we examined in some depth the various reasons why popular participation is considered desirable, including the fact that it is regarded by many political leaders as a basic democratic right. But we avoided the fundamental question of whether or not the people themselves actually want to be involved in planning.

This is not an easy question to answer. On the one hand, if one were simply to ask the people in an area whether they wanted to be involved in decisions about the development of the area, they would probably say that they would. Similarly, one often hears complaints from local communities that decisions were forced upon them by the authorities or that they were not consulted in planning a local development programme. But, on the other hand, there is also considerable evidence to suggest that on many occasions people do not participate actively in local planning if given the opportunity to do so. For example, one often hears that a meeting held to discuss a proposed project was poorly attended, a community organization set up to make decisions about local development has collapsed through lack of support, or the turnout at local government elections was very poor. In many countries the cynics also complain that local government councillors only attend meetings because they receive a salary for doing so. It should, incidentally, be pointed out that these problems are not unique to the Third World. The apparent apathy and lack of interest in local affairs among the citizens of developed countries is a constant source of frustration for planners, politicians, and community leaders.

Studies of successes and failures in community participation suggest that two factors are particularly important in determining whether or not people really do want to be involved in planning. One factor is the likely outcome of their involvement. It is fairly obvious that people are unlikely to participate willingly or enthusiastically in a planning exercise if they feel that their participation will have no significant effect on the final plans. We shall return to this issue a little later when we consider the problems of meeting local expectations.

The other factor is that, again fairly obviously, people are reluctant to participate in activities in which they have no particular interest or which are unlikely to affect them directly. For example, one of the apparent reasons for the lack of support for local governments in many countries is that a large proportion of the matters discussed in local government meetings are of only marginal concern to most of the members—or to the people in their electorates. Part of the problem is, of course, that people are sometimes not aware that a proposed development project or programme will affect them until it is too late. How, for example, can the Papua New Guinea government convince the people in the remote Ok Tedi area that their lives will be completely transformed by the forthcoming copper mine until the project is already under way, by which time it will be too late for them to play an active part in its planning?

Nevertheless, this evidence does suggest that people are more likely to participate voluntarily if planning is decentralized as far as possible, but confined to activities with which people are directly concerned. Unfortunately, this sometimes causes frustration among planners and administrators, who feel that the people are 'wasting their time' discussing trivial matters while much more important issues are ignored. This problem arose in the Eastern Highlands Province of Papua New Guinea, where a new form of community level government was established during the 1970s (Conyers and Simpson, 1978). Provincial and national authorities were disappointed because the community governments seemed to take very little interest in development activities such as agricultural improvement, roads, or schools. They spent most of their time—and money—on small-scale commercial enterprises (many of which never became economically viable) and on resolving local disputes. However, for the people in the area these were the most important issues and so, in their eyes, the community governments were relatively successful institutions. In effect, this means that planners and administrators have to adjust their attitudes about what is and is not important—but is that not what local participation should be all about?

Do the people know what they want?

The above example from the Eastern Highlands of Papua New Guinea also illustrates another problem faced by planners. This is the question of whether people really know what they want—or to put it in a slightly different way, whether they 'know what is good for them'. Planners often complain that when they ask local people what sort of development they would like to see in the area, their answers are of little value. For example, sometimes they ask for the impossible (such as large-scale industrial employment in a rural area or a high school in every village), sometimes they merely repeat a long list of 'conventional' development projects (schools, roads, health centres, and so on) which they have been told by the authorities that they *should* want, and sometimes they say that they do not want anything to change.

There is a genuine problem here in that the average citizen in a developing country—particularly in the rural areas—has very little idea of the range of options open to him or of the implications of these various options. Consequently, it is not surprising that he will often ask for the impossible or for what others have told him he should want. It is also natural that, because of a very understandable fear of the unknown, he may say that he wants things to stay as they are, particularly if there is any form of risk attached to a proposed new development. There is therefore some truth in the statement sometimes made by planners that they know what is good for the people better than they do themselves.

However, it is also partly a question of the approach and attitude adopted by the planners. Thus, if the planners take time to educate the people about the alternative forms of development available to them, they are more likely to obtain reasonable answers to their questions. But this takes a great deal of time, patience, and understanding on the part of the planners, or those people who are given the task of obtaining information on their behalf. It is unlikely that the brief surveys undertaken by 'outsiders' for many development projects will be adequate for this purpose. The process of community education is more likely to take place through the use of good extension workers or some form of decentralized planning or community development which allows government officials and local representatives to interact and exchange ideas over a relatively long period of time.

Equally important is the fact that the planners must be prepared to accept that, even if the people are fully informed about the options available to them, their priorities may be different from those of the planners. For example, it is likely that the people of the Eastern Highlands would have chosen to concentrate their efforts on commercial ventures and the resolution of disputes, however much information they had on alternative activities. Moreover, the fact that the commercial ventures were seldom economically viable was not nearly as important as one might think because to the Eastern Highlanders (like many other Papua New Guineans) the main purpose of having a business—such as a shop or a commercial vehicle—is often not to make money but to gain status or prestige. Owning a business is not only a status symbol itself but it also enables the owner to do favours for his neighbours—for example, supply goods on credit or give free rides in the vehicle—and thus build up a chain of social obligations which also adds to his status. This attitude can only be explained in terms of the local social organization and customs, but this does not make it any less important, and the fact that planners may encounter such attitudes is one of the risks they take if they advocate local participation.

What is a community?

In our discussions of participatory planning we have used the word 'community' many times without actually defining it. We have used terms such as 'popular participation' and 'community involvement' more or less interchangeably and we have discussed at some length the concept of 'community development' as one possible way of achieving participation. This has been possible because most people have some general understanding of the term and tend to assume that the population can be divided into recognizable communities which can provide a basis for communication between planners and people. At this point, however, it is necessary to look more carefully at the concept of a community and question whether, in fact, it is possible to use communities as a basis for participatory planning in this way.

The United Nations, in a report on community development from which we quoted in Chapter 6, states that:

Implicit in the theory that has been built up in relation to community development is an organic and physical concept of community—a group in face-to-face contact, bound by common values and objectives, with a basic harmony of interest and aspirations. (United Nations, 1971, p. 12)

This statement suggests three important criteria which we may consider when looking for a definition of the term community—and when trying to identify communities on the ground.

Firstly, the concept of community has a physical component. It implies a group of people living in a geographically defined area and interacting with each other. The concepts of geographic space and 'face-to-face' interaction are both important. Thus, for example, one would not normally say that the present inhabitants of a village and former residents who have migrated elsewhere belong to the same community because, although they would still have many things in common, they would not be living in the same area. And neither would the word 'community' be used to describe a typical middle- or upper-class suburb of a large town because the inhabitants would have very little direct contact with each other. Interaction between members of a community may result from economic interdependence, social cohesion, or the existence of some form of political organization within the community—or some combination of these.

Secondly, the members of a community usually have a number of characteristics in common, which enable them to be identified as a group. It is not possible to generalize about which characteristics are important, since these will vary from one community to another; but language, tribal or racial origins, religion, culture, values, and life style are often significant factors.

Thirdly, and largely because of the other criteria, a community should have what the United Nations describes as a 'basic harmony of interest and aspirations'. This is particularly important from the planner's point of view because it means that the members of a community are more likely to have similar views of future development needs and proposals in their area. Consequently, it is easier for the planner to consult the local people and to obtain some sort of consensus of opinion if he works through recognized communities.

The United Nations concept of a community thus provides a basis for defining what is meant by the term and for determining criteria which can be used in identifying communities. In practice, however, the task of actually identifying communities which can provide a basis for community development and community involvement in planning is much more difficult than this definition suggests.

The extent of the problem varies considerably from one place to another. In some areas it is possible to find communities which are fairly clearly defined and recognized as such by their members. For example, in some rural areas traditional villages are relatively cohesive and clearly defined units which can be regarded as communities for most purposes. This is the case in India, where traditional villages have been used as the basis for the country's community development programme. In some countries the boundaries of local communities have been officially recognized and they are used for a variety of political, administrative, and planning purposes, thus making them easier to identify on the ground and more generally recognized by national authorities and the general public. China's success in mobilizing local community activity can be attributed partly to this.

Elsewhere, however, it is much more difficult to identify any form of community structure. For example, in many rural areas people do not live in clearly defined nuclear settlements which can be called villages, but in scattered hamlets of perhaps only two or three related families. The resettlement of millions of people in Tanzania during the 1970s was designed to overcome this problem by relocating people in nuclear villages which could then be officially recognized and used for a variety of developmental purposes. The identification of communities in many urban areas is even more difficult because of the mobility of the population and the absence of any traditional community organization.

One of the main problems in identifying communities, especially for planning purposes, is how to determine the size of the communities. The optimum size is likely to vary, depending on various factors—including the purpose for which they will be used. For example, communities which are to be used as the basis for planning and organizing small self-help projects should be considerably smaller than those which are expected to function as local government bodies, employing professional staff and controlling considerable sums of money. Most traditional societies recognize the need for different levels of community organization for different purposes. Thus, for some purposes the extended family may be the only functional community organization, while for other purposes the concept of community may be extended to include a clan or village or even a whole tribal or regional grouping. Similarly, for community development and planning purposes it is often necessary to identify a hierarchy of community organizations.

Another serious problem is that not even the most clearly defined communities are entirely homogeneous or free from internal conflict and disunity. The degree of conflict does, of course, vary considerably. For instance, it is much higher in a caste-ridden Indian village than in an isolated subsistence community in Africa or a Chinese commune. However, in all communities there are individuals and interest groups with different, and often competing or conflicting, aspirations and objectives; in fact, the existence of such conflict or competition often helps to maintain the viability of the community as a functional unit. In this respect, the 'basic harmony of interest and aspirations' inherent in the United Nations concept of a community represents the ideal rather than the real situation. This not only complicates the process of identifying viable communities but also makes the work of the planner—and the community development worker—more difficult. It means that one cannot assume that all members of the community share the same views about future development in the area or are likely to benefit equally from it. We shall look at some of the implications of this in the next section.

We may therefore conclude that there is no ideal—or easy—way of identifying communities. Although the concept of a community remains a useful tool for planners concerned about popular participation, the criteria used to define communities will vary greatly, depending on the particular characteristics of the area and the specific planning purpose for which the communities are required; in many cases it may be necessary to recognize a hierarchy of communities to meet different needs. Moreover, although the identification and use of communities for planning purposes is likely to be easier if community boundaries are officially recognized and incorporated into local administrative or political structures and if they are accepted as such by the people themselves, it should be remembered that these boundaries will still be to some extent arbitrary and the communities which they define will not be entirely homogeneous or united.

Problems of representation, conflict, and inequality

The fact that no community is entirely homogeneous or free from internal conflict is related to a more general problem faced by planners: that of deciding which members of the community should actually be involved in the planning process. This problem is particularly obvious when participation is sought through community development programmes, which are highly dependent on community leaders whose role it is to mobilize the rest of the population and act as a channel of communication between the community and outside agencies. However, it also arises in other forms of participatory planning, since whatever method is used, it is very seldom possible to involve every member of the community directly and so some people have to be selected as representatives. Thus, when carrying out surveys of a project area, the social scientist has to decide whether he is going to interview a random sample of the population, rely on information provided by community leaders (which then raises the same questions as in the case of community development programmes), or hold public meetings at which anyone can air his views. Similarly, extension workers have to decide which members of the community they will work through, while local government is based on the principle of representation, either through direct elections or through some form of indirect selection process.

The problem is that whatever method is used to select the representatives, one cannot guarantee that those selected will adequately represent the views of the community as a whole, or even of the majority of its members. There are obviously some basic rules which can be followed in order to obtain the best possible representation. For example, in Chapter 8 we shall look at ways of selecting a representative sample of the population to interview in a social survey, while the community development worker or other extension officer should try to work through those people who are regarded as leaders by the majority of the population. Similarly, in the case of local government, there are 'good' and 'bad' ways of conducting elections. But beyond this point it is difficult to make any generalizations. For example, in the section on local government we pointed out that direct elections do not necessarily produce more effective representatives than some form of indirect selection process.

Another problem is that rules or methods which are valid in developed countries do not always apply in countries of the Third World. Thus, if one wishes to interview sample households as part of a social survey, one has to decide first how to define a 'household' because concepts such as 'household' and 'family' vary considerably from one society to another in the Third World and are usually very different from those in the developed world. Similarly, direct elections are more difficult to conduct and their value is more dubious in developing countries because people are less accustomed to choosing their leaders by secret ballot. One of the significant features of the community governments in the Eastern Highlands of Papua New Guinea was that their members could be chosen by traditional methods rather than by ballot if the people so desired.

The situation is even more complex when—as is so often the case—the community or area from which representatives must be selected is composed of several different, and perhaps conflicting, interest groups, each with its own leadership structure. If a local government council ward covers two different clans or linguistic groups, for example, it may well be impossible to elect one person who can adequately represent the whole area. In such cases it is usually wise to divide the ward into two, even if it means that these wards are much smaller than the average. Similarly, the community development worker or other extension officer is faced with serious problems if there are two rival leaders in the community in which he is working. It may be impossible to approach one leader without automatically alienating himself from the other.

This problem has most serious effects where there are significant inequalities within communities, notably in many parts of Latin America and Asia, but to a lesser extent in many other countries. In such situations the danger is that those people who are selected to represent the community are those who are economically and socially better off, and they then use their positions as community representatives to further their own interests, thus merely increasing the existing inequalities. This is a common problem for extension workers, who often find it easier to work with the more progressive members of the community, who are likely to be those who are already in a better socio-economic position. Similarly, in most countries members of local government bodies tend to be better off than most people in the community, and they frequently use their positions in local government to increase their personal wealth and status even further.

India provides a good example of the problems of trying to achieve participatory planning in this sort of environment. Thus, in Chapter 4 we saw how the so-called 'green revolution' really only benefited the wealthier, more progressive, farmers; while in Chapter 6 we pointed out that one of the most significant criticisms of the Indian community development programme is that it has not reduced social and economic inequalities because the programme has been manipulated by the more affluent members of the community who are in most cases the established political leaders.

In these circumstances it is certainly very difficult to be optimistic about participatory planning, and in particular about any attempt to obtain participation through conventional community development methods. One is able to sympathize with critics like André Gunder Frank, who points out that in countries like those of Latin America, where 'the rural community is entirely conflict ridden because it is an integral part of the exploitative class structure of the capitalist system', conventional approaches to community development are of no value. Frank maintains that 'community development programmes must aid peasants and mobilize them to confront the landowners, merchants and political–military authorities that exploit and oppress them' (Frank, 1969, p. 251). As we saw in Chapter 6, this was the approach adopted in countries like China.

The communication gap

We have already referred on several occasions to what may be called a 'communication gap' between the planners or administrators who prepare plans or collect the information on which plans are based, and the ordinary people who they try to involve in the planning process. For example, in Chapter 6 we pointed out that social scientists making a brief study of an area are seldom able in the limited time available to communicate effectively with the local people, and even extension workers resident in the area are often still regarded as 'outsiders' by the rest of the community. We also suggested that systems of local government established during the colonial era have not been accepted as a means of participation by many communities because they were based on alien concepts of political organization and decision-making. And we mentioned that one of the main problems faced by the community development worker is that of his role in relation to members of the community in which he is working.

There is no easy solution to this problem because the underlying cause is the enormous gap between the environment of the planners, administrators, or extension workers and that of the people whose participation they seek to obtain. This gap leads not only to practical difficulties in communication, such as language problems, but also to differences in attitudes and expectations and to mutual feelings of suspicion, mistrust, resentment, and even derision.

The only way of overcoming the problem is to try to bridge the gap in some way. Anthropologists try to do this by living in a community until they feel that they are, at least to a certain extent, accepted into it. However, it appears that even if the anthropologist feels he has been accepted, there is still a social and cultural gap, at least in the eyes of the local people. In the case of extension workers, there is—as we have seen—a move in some countries to improve the effectiveness of extension workers by careful selection and training and by encouraging them to live as members of the community. However, again there are problems, particularly since in most parts of the world extension staff are government employees who have all sorts of expectations and ambitions regarding their salary, living conditions, status, promotion prospects, and so on. There are also moves in many countries to develop more appropriate systems of village or community level government; but again there is no ideal system.

A community development approach probably offers the greatest potential for at least reducing, if not entirely removing, the gap—especially if it can be combined with a system of local government and administrative decentralization. However, as our brief discussion of the Indian community development programme revealed, such programmes are very difficult to establish and operate effectively, and even countries like India have not solved the problem of the gap between members of the community and those providing organizational or technical assistance.

Once again the Chinese have perhaps made more progress than many countries in bridging the gap between planners and people. This has been achieved partly through the unique combination of 'top down' and 'bottom up' planning, and partly by the fact that local planners, extension workers, and administrators are far more integrated into the community than they are in most countries. China's 'barefoot doctors' have become a model for community-based health workers throughout the developing world; but it is less widely known that in China a wide range of administrative jobs which elsewhere would be done by a separate 'class' of government employees are also performed by members of the local community (Conyers, 1977). Although this is one of the areas where changes appear to be occurring since the death of Chairman Mao, there is as yet no evidence to suggest that China is likely to abandon this community development approach to development and planning entirely. However, as we have already emphasized on several occasions, there are major obstacles to the reproduction of the Chinese system in other countries.

The problem of unfulfilled expectations

We mentioned earlier that, for fairly obvious reasons, people are normally reluctant to participate in planning if they feel that their participation will have little or no effect on what actually happens. Sometimes they may feel this way simply because they do not understand the decision-making process and so do not see how their participation can have any effect. More often, however, the feeling can be attributed to past experience in which they have participated but have not had any noticeable effect on the course of events. In other words, people are reluctant to participate because in the past their expectations have not been fulfilled.

The main problem from the planners' point of view is that this attitude is quite often justifiable because on many occasions it is not possible to meet people's expectations. There are several reasons why this may be so. The most obvious one is that because of inadequate information people often ask for things which cannot possibly be provided. This is related to the question we raised earlier of whether people really know what they want and, as we suggested then, the only solution is to try to explain what options are—and are not—open to them so that they are less likely to demand the impossible.

Another reason, which is also due to inadequate information or knowledge, is that sometimes people think their participation will achieve much more than it actually will. For example, a common problem faced by local governments is that if people are required to pay an annual tax or rate, they regard this as payment for some sort of development project or service (such as a road or a school) in their own area, and when after a few years they see no result they begin to lose interest in the local government and refuse to pay the tax. Again, the most obvious answer to such a problem is to try to explain how the system works, so that people understand where their money goes. However, in some cases it may also be possible to change the system so that it makes more sense to the people. Thus, in the above example, it may be possible to replace all or part of the compulsory local government tax with a system of voluntary contributions for specific development projects so that the people see a direct result for their money.

A third reason why expectations are often unfulfilled is that, although requests or suggestions made by the people are perfectly reasonable, they are not incorporated into the plans. This may occur because the planners have weighed up the views of the people against other conflicting factors and eventually decided that the other factors are more important. For instance, a decision to go ahead with a new mining venture may be made despite opposition from the people in the area because the project is of vital importance for the country's economic development. However, it may also occur because the planners simply ignore the views of the people altogether. In some cases, 'consulting the people' is merely a gesture made by planners to satisfy the demands of politicians or other advocates of participatory planning when, in fact, they have no intention of taking any notice of the results of such consultation. In order to avoid such situations, it is very important that planners do not ask for people's views unless they are prepared to give them very serious consideration, and if after such consideration they find it is really impossible to meet their demands, they should make an effort to explain to the people why this is so.

In some cases, the demands or suggestions made by the people are incorporated into the plans for a project, but the people are still disillusioned because, for some reason or other, the project subsequently fails. For example, following requests from the people in an area, the government may provide financial and technical assistance for the establishment of a local business venture which later collapses. Although the project's failure may have nothing to do with the fact that the people were involved in the planning stages, they may still feel that it is not worth making any further efforts.

A similar result may occur if people do not see the results of their participation quickly. Thus, local government councillors are usually asked fairly early in the year to suggest projects for inclusion in the next year's budget—or even in a plan for the next five years. Many councillors are confused by this because, having suggested a project, they expect work to start on it almost immediately. This is a fairly common problem in planning because the ordinary person tends to think in terms of immediate needs, while planning—by definition—involves making decisions about the future, and sometimes the future may mean several years ahead.

The problem of how to meet people's expectations so that they do not become disillusioned is, therefore, a fairly complex one and there is no simple solution. However, our discussion suggests that there are two particularly important lessons for the planner. Firstly, people should not be asked to participate unless their views will be given serious consideration. And secondly, any decision-making system which involves participation should be kept as simple as possible and time should be taken to explain it to the people, so that they are able to participate effectively.

Participation versus speed and efficiency

One factor which sometimes discourages a participatory approach to planning is that it is not usually the easiest or most 'efficient' way of planning—if 'efficiency' is measured in terms of the amount of time, money, and effort required to meet a particular objective. Involving local communities in the planning process requires a considerable amount of time, money, and manpower, particularly if it is done properly. Time is an especially important consideration; throughout this chapter and Chapter 6 we have emphasized the need to take time to get to know and be accepted by a community and to explain to people how the decision-making system works and what options are available to them. Popular participation thus increases the length and cost of a planning exercise and so is regarded by some planners as an inefficient way of making decisions, particularly if the decisions have to be made quickly.

Participatory planning also requires considerable organizational capacity. The success of any attempt to improve the quality of extension workers, decentralize planning, or establish an effective local government system or community development programme is dependent, at least in part, on the existence of an effective organizational structure. And the creation of such a structure requires time, expense, and political organization. We have pointed out on several occasions that China's achievements can be attributed to a great extent to its political and administrative organization and it is this which is so difficult to reproduce elsewhere.

Finally, popular participation also complicates the planning process considerably. It raises new issues which have to be taken into consideration, results in all sorts of demands which cannot easily be met, and may even threaten the existence of a proposed project or programme. In other words, it is usually much simpler to make decisions without trying to involve or consult the local population, especially if there is any likelihood that their views will differ from those of others involved in the planning process.

The obvious answer to these arguments is that this is the price one has to pay for popular participation. The purpose of participatory planning is not to make the planning process simpler or more 'efficient'—at least not in the sense that we have been using the term 'efficient' here—but to make sure that local conditions and needs are taken into account and to allow people to have some say in their own development. If planners are genuine about advocating popular participation, they must be prepared to accept the costs which go with it.

Local versus national interests

The final problem which we shall consider in this chapter is that of conflict between national and local interests. It is inevitable that if local communities are involved in the planning process there will sooner or later be a conflict of interest between local needs and demands and the priorities and goals of the national government.

More often than not this conflict is due simply to a difference in viewpoint. The local community sees the situation only from its own point of view while the planners at the national level have to consider the needs of the country as a whole. For example, in the case of education planning, every community is likely to ask for a new or better school, while the national government, aware of the limited resources available, has to consider which areas have the greatest need. However, sometimes there may be a more fundamental difference in policy between the two interest groups. To use the example of education planning again, a local community may have different ideas about curriculum or the language to be used in schools. In extreme cases, local community organizations may become political pressure groups, with the aim of thwarting or even overthrowing the national government.

When such a conflict arises the planners are faced with a dilemma. If they give in to the demands of the local community, they have to sacrifice national goals—and in a country which is trying to achieve rapid socio-economic development with very limited resources, this is not easy to do. Moreover, sometimes it is just not possible to meet local demands. For example, there is no way that every community can be provided with a school at the same time. However, as we saw in the previous section, if the planners ignore local demands the people soon become frustrated and disillusioned and the concept of participatory planning becomes a farce.

The conflict between national and local interests is potentially greatest when planning is decentralized to the extent that local communities not only have the right to make suggestions about the type of development they would like in their area but also to put these suggestions into effect. As we indicated in the section on decentralized planning in Chapter 6, participation is likely to be much more effective if people can implement their own plans; but the threat to national goals and policies is also that much greater. We have already seen that countries react differently when faced with this situation, depending at least in part on the relative importance of national goals and local interests. Many countries tend to reduce the powers of local decision-making bodies, or ensure that national government interests are adequately represented on them; while others are prepared to increase local decision-making powers, at the possible expense of national interests.

Once again there is no easy or universal solution to the problem, and a great deal depends on the particular political situation and development priorities of each country. The conflict between national and local interests can generally be reduced by establishing an effective organizational structure extending from village to national level, through which local planning can as far as possible be integrated into the national planning system. However, this will only reduce rather than eliminate the problem and planners have to accept that some degree of conflict is inevitable in decentralized planning.

Conclusion: the future of participatory planning

Having considered all the problems involved in participatory planning, it is fairly easy to understand why many planners have grave doubts about its practicality or even its value. Their doubts are based on the enormous difficulties of obtaining effective popular participation and the fact that it adds considerably to the complexities of the planning process. Nevertheless, in spite of these formidable obstacles, the arguments in favour of participation, which we discussed at the beginning of Chapter 6, are such that in most countries it continues to be an important stated objective, even if in practice relatively little effort is made to achieve it.

Since many planners are likely to be faced with the situation of having to try to involve local communities as much as possible in the planning process, in spite of the problems of doing so, it may be useful to summarize very briefly the main conclusions we have reached in this chapter.

Firstly, we have mentioned several times the need for an organizational structure extending from the national to the local level, through which communication on planning issues can take place. Each level should be given the power to make decisions about issues which are most effectively resolved at that level and should, if possible, also have some power to implement these decisions. This will help to integrate local plans into the national planning process, thus minimizing conflict between national and local interests, and increase the chances that local needs and demands will actually be met.

Secondly, the most important level of local participation is probably that of the 'community' or village, where as many people as possible can be directly involved. However, it should be remembered that there is no easy way of defining community boundaries and that no communities are simple or homogeneous entities.

Thirdly, it is essential that people should be involved in making—and implementing—decisions about things which they think are important, even if these things seem unimportant to authorities at higher levels. This is related to the fact that popular participation must be taken seriously by these authorities. There is no point in asking people to participate in planning if there is no intention of taking their views seriously and incorporating them into the plans.

Fourthly, planners should give adequate consideration to the problems of communicating effectively with local communities, recognizing both the difficulties of finding people who genuinely represent community interests and the inevitable communication gap between planners and people. They should make every effort to overcome these problems in the ways we have discussed, and at the same time recognize that much of the information they obtain from local communities may be somewhat biased because of these obstacles.

Planners should also remember that there has to be an important educational component in any form of participatory planning. This education should be a two-way process. The people must be made aware of how the decision-making system works and what options are available to them so that they can participate effectively; and at the same time the planners must learn to understand and appreciate local needs and attitudes.

The next point which planners may wish to bear in mind is that participation will inevitably result in some conflict between local and national interests. Although such conflict can be reduced to some extent, it cannot be eliminated completely because local and national interests are bound to differ sometimes. It is important to remember that the whole purpose of participatory planning is to enable local views to be taken into consideration, and so some conflict is inevitable. In this context, it may be useful to remind ourselves that planning is above all a political process in which different interest groups compete to have some influence over the decisions that are made and so to benefit from them. In these terms, local participation may be seen as the introduction of additional interest groups into the planning process, thus increasing the amount of competition—and potential conflict—involved.

Finally, it is important to recognize that participatory planning is not the most efficient way of making decisions, in the sense that it inevitably makes the planning process longer, more expensive, and more complex. Rather than resent this, planners should accept it as a necessary price to pay for the benefits of achieving popular participation. As in so many other aspects of social planning, one cannot measure its benefits purely in terms of monetary gain or concepts such as 'efficiency'.

In conclusion, we quote from two writers who see the problems of participation from very different viewpoints, but have come to remarkably similar conclusions. An American political scientist, Milton Esman, in an article on administration and development, points out that:

The romance of 'participation' should not lead administrators to expect that the results will be painless either to themselves or to citizens. Participation will generate conflict. It will make more work for officials, but hopefully it will improve the relevance and the effectiveness of developmental public services. (Esman, 1974, p. 23)

While President Kaunda of Zambia, in explaining the importance of decentralization in his country, writes:

We need to remember that efficiency cannot be measured wholly or even chiefly in terms of results that can be reduced to quantifiable terms. The mere fact of decentralization and the winning of power by the people to do things for themselves and to run their own affairs produce results in terms of human dignity and human self-fulfilment which are incapable of being expressed in any statistical form at all. Yet they remain things of profound importance in terms of the quality of life of our people. (Kaunda, 1974, p. 36)

Guide to further reading to chapters 6 and 7

For a general survey of the practice and problems of popular participation in planning in the developing world, the most useful general work is probably the United Nations publication entitled *Popular Participation in Decision Making for Development* (New York, 1975). Also useful is Chapter 18 of G. Myrdal's book *Asian Drama: an Enquiry into the Poverty of Nations* (Harmondsworth, Penguin Books, 1968). Although this book is now rather dated and refers specifically to South Asia, most of Myrdal's comments are still relevant today and apply to most parts of the Third World. More recently, the International Labour Organization (ILO) has produced a series of working papers on various aspects of participation in development as part of its World Employment Programme Research. Details can be obtained from the ILO headquarters in Geneva or from any of its regional offices.

For comparative purposes, the reader may also like to refer to some of the parallel works on participation in planning in developed countries. A useful example is *The Planner in Society* by D. Eversley (London, Faber, 1973).

There is a considerable amount of written material on the various ways of achieving participation described in Chapter 6. Some of the more useful general works are listed below; these should be used in conjunction with the references given in the text.

Surveys and consultation

Bulmer, M., and D. P. Warwick (eds.), *Social Research in Developing Countries* (Chichester, Wiley, forthcoming).

Cochrane, G., *The Cultural Appraisal of Development Projects* (New York, Praeger, 1979).

O'Barr, W., *et al.* (eds.), *Survey Research in Africa: its Applications and Limits* (Evanston, Illinois, Northwestern University Press, 1973).

See also the guide to further reading on 'data collection' at the end of Chapter 8.

Extension services

Cliffe, L. *et al.* (eds.), *Government and Rural Development in East Africa: Essays on Political Penetration* (The Hague, Martinus Nijhoff, 1977), especially chapters by Chambers, Sharman, van Velzen, and Leonard.

Crouch, B. R., and S. Chamala (eds.), *Extension Education and Rural Development* (Chichester, Wiley, 1981, 2 vols.).
Hunter, G. *et al., Policy and Practice in Rural Development* (London, Croom Helm, 1976), Part IV.
Leonard, D. K., *Rural Administration in Kenya* (Nairobi, East African Literature Bureau, 1973).
See also the guide to further reading on 'working with communities' at the end of Chapter 9.

Decentralized planning

Hyden, G. *et al.* (eds.), *Development Administration: the Kenyan Experience* (Nairobi, Oxford University Press, 1970).
Maddick, H., *Democracy, Decentralization and Development* (Bombay, Asia Publishing House, 1963).
Saxena, A. P. (ed.), *Administrative Reforms for Decentralised Development* (Kuala Lumpur, Asian and Pacific Development Administration Centre, 1980).
Taylor, D. R. F., and W. Stohr (eds.), *Development from Above or Below? Radical Approaches to Spatial Planning in Developing Countries* (Chichester, Wiley, 1981).
The ILO is also producing a series of working papers on decentralized planning in particular countries as part of its World Employment Programme Research. Details can be obtained from ILO offices.

Local government

Hicks, U. K., *Devlopment from Below* (Oxford, Clarendon Press, 1961).
United Nations, *Local Government Reform: an Analysis of Experience in Selected Countries* (New York, 1975).

Community development

For a general survey of community development programmes, the United Nations publication, *Popular Participation in Development: Emerging Trends in Community Development* (New York, 1971) provides a comprehensive but rather uncritical review. Other general surveys tend to be much briefer but more critical; three examples are:
Alldred, A., 'Some contradictions in community development: the need for a stronger community approach', *Community Development Journal*, 11 (1976), 134–140.
Manghezi, A., *Class, Elite and Community in African Development* (Uppsala, Scandinavian Institute of African Studies, 1976), Ch. 3.
Mayo, M., 'Community development: a radical alternative?' in Bailey, R., and M. Brake (eds.), *Radical Social Work* (London, Edward Arnold, 1975), 129–143.
Several case studies of particular community development programmes are documented in Chapter 6 of *Attacking Rural Poverty* by P. H. Coombs with M. Ahmed (Baltimore, Johns Hopkins Press, 1974) and in Coombs, P. H. (ed.), *Meeting the Basic Needs of the Rural Poor: the Integrated Community Based Approach* (New York, Pergamon Press, 1981).
Further details of the Indian community development programme can be found in the following:
Jain, S. C., *Community Development and Panchayati Raj in India* (Calcutta, Allied Publishers, 1967).
Karunaratne, G., 'The failure of the community development programme in India', *Community Development Journal*, 11 (1976), 95–118.

Maddick, H., *Panchayati Raj: a Study of Rural Local Government in India* (London, Longman, 1970).

The problems of using a successful pilot project as a model for a nationwide community development programme in the Indian context are documented in Sussman, G. E., 'The pilot project and the choice of an implementing strategy: community development in India' in Grindle, M. S. (ed.), *Politics and Policy Implementation in the Third World* (Princeton, Princeton University Press, 1980), Chapter 4.

And for further details of the Chinese approach see:

Aziz, S., *Rural Development: Learning from China* (London, Macmillan, 1978).

Burchett, W., and R. Alley, *China: the Quality of Life* (Harmondsworth, Penguin, 1976), especially Chapter 12.

Gek-boo, N., *Mass Participation and Basic Needs Satisfaction: the Chinese approach* (Geneva, International Labour Organization, World Employment Programme Research, WEP 2-32/WP 14, 1979).

PART THREE

ORGANIZATION AND METHODS

CHAPTER 8

INFORMATION FOR SOCIAL PLANNING

Part Two described the various fields of social planning as they are practised in the Third World. In this part of the book, attention is focused on the methods used in social planning, the skills required by the social planner, and the organizational structure within which social planning occurs. We begin in this chapter with an examination of the information needs of social planning.

Any form of planning is dependent on information, since planning is essentially a process of decision-making and it is impossible to make rational decisions—as opposed to mere guesses—without information. Social planning is no exception in this respect; but the purposes for which information is required and the methods and problems of collecting, analysing, and storing it require special understanding and skills. These are the topics to be discussed in this chapter.

Measuring social development

The information needs of social planning are related to the basic issue of measuring social development. References have often been made in earlier chapters to the need for information on social conditions—the social structure of society, the availability of social services, social customs and attitudes, inequalities between different social groups, and so on. In other words, we have expressed the need to be able to measure various aspects of 'social development'. In this section of the chapter we consider why the social planner often needs to measure social development, what he should actually measure, and the problems which may actually arise in so doing.

(i) *Why measure social development?*

There are three main reasons why it may be useful or necessary to measure social development. Firstly, it may be necessary to have information on existing social conditions, or the existing state of social development. This may be required purely for descriptive purposes or, more often, to assist in identifying problems or formulating policies or programmes. For example, when preparing plans for the future development of health services it is necessary to have information on the present health status of the population and on the existing availability of health services. Similarly, before tackling problems such as urban crime or unemployment among school-leavers, it is necessary to have information which indicates the extent of these problems.

Secondly, it may be necessary to measure social development in order to indicate variations in social conditions between different sectors of the population; for instance, between different geographical regions or between different social classes. Again, this information may be used for purely descriptive purposes or to assist in planning and policy formulation. To use the example of health planning again, it is essential to have information on the extent to which disease patterns and access to health services vary between different parts of the country and between different socio-economic groups. This sort of information is obviously particularly important in situations where there is a specific concern to reduce social inequalities.

Thirdly, it may be necessary to measure changes in social conditions which occur over time. Sometimes the planner may wish to record changes which occur without any particular intervention by the government or other agencies. Thus, in Chapter 4 we described the role of the social planner in monitoring aspects of social change, such as changes in family size and structure or trends in rural–urban migration. More often, however, he is concerned in measuring changes which have occurred, or are likely to occur in the future, as a result of specific policies, programmes, or projects. This is perhaps the most common reason for measuring social development, and in previous chapters we often referred to the need for this sort of information. For example, it may be necessary to measure the impact of a family planning programme on birth-rates, the effects of the 'green revolution' on rural inequalities in India, or the impact of a new approach to community development on participation in planning. Similarly, the planner may have to measure the social impact of a major economic development project or predict the likely impact of a proposed project, such as the Ok Tedi mine in Papua New Guinea, described in Chapter 5.

Two factors have contributed to the importance of this form of social measurement. One is the increasing emphasis which, as we have noted in earlier chapters, is now placed on monitoring the implementation of development plans in order to make sure that objectives are actually achieved and to identify problems as they arise. This means that the social planner has to pay more attention to monitoring the impact of programmes or projects, both during and after implementation. The other is the greater importance now attached to measuring the likely *social* costs and benefits of proposed projects, before deciding whether or not to go ahead with them or choosing between alternative projects. Cost–benefit analysis is a technique which has long been used by economists in evaluating projects, but it is only fairly recently that social factors have also received significant attention. We shall consider the problems involved in this in Chapter 9.

(ii) *What should be measured?—the concept of social indicators*

Although the need to measure social development is thus fairly obvious, it is much more difficult to decide exactly what to measure. The normal practice is to identify specific criteria which indicate the particular aspect of social development with which one is concerned and then to measure these criteria. The fact that the criteria which one actually measures *indicate* the type of social development or change with which one is concerned, has led to the use of the term *social indicators* to refer to these criteria. For example, measurements such as life expectancy, infant mortality, causes of death, and the number of people recorded as suffering from particular illnesses are some of the *indicators* which may be used to measure the health status of a population.

Because the scope of social planning is so wide, the number and variety of possible social indicators is enormous. Apthorpe, in a useful handbook on social indicators, points out the problem of defining what is and is not a social indicator and recognizes several different kinds of indicator, which reflect different interpretations of the term 'social indicator' and, in fact, different interpretations of the content and scope of social planning (Apthorpe, 1978, pp. 3–16). The various kinds of indicator recognized by Apthorpe may be grouped into three broad categories:

(i) indicators which measure the 'non-economic' aspects of development, including demographic data, information on health, education, and other aspects of 'social' well-being, and information on the availability of and access to social services;

(ii) indicators which measure the 'quality of life' or the degree of contentment or general well-being of the population, using either some supposedly 'objective' criteria of what constitutes a 'good' life or attempting to identify the 'felt' needs and aspirations of the people concerned;

(iii) indicators which measure variations in the quality of life between different sectors of the population and thus indicate the existence of social inequalities.

It should be noted that these three kinds of social indicator are not mutually exclusive. For example, there are many individual indicators—such as those related to health, education, or the quality of housing—which would be included in each of the three categories. There is, however, a difference in the scope of the three categories, the second being considerably broader in scope than the first, and the third even broader. Apthorpe points out that if the term 'social indicator' is interpreted to mean an indicator of social inequalities, social indicators are concerned with 'the distributional aspects of anything and everything, whatever it may be, that has a distribution in society and can be represented on spatial, temporal and other interval bases' (Apthorpe, 1978, p. 14). We shall see later that this makes it very difficult to identify specific indicators and to distinguish social indicators from any other sort, such as indicators of the 'economic' aspects of development. For the time being, however, we shall merely conclude that social indicators may include anything which the social planner may wish to measure, although there are certain indicators—such as those related to population, health, education, and other indisputably 'social' characteristics—which are more generally agreed to be social indicators than others.

Social scientists have devoted considerable attention to the question of what constitutes a 'good' social indicator. Three qualities emerge as of particular importance. Firstly, a good indicator should accurately reflect whatever it is one is trying to measure. This may appear to be merely stating the obvious, but it is a consideration which is not always given sufficient attention. It is not enough to simply select the first available statistic which bears some relation to what one is trying to measure. For example, if one wanted to measure variations in the availability of health services, it would not normally be adequate just to use data on the number of persons per doctor, since this would ignore many other considerations—such as how many of these people actually have access to the doctors (the doctors may all be based in one urban hospital or some may be private practitioners only available to those who can afford to pay) and the availability of other health services, such as rural health centres or village medical aides. In other words, when deciding what indicators to use it is necessary first to decide exactly what it is one wishes to measure and then to find indicators which really do measure this.

Secondly, when selecting indicators one should ensure that the necessary data are available in the form required and of a reasonable degree of accuracy, or that such data can be made available without the expenditure of an unreasonable amount of time and money. For example, there would be no use in selecting adult literacy as a measure of social development if there were no statistics available on adult literacy or if the statistics were known to be particularly unreliable. Furthermore, if one wishes to make comparisons between areas or over time, one must ensure that the data are broken down by appropriate areal units and available in the form of a time series extending over the period of time with which one is concerned.

Thirdly, indicators should be quantifiable or, to quote Apthorpe, 'scalable' (Apthorpe, 1978, p. 20), so that comparisons can be made. This does not mean that they must necessarily be measurable in precise numerical terms. Some indicators, such as people's attitudes, may be measured on an ordinal scale (for example, they may be measured as 'high', 'medium', or 'low'); while others, such as the availability of certain facilities, may be measured simply by a positive or negative 'score' which indicates whether or not the facility exists.

The importance of having 'good' indicators has encouraged individual governments and international agencies, such as the United Nations, to make efforts to improve the quality of 'social statistics' available in developing countries. Bodies responsible for collecting statistics in these countries have been encouraged to collect those which will be of direct use in planning and policy-making, to make sure they are available in the form required, and to improve their reliability.

Considerable effort has also been devoted to the search for certain 'key' or 'core' indicators which reflect a fairly wide range of related social conditions. For example, infant mortality is often used as an indicator of the general level of social well-being or quality of life because it indicates not only the number of babies who die but also various other related factors, such as nutrition levels, the availability of health services, and the quality of housing. Table 11 compares the level of social and economic development in 125 countries as measured by a few 'key' indicators (gross national product per capita, annual rate of inflation, adult literacy, life expectancy at birth, and food production per capita) used by the World Bank. In order to identify key indicators, studies are made of the pattern of correlation between a large number of different indicators, using data from many different countries. Those indicators which reveal a high degree of correlation with many other indicators are then adopted as the key indicators.

(iii) Some measurement problems

A number of problems arise in relation to the use of social indicators. Some of these are problems which would arise when trying to measure social development in any part of the world; others are peculiar to developing countries.

One of the most obvious problems, which occurs in developed and developing countries, is that of defining exactly what is meant by social indicators. As we have already suggested, the scope of social planning is so broad that almost anything can be included as a social indicator. The task is easiest if one adopts the relatively narrow definition of social indicators as indicators which measure the 'non-economic' aspects of development. But even then problems arise since, as we saw in Chapter 1, many aspects of development cannot be clearly classified as either 'economic' or 'social'. For example, roads bring both economic and social benefits, so should the quality of the road network be regarded as a social indicator or not? Even income, which would normally be considered an economic rather than a social indicator, has important social implications because it is a major factor in determining people's access to social services and to many other goods and services which generally enhance their social well-being. It is dilemmas such as these which are partly responsible for the fact that concepts such as 'social development' tend to increase in scope, which in turn makes the problem of defining social indicators even more difficult.

This problem can be reduced if particular care is taken to define exactly what it is one wants to measure—in other words, what sort of social development one is aiming to achieve and, therefore, to measure—and only then to look for indicators which will actually measure it. However, this raises another serious problem since, as one writer on social indicators points out: 'This raises immediately the question of whose values and goals are to be taken into account in assessing development. Planners' values or people's values? Market values or politically determined values?' (Baster, 1972, p. 2.)

Let us take the example of measuring the 'quality of life'. In theory this is

Table 11 Key indicators used by the World Bank

| | Popula-tion (millions) mid-1978[a] | Area (thousands of square kilometres) | GNP per capita | | Average annual rate of inflation (%) | | Adult literacy rate (%) 1975[e] | Life ex-pectancy at birth (years) 1978 | Average index of food production per capita (1969–71 = 100) 1976–78 |
			Dollars 1978[a]	Average annual growth (%) 1960–78[b]	1960–70[c]	1970–78[d]			
Low-income countries	1,293.9 t	26,313 t	200 w	1.6 w	3.0 m	10.6 m	38 w	50 w	97 w
1 Kampuchea, Dem. Rep.	8.4	181	—	—	3.8	—	—	—	57
2 Bangladesh	84.7	144	90	−0.4	3.7	17.9	26	47	90
3 Lao PDR	3.3	237	90	—	—	—	—	42	96
4 Bhutan	1.2	47	100	−0.3	—	—	—	41	100
5 Ethiopia	31.0	1,222	120	1.5	2.1	4.0	10	39	84
6 Mali	6.3	1,240	120	1.0	5.0	7.8	10	42	90
7 Nepal	13.6	141	120	0.8	7.7	9.1	19	43	92
8 Somalia	3.7	638	130	−0.5	4.5	10.7	60	43	87
9 Burundi	4.5	28	140	2.2	2.8	10.1	25	45	107
10 Chad	4.3	1,284	140	−1.0	4.6	7.4	15	43	89
11 Mozambique	9.9	783	140	0.4	2.8	10.9	—	46	81
12 Burma	32.2	677	150	1.0	2.7	13.7	67	53	96
13 Upper Volta	5.6	274	160	1.3	1.3	9.6	5	42	95
14 Viet Nam	51.7	330	170	—	—	—	87	62	102
15 India	643.9	3,288	180	1.4	7.1	8.2	36	51	100
16 Malawi	5.7	118	180	2.9	2.4	9.1	25	46	99
17 Rwanda	4.5	26	180	1.4	13.1	14.7	23	46	103
18 Sri Lanka	14.3	66	190	2.0	1.8	11.8	78	69	114
19 Guinea	5.1	246	210	0.6	1.7	6.4	—	43	86
20 Sierra Leone	3.3	72	210	0.5	2.9	10.8	15	46	93
21 Zaire	26.8	2,345	210	1.1	29.9	26.2	15	46	94
22 Niger	5.0	1,267	220	−1.4	2.1	10.7	8	42	87
23 Benin	3.3	113	230	0.4	1.9	7.4	11	46	92

24 Pakistan	77.3	804	230	2.8	3.3	14.6	21	52	101
25 Tanzania	16.9	945	230	2.7	1.8	12.3	66	51	93
26 Afghanistan	14.6	647	240	0.4	11.9	4.4	12	42	100
27 Central African Rep.	1.9	623	250	0.7	4.1	9.0	—	46	102
28 Madagascar	8.3	587	250	−0.3	3.2	9.6	50	46	95
29 Haiti	4.8	28	260	0.2	4.1	12.2	23	51	91
30 Mauritania	1.5	1,031	270	3.6	1.6	10.4	17	42	71
31 Lesotho	1.3	30	280	5.9	2.5	11.2	55	50	90
32 Uganda	12.4	236	280	0.7	3.0	27.3	—	53	90
33 Angola	6.7	1,247	300	1.2	3.3	22.0	20	41	88
34 Sudan	17.4	2,506	320	0.1	3.7	7.4	18	46	108
35 Togo	2.4	56	320	5.0	1.7	7.4	40	46	80
36 Kenya	14.7	583	330	2.2	1.5	12.0	10	53	91
37 Senegal	5.4	196	340	−0.4	1.7	8.0	—	42	96
38 Indonesia	136.0	2,027	360	4.1	—	20.0	62	47	100
Middle-income countries	872.8 t	32,998 t	1,250 w	3.7 w	3.1 m	13.1 m	71 w	61 w	106 w
39 Egypt	39.9	1,001	390	3.3	2.7	7.0	44	54	93
40 Ghana	11.0	239	390	−0.5	7.6	35.9	30	48	79
41 Yemen, PDR	1.8	333	420	—	—	—	27	44	108
42 Cameroon	8.1	475	460	2.9	3.7	9.8	30	46	112
43 Liberia	1.7	111	460	2.0	1.9	9.7	57	48	96
44 Honduras	3.4	112	480	1.1	3.0	8.0	39	57	84
45 Zambia	5.3	753	480	1.2	7.6	5.7	—	48	109
46 Zimbabwe	6.9	391	480	1.2	1.3	7.6	84	54	102
47 Thailand	44.5	514	490	4.6	1.9	9.1	63	61	122
48 Bolivia	5.3	1,099	510	2.2	3.5	22.7	87	52	111
49 Philippines	45.6	300	510	2.6	5.8	13.4	13	60	115
50 Yemen Arab Rep.	5.6	195	520	—	—	—	50	39	98
51 Congo, People's Rep.	1.5	342	540	1.0	5.4	10.6	32	46	82
52 Nigeria	80.6	924	560	3.6	2.6	18.2	—	48	89
53 Papua New Guinea	2.9	462	560	3.6	3.6	8.8	62	50	106
54 El Salvador	4.3	21	660	1.8	0.5	10.3	28	63	111
55 Morocco	18.9	447	670	2.5	2.0	7.1	28	55	80

Table 11 (continued)

| | Popula-tion (millions) mid-1978[a] | Area (thousands of square kilometres) | GNP per capita | | Average annual rate of inflation (%) | | Adult literacy rate (%) 1975[e] | Life ex-pectancy at birth (years) 1978 | Average index of food production per capita (1969–71 =100) 1976–78 |
			Dollars 1978[a]	Average annual growth (%) 1960–78[b]	1960–70[c]	1970–78[d]			
56 Peru	16.8	1,285	740	2.0	9.9	22.2	72	56	90
57 Ivory Coast	7.8	322	840	2.5	2.8	13.9	20	46	104
58 Nicaragua	2.5	130	840	2.3	1.9	11.0	57	55	102
59 Colombia	25.6	1,139	850	3.0	11.9	21.7	81	62	114
60 Paraguay	2.9	407	850	2.6	3.0	12.3	81	63	103
61 Ecuador	7.8	284	880	4.3	—	14.8	74	60	103
62 Dominican Rep.	5.1	49	910	3.5	2.1	8.6	67	60	93
63 Guatemala	6.6	109	910	2.9	0.1	10.8	47	57	108
64 Syrian Arab Rep.	8.1	185	930	3.8	1.9	12.7	53	57	150
65 Tunisia	6.0	164	950	4.8	3.7	7.1	55	57	128
66 Jordan	3.0	98	1,050	—	—	—	70	56	77
67 Malaysia	13.3	330	1,090	3.9	-0.3	7.2	60	67	110
68 Jamaica	2.1	11	1,110	2.0	3.8	16.9	86	70	98
69 Lebanon	3.0	10	—	1.4	—	—	—	65	85
70 Korea, Rep. of	36.6	99	1,160	6.9	17.5	19.3	93	63	116
71 Turkey	43.1	781	1,200	4.0	5.6	21.5	60	61	110
72 Algeria	17.6	2,382	1,260	2.3	2.3	13.4	37	56	82
73 Mexico	65.4	1,973	1,290	2.7	3.5	17.5	76	65	99
74 Panama	1.8	76	1,290	2.9	1.6	7.5	78	70	103
75 Taiwan	17.1	36	1,400	6.6	4.1	10.3	82	72	105
76 Chile	10.7	757	1,410	1.0	32.9	242.6	88	67	94
77 South Africa	27.7	1,221	1,480	2.5	3.0	11.7	—	60	100

	667.8 t	30,429 t	8,070 w	3.7 w	4.2 m	9.4 m	99 w	74 w	108 w
78 Costa Rica	2.1	51	1,540	3.3	1.9	15.7	90	70	114
79 Brazil	119.5	8,512	1,570	4.9	46.1	30.3	76	62	117
80 Uruguay	2.9	176	1,610	0.7	51.1	65.6	94	71	105
81 Argentina	26.4	2,767	1,910	2.6	21.8	120.4	94	71	114
82 Portugal	9.8	92	1,990	5.9	3.0	15.2	70	69	82
83 Yugoslavia	22.0	256	2,380	5.4	12.6	17.3	85	69	117
84 Trinidad and Tobago	1.1	5	2,910	2.2	3.2	21.3	95	70	94
85 Venezuela	14.0	912	2,910	2.7	1.3	11.1	82	66	97
86 Hong Kong	4.6	1	3,040	6.5	2.3	7.7	90	72	30
87 Greece	9.4	132	3,250	6.0	3.2	13.8	—	73	120
88 Singapore	2.3	1	3,290	7.4	1.1	6.1	75	70	112
89 Spain	37.1	505	3,470	5.0	6.3	15.0	—	73	122
90 Israel	3.7	21	3,500	4.2	6.2	31.0	88	72	113
Industrialized countries	667.8 t	30,429 t	8,070 w	3.7 w	4.2 m	9.4 m	99 w	74 w	108 w
91 Ireland	3.2	70	3,470	3.3	5.2	14.7	98	73	128
92 Italy	56.7	301	3,850	3.6	4.4	14.0	98	73	100
93 New Zealand	3.2	269	4,790	1.7	3.3	11.0	99	73	107
94 United Kingdom	55.8	244	5,030	2.1	4.1	14.1	99	73	111
95 Finland	4.8	337	6,820	4.1	5.6	13.2	100	72	107
96 Austria	7.5	84	7,030	4.2	3.6	7.6	99	72	109
97 Japan	114.9	372	7,280	7.6	4.8	9.6	99	76	97
98 Australia	14.2	7,687	7,990	2.9	3.1	12.8	100	73	121
99 France	53.3	547	8,260	4.0	4.1	9.3	99	73	106
100 Netherlands	13.9	41	8,410	3.4	5.3	8.8	99	74	118
101 Belgium	9.8	31	9,090	4.1	3.6	8.6	99	72	105
102 Canada	23.5	9,976	9,180	3.5	3.1	9.4	98	74	112
103 Norway	4.1	324	9,510	4.0	4.2	8.6	99	75	108
104 Germany, Fed. Rep.	61.3	249	9,580	3.3	3.2	5.9	99	72	104
105 United States	221.9	9,363	9,590	2.4	2.8	6.8	99	73	114
106 Denmark	5.1	43	9,920	3.2	6.0	9.8	99	74	102
107 Sweden	8.3	450	10,210	2.5	4.3	9.3	99	75	113
108 Switzerland	6.3	41	12,100	2.2	4.6	6.6	99	74	113

Table 11   (continued)

| | Popula-tion (millions) mid-1978^a | Area (thousands of square kilometres) | GNP per capita | | Average annual rate of inflation (%) | | Adult literacy rate (%) 1975^e | Life ex-pectancy at birth (years) 1978 | Average index of food production per capita (1969-71 = 100) 1976-78 |
			Dollars 1978^a	Average annual growth (%) 1960-78^b	1960-70^c	1970-78^d			
	60.1 t	6,011 t	3,340 w	7.1 w	1.2 m	22.2 m	50 w	53 w	111 w
Capital-surplus oil exporters									
109 Iraq	12.2	435	1,860	4.1	1.7	—	—	55	84
110 Iran	35.8	1,648	2,160	7.9	-0.5	23.7	50	52	113
111 Libya	2.7	1,760	6,910	6.2	5.2	20.7	50	55	123
112 Saudia Arabia	8.2	2,150	7,690	9.7	—	28.4	—	53	135
113 Kuwait	1.2	18	14,890	-2.3	0.6	19.8	60	69	—

Table 11   (continued)

| | Popula-tion (millions) mid-1978[a] | Area (thousands of square kilometres) | GNP per capita | | Average annual rate of inflation (%) | | Adult literacy rate (%) 1975[e] | Life ex-pectancy at birth (years) 1978 | Average index of food production per capita (1969–71 =100) 1976–78 |
			Dollars 1978[a]	Average annual growth (%) 1960–78[b]	1960–70[c]	1970–78[d]			
	1,352.4 t	34,826 t	1,190 w	4.0 w	—	—	—	70 w	112 w
Centrally planned economies									
114 China	952.2	9,597	230[f]	3.7	—	—	—	70	111
115 Korea, Dem. Rep.	17.1	121	730	4.5	—	—	—	63	130
116 Albania	2.6	29	740	4.1	—	—	—	69	107
117 Cuba	9.7	115	810	–1.2	—	—	96	72	96
118 Mongolia	1.6	1,565	940	1.5	—	—	—	63	94
119 Romania	21.9	238	1,750	8.6	—	—	98	70	148
120 Bulgaria	8.8	111	3,230	5.7	—	—	—	72	113
121 Hungary	10.7	93	3,450	5.0	—	—	98	70	122
122 Poland	35.0	313	3,670	5.9	—	—	98	71	104
123 USSR	261.0	22,402	3,700	4.3	—	—	99	70	111
124 Czechoslovakia	15.1	128	4,720	4.3	—	—	—	70	118
125 German Dem. Rep.	16.7	108	5,710	4.8	—	—	—	72	127

[a] Figures in italics are for 1977, not 1978.
[b] Figures in italics are for 1960–77, not 1960–78.
[c] Figures in italics are for 1961–70, not 1960–70.
[d] Figures in italics are for 1970–77, not 1970–78.
[e] Figures in italics are for years other than 1975.
[f] Preliminary estimate based on partial official information.

[t] total
[w] weighted average
[m] median

Source: World Bank, 1980a, pp. 110–111. Reproduced by permission of Oxford University Press.

obviously a very desirable thing to measure; but in practice how does one begin to determine what constitutes a 'good' life? Furthermore, because values and goals differ so much between—and even within—countries, it becomes very difficult to use social indicators as a means of comparing conditions in different countries, or even different regions or different social groups within the same country.

The difficulties of determining what indicators to use in measuring social development are demonstrated by the problems which have arisen in connection with the 'basic needs' approach to development, to which we referred in Chapter 2. Few people would dispute the concepts behind the basic needs approach, but the problems arise when one attempts to define exactly what is and what is not a basic need in any particular country and even more so if one attempts to define basic needs for the world as a whole.

Related to this is the problem of defining a small number of key indicators. The interrelationship between different aspects of development is so complex and varies so much from one place to another that, however rigorous the process of statistical analysis used to identify key indicators, the final choice is bound to oversimplify the real situation. Furthermore, as when identifying indicators in general, the selection of key indicators reflects very much the goals and biases of those making the selection. For example, national income is still probably used more often than any other single indicator of development, particularly when making comparisons between nations. Thus, in Table 11 the countries are ranked according to per capita income rather than to any of the other indicators used in the table. This is partly due to the fact that income does have a major impact on other aspects of development and is therefore closely correlated with many other indicators. However, it also reflects the continuing tendency in many countries and international agencies to associate development with economic growth and to measure economic growth in terms of per capita income.

Another problem is that of finding indicators which actually measure what one wants to measure. There are two sides to this problem. Firstly, there are some aspects of development which it is very difficult to measure in any way. For example, if one is trying to measure the quality of people's lives, an important consideration should be how 'happy' they are. But how does one measure 'happiness'? Since few people would agree on what constitutes happiness it would be very difficult to obtain an objective definition of it, let alone find any way of measuring it.

The other side of the problem is that there may be indicators which would provide the necessary information, but either there is no data available on these indicators or the data are not available in the right form or are not sufficiently reliable. This is often the case when one attempts to measure variations in the quality of life between social groups or regions. For instance, it is often very difficult to obtain information on the distribution of income between different social groups. In Chapter 2 we presented some summary data on differences in income distribution between developed and developing nations (see Table 1,

p. 23), but warned that the original data from which they were obtained were rather inadequate. The original data, which were collected by the World Bank, are reproduced in full in Table 12. It will be noted that data are available for only 28 of the 125 countries listed and, in notes accompanying the table, the Bank warns that:

Because the collection of data on income distribution has not been systematically organized and integrated into the official statistical system in many countries, estimates were typically derived from surveys designed for other purposes. . . . These surveys use a variety of income concepts and sample designs. . . . Furthermore, the coverage of many of these surveys is too limited to provide reliable nationwide estimates of income distribution. Thus, although the estimates are considered the best available, they do not avoid all these problems and should be treated with extreme caution. (World Bank, 1980a, p. 165)

This problem arises particularly—although not only—in developing countries, because it tends to be more difficult to obtain data of the quantity and quality required. Thus, in Table 12, most of the countries for which data on income distribution are not available are developing countries. This is partly due to the fact that statistical services tend to be less well developed in the Third World but also to the much greater problems of gathering basic social data in countries where a large part of the population lives in inaccessible rural areas, does not earn a fixed monetary income, and is wholly or partially illiterate. As indicated earlier, major efforts are being made to improve statistical services in most countries, but it will be some time before the full benefits of these efforts are felt.

Finally, there is the problem that much of the information on social conditions is not easily quantifiable or scalable, and so does not provide very good indicators. Many aspects of social development are very difficult to measure in quantifiable terms, even by the use of an ordinal scale (such as 'high', 'medium', 'low', or 'very good', 'good', 'average', 'bad', 'very bad'). This is a particular problem when trying to measure people's attitudes or opinions.

Scalability is important because it enables comparisons to be made. Sometimes it may be necessary to compare variations in one particular indicator, or set of related indicators, which occur over time or space. For example, if one is able to measure the availability of health services in some sort of numerical terms (such as average distance to the nearest health centre or population per doctor) one is able to compare health services between different countries or regions or to record changes over time in one particular area.

However, sometimes it is also necessary to compare different indicators of development. Thus, one may want to consider whether an area which has good health services but poor education services is better or worse off than an area with good education but poor health services. Or it may be necessary to decide whether the advantages of a new irrigation scheme in terms of increased agricultural production outweigh the disadvantage of a consequent increase in the incidence of the disease bilharzia. In order to make this sort of comparison, both indicators have to be expressed in the same terms, and in the case of

Table 12   International data on income distribution

| | | Percentage share of household income, by percentile groups of households[a] | | | | | |
	Year	Lowest 20%	Second quintile	Third quintile	Fourth quintile	Highest 20%	Highest 10%
Low-income countries							
1 Kampuchea, Dem. Rep.		—	—	—	—	—	—
2 Bangladesh		—	—	—	—	—	—
3 Lao PDR		—	—	—	—	—	—
4 Bhutan		—	—	—	—	—	—
5 Ethiopia		—	—	—	—	—	—
6 Mali		—	—	—	—	—	—
7 Nepal		—	—	—	—	—	—
8 Somalia		—	—	—	—	—	—
9 Burundi		—	—	—	—	—	—
10 Chad		—	—	—	—	—	—
11 Mozambique		—	—	—	—	—	—
12 Burma		—	—	—	—	—	—
13 Upper Volta		—	—	—	—	—	—
14 Viet Nam		—	—	—	—	—	—
15 India	1964–65	6.7	10.5	14.3	19.6	48.9	35.2
16 Malawi		—	—	—	—	—	—
17 Rwanda		—	—	—	—	—	—
18 Sri Lanka	1969–70	7.5	11.7	15.7	21.7	43.4	28.2
19 Guinea		—	—	—	—	—	—
20 Sierra Leone		—	—	—	—	—	—
21 Zaïre		—	—	—	—	—	—
22 Niger		—	—	—	—	—	—
23 Benin		—	—	—	—	—	—
24 Pakistan		—	—	—	—	—	—
25 Tanzania		—	—	—	—	—	—
26 Afghanistan		—	—	—	—	—	—
27 Central African Rep.		—	—	—	—	—	—
28 Madagascar		—	—	—	—	—	—
29 Haiti		—	—	—	—	—	—
30 Mauritania		—	—	—	—	—	—
31 Lesotho		—	—	—	—	—	—
32 Uganda		—	—	—	—	—	—
33 Angola		—	—	—	—	—	—
34 Sudan		—	—	—	—	—	—
35 Togo		—	—	—	—	—	—
36 Kenya		—	—	—	—	—	—
37 Senegal		—	—	—	—	—	—
38 Indonesia		—	—	—	—	—	—
Middle-income countries							
39 Egypt		—	—	—	—	—	—
40 Ghana		—	—	—	—	—	—
41 Yemen, PDR		—	—	—	—	—	—
42 Cameroon		—	—	—	—	—	—
43 Liberia		—	—	—	—	—	—

Table 12   (continued)

		Percentage share of household income, by percentile groups of households[a]					
	Year	Lowest 20%	Second quintile	Third quintile	Fourth quintile	Highest 20%	Highest 10%
44 Honduras	1967	2.3	5.0	8.0	16.9	67.8	50.0
45 Zambia	—	—	—	—	—	—	—
46 Zimbabwe	—	—	—	—	—	—	—
47 Thailand	—	—	—	—	—	—	—
48 Bolivia	—	—	—	—	—	—	—
49 Philippines	1970–71	3.7	8.2	13.2	21.0	53.9	—
50 Yemen Arab Rep.	—	—	—	—	—	—	—
51 Congo, People's Rep.	—	—	—	—	—	—	—
52 Nigeria	—	—	—	—	—	—	—
53 Papua New Guinea	—	—	—	—	—	—	—
54 El Salvador	—	—	—	—	—	—	—
55 Morocco	—	—	—	—	—	—	—
56 Peru	1972	1.9	5.1	11.0	21.0	61.0	42.9
57 Ivory Coast	—	—	—	—	—	—	—
58 Nicaragua	—	—	—	—	—	—	—
59 Colombia	—	—	—	—	—	—	—
60 Paraguay	—	—	—	—	—	—	—
61 Ecuador	—	—	—	—	—	—	—
62 Dominican Rep.	—	—	—	—	—	—	—
63 Guatemala	—	—	—	—	—	—	—
64 Syrian Arab Rep.	—	—	—	—	—	—	—
65 Tunisia	—	—	—	—	—	—	—
66 Jordan	—	—	—	—	—	—	—
67 Malaysia	1970	3.3	7.3	12.2	20.7	56.6	39.6
68 Jamaica	—	—	—	—	—	—	—
69 Lebanon	—	—	—	—	—	—	—
70 Korea, Rep. of	1976	5.7	11.2	15.4	22.4	45.3	27.5
71 Turkey	1973	3.4	8.0	12.5	19.5	56.5	40.7
72 Algeria	—	—	—	—	—	—	—
73 Mexico	1977	2.9	7.0	12.0	20.4	57.7	40.6
74 Panama	—	—	—	—	—	—	—
75 Taiwan	1971	8.7	13.2	16.6	22.3	39.2	24.7
76 Chile	1968	4.4	9.0	13.8	21.4	51.4	34.8
77 South Africa	—	—	—	—	—	—	—
78 Costa Rica	1971	3.3	8.7	13.3	19.9	54.8	39.5
79 Brazil	1972	2.0	5.0	9.4	17.0	66.6	50.6
80 Uruguay	—	—	—	—	—	—	—
81 Argentina	1970	4.4	9.7	14.1	21.5	50.3	35.2
82 Portugal	—	—	—	—	—	—	—
83 Yugoslavia	1973	6.5	11.9	17.6	24.0	40.0	22.5
84 Trinidad and Tobago	—	—	—	—	—	—	—
85 Venezuela	1970	3.0	7.3	12.9	22.8	54.0	35.7
86 Hong Kong	—	—	—	—	—	—	—
87 Greece	—	—	—	—	—	—	—
88 Singapore	—	—	—	—	—	—	—
89 Spain	1974	6.0	11.8	16.9	23.1	42.2	26.7
90 Israel	—	—	—	—	—	—	—

Table 12   (continued)

		Percentage share of household income, by percentile groups of households[a]					
	Year	Lowest 20%	Second quintile	Third quintile	Fourth quintile	Highest 20%	Highest 10%
Industrialized countries							
91 Ireland	—	—	—	—	—	—	—
92 Italy	1969	5.1	10.5	16.2	21.7	46.5	30.9
93 New Zealand	—	—	—	—	—	—	—
94 United Kingdom	1973	6.3	12.6	18.4	23.9	38.8	23.5
95 Finland	—	—	—	—	—	—	—
96 Austria	—	—	—	—	—	—	—
97 Japan	1969	7.9	13.1	16.8	21.2	41.0	27.2
98 Australia	1966–67	6.6	13.5	17.8	23.4	38.8	23.7
99 France	1970	4.3	9.8	16.3	22.7	46.9	30.4
100 Netherlands	1967	6.5	11.6	16.4	22.7	42.9	27.7
101 Belgium	—	—	—	—	—	—	—
102 Canada	1969	5.0	11.8	17.9	24.3	41.0	25.1
103 Norway	1970	6.3	12.9	18.8	24.7	37.3	22.2
104 Germany, Fed. Rep.	1973	6.5	10.3	15.0	22.0	46.2	30.3
105 United States	1972	4.5	10.7	17.3	24.7	42.8	26.6
106 Denmark	—	—	—	—	—	—	—
107 Sweden	1972	6.6	13.1	18.5	24.8	37.0	21.3
108 Switzerland	—	—	—	—	—	—	—
Capital-surplus oil exporters							
109 Iraq		—	—	—	—	—	—
110 Iran		—	—	—	—	—	—
111 Libya		—	—	—	—	—	—
112 Saudi Arabia		—	—	—	—	—	—
113 Kuwait		—	—	—	—	—	—
Centrally planned economies							
114 China		—	—	—	—	—	—
115 Korea, Dem. Rep.		—	—	—	—	—	—
116 Albania		—	—	—	—	—	—
117 Cuba		—	—	—	—	—	—
118 Mongolia		—	—	—	—	—	—
119 Romania		—	—	—	—	—	—
120 Bulgaria		—	—	—	—	—	—
121 Hungary		—	—	—	—	—	—
122 Poland		—	—	—	—	—	—
123 USSR		—	—	—	—	—	—
124 Czechoslovakia		—	—	—	—	—	—
125 German Dem. Rep.		—	—	—	—	—	—

[a] These estimates should be treated with caution.
Source: World Bank, 1980a, pp. 156–157. Reproduced by permission of Oxford University Press.

social indicators this is often not possible. The usual method of comparison is to express both indicators in monetary terms, but many social indicators cannot be expressed in this way. For example, one cannot attach a simple monetary value to the benefits of either health or extension services or to the costs incurred by an increase in the incidence of bilharzia. We shall see in Chapter 9 that this is one of the main problems of using conventional methods of cost–benefit analysis in social planning.

Data collection

Data collection is an essential component of any form of planning because planning decisions should only be made after considering any available relevant data. Social planners are particularly, although by no means exclusively, concerned with collecting information about people—their number, their physical and social attributes, the conditions in which they live, and their attitudes and opinions. It is impossible in one section of one chapter to cover all aspects of data collection relevant to social planners. This section is not, therefore, intended in any way as a substitute for a textbook on social survey methods. Those readers who are unfamiliar with this field of study, or feel the need to refresh their memories about particular aspects of data collection, are referred to the guide to further reading at the end of this chapter.

In this section we shall merely examine briefly the advantages and disadvantages of a number of important methods of data collection, namely:

(i)   the use of existing data;
(ii) censuses;
(iii) sample surveys;
(iv) interviewing key people;
(v)   group interviews;
(vi) participant observation.

In each case, we shall be particularly concerned with the suitability of the method for use in developing countries, since most of the available textbooks are based on conditions and needs in developed countries and so are not entirely relevant to the Third World planner.

Before examining each method of data collection individually, let us consider some general characteristics of data collection in developing countries. In general terms, it is probably true to say that data collection is more difficult than it is in the developed world. In the first place, existing data (such as published statistical series) are less likely to be available, especially in the form required by the planner. Secondly, original data are more difficult—and expensive—to collect for a variety of reasons. These include the physical problems of communication in most developing countries, which make it difficult to reach the people from whom information is required; other problems of communication between interviewers and interviewees, such as language or cultural barriers and the illiteracy or innumeracy of interviewees; and the fact that it is generally more difficult to measure data in quantitative terms.

Thirdly, the resources available for data collection, particularly finance and skilled manpower, are more limited. And finally, there is often very little time available for collecting the data, since the planners are under great pressure from politicians and other decision-makers to produce results immediately. This last problem is shared by planners throughout the world; but it tends to be particularly acute in developing countries because of the speed with which change and 'development' are so often required.

Because of these constraints, some principles and methods of data collection and usage designed in Europe or North America have to be modified for use in the Third World. For example, planning decisions often have to be made on the basis of data which elsewhere would be considered inadequate. The spatial or temporal coverage of the data may be inadequate, its accuracy may be rather dubious, or there may be some aspects of the issue for which no data are available at all. Similarly, it is often necessary to look for 'short-cut' methods of collecting data. We shall examine some of these when we consider specific methods of data collection.

This does not mean that social planners in the Third World should abandon all principles when collecting and using data. For example, recommendations should not be made without trying to collect any information at all, and surveys should not be conducted by interviewing the first people one meets instead of selecting some kind of sample. Furthermore, any deficiencies in the data should be clearly pointed out to the decision-makers, so that they are aware of the basis on which they are making decisions. What it does mean is that there is a need to modify standards and methods developed in Europe or North America to meet the needs and conditions of the Third World.

Another implication of the constraints which affect data collection in developing countries is that any data-collection exercise should be 'action oriented', in the sense that it should be designed to meet very specific needs. The collection of large quantities of data which will not actually be used—as in many surveys conducted in the Third World by overseas consultants—or data collection 'for its own sake' cannot be justified in a situation where there is an acute shortage of essential data and the resources available for their collection are severely limited.

With these points in mind, let us now look at some of the more important methods of data collection in rather more detail.

(i) *Existing data*

When looking for information on a particular topic, planners may be able to make use of data which have already been collected. For example, they may obtain demographic data from previous population censuses, they may find information on disease patterns and the availability of health services from the reports of the ministry of health, and they may use anthropological studies to learn more about the culture and mode of life of a particular community. This kind of data is very varied in both form and availability. Some may be published and so fairly readily available in libraries or government offices; but much is unpublished material, which may be buried away in government files or other obscure places.

There are two main problems in using existing data for planning purposes. Firstly, it is often difficult to find, especially in the case of unpublished material. This is a common problem in both developed and developing countries, and planners often choose to go out and collect their own data rather than face the rather tedious task of searching through libraries, government files, and other sources of information to find the particular material which they require. Secondly, it is not always available in the form required for the specific purpose at hand. This is particularly likely in developing countries, because there are generally less data available. For example, as we saw earlier in this chapter, it is usually more difficult to obtain reliable social statistics, particularly if data are required over a considerable period of time.

On the other hand, the use of existing data has some significant advantages. It is the only way of obtaining historical data, that is, information on social conditions at some time in the past or information on the way in which conditions have changed over time. Furthermore, although the process of locating existing data can be rather tedious and time-consuming, it is generally considerably quicker and less expensive than going out and collecting data oneself. This is particularly important in developing countries, in view of the lack of resources available for data collection.

On the whole, it is probably true to say that planners in the Third World do not make full use of the—admittedly limited—data which does already exist. There is always a tendency, especially among the more academically oriented researchers and planners, to go and collect original data before checking to see whether the information could be obtained from existing data sources. In this respect, improvements in the storage and retrieval of existing data are important, so that the information is more easily accessible. We shall look briefly at this in the next section of this chapter.

(ii) *Censuses*

A census is one of the means which planners may use to obtain information about people; in other words, it is one form of social survey. The term 'census' is used to refer to a survey which covers the whole population. In this context, the word 'population' is used in its statistical sense; that is, it means all the people who are relevant to, or included in, a particular study. In some cases, it may in fact mean all the inhabitants of a country, as in the case of a national population census. But this is not necessarily so. For example, if one was studying the attitudes of doctors towards proposed changes in health services, the relevant 'population' would merely be all doctors. Censuses are normally used when it is necessary to find out the total size of the population or to have information about every individual in the population rather than merely a representative sample.

The conduct of a census tends to be more difficult in developing countries, especially when the population to be surveyed is very large or the information required is particularly extensive or complex. This is because of the problems of communication mentioned earlier and the limited resources available. Conducting a census of the whole population obviously creates more communication problems and requires more resources than merely surveying a sample of the population. Consequently, sample surveys are often used in place of full censuses, even when it is really desirable to have information about the whole population, as in the case of national population censuses. During the colonial era it was common practice to conduct a complete census of the European population of a colonial territory, but only a sample survey of the indigenous population. Furthermore, when censuses are conducted they are often subject to considerable error because of the difficulties of obtaining accurate information about the whole population.

(iii) *Sample surveys*

Sample surveys are surveys which cover only a portion, or *sample*, of the population. They are usually conducted when information about the population is required, but it is either not possible or not necessary to survey the whole population. Most books on social survey methods devote a significant part to a discussion of sample surveys, including their uses (and abuses), methods of selecting samples, and ways of obtaining information from those people who are selected. We shall not attempt to consider any of these aspects in depth here, but merely to consider some particular points about conducting sample surveys in developing countries.

The selection of a representative sample of the population tends to be more difficult in developing countries, particularly in the case of rural surveys, because it is often difficult to obtain a sampling frame. For instance, one may wish to interview a random sample of 10 per cent of the households in a rural district, but one may not be able to obtain a complete list of all households from which to select the 10 per cent sample. The situation becomes even more difficult if one requires a stratified sample; for example, if one wishes to interview equal numbers of large and small landowners or those with non-farm income and those without. Furthermore, there is also the fundamental problem of how one should define a 'household'. Aerial photographs can sometimes be used to identify a sampling frame if lists of households are not available; but this requires up-to-date air photography, a reasonable knowledge of air photographic interpretation, and preferably some first-hand experience of the area itself and it is not usually much use in selecting a stratified sample.

Because of these problems, samples are often selected in a rather arbitrary fashion. In many cases this is inevitable because it is a question of collecting the information in this way or not at all. However, the implications of this in terms of the accuracy of the data thus collected should be remembered when analysing and interpreting the data. Furthermore, this should not be used as an excuse for not selecting a proper sample if it is possible to do so.

The most common method of obtaining information from those people selected for survey is to use a questionnaire. The main advantage of this method is that it standardizes the information collected, thereby minimizing interviewer bias and facilitating comparative analysis of the data. However, the use of questionnaires also presents a number of problems, some of which are particularly evident in developing countries.

Firstly, when using questionnaires in the Third World it is very important that they be relatively short and simple, because both interviewers and interviewees are likely to be discouraged by long, complex questionnaires. Moreover, the longer the questionnaire, the more expensive the survey becomes in terms of the input of time and, therefore, manpower and money.

Secondly, the question of language presents particular problems, since in many developing countries the language used by the people being interviewed is not the same as that used by those designing the questionnaire. In such cases, the questionnaire should be written in the language of the people being interviewed; if it is written in the language of those designing the questionnaire and then translated on the spot by the interviewer, there is likely to be a great deal of error due to inconsistencies in translation.

Designing a questionnaire which is clear, unambiguous, and produces the kind of answers required is not an easy task in any language, and it is particularly difficult when it has to be translated into another language. It requires a very thorough working knowledge of both languages, not merely a 'dictionary' knowledge. This problem is illustrated in an article on cross-cultural interviewing by Deutscher. He uses the example of the difficulty of translating the word 'friend':

The word friend . . . translates easily back and forth with the German cognate *Freund*. But is *ein Freund* in fact a friend? Hardly! For the German, the term is reserved for a very few intimate associates of long standing. For the American, the English cognate has a much broader reference to a much wider assortment of acquaintances. . . . The Spanish word which would provide a reliable back translation for the English 'friend' is *amigo*. Yet among Mexicans that term is employed both as a form of direct address and as indirect reference to strangers with whom the speaker may have had only the most casual and superficial encounter. (Deutscher, 1973, p. 169)

To this we may add the case of Papua New Guinea, where the English word 'friend' has been adopted into Melanesian Pidgin, but with the specific meaning of a close friend of the opposite sex (as in the English usage of the words 'boyfriend' and 'girlfriend'). In Pidgin the word *wantok* (meaning literally someone speaking the same language) is usually a more accurate translation of the word 'friend'.

Incidentally, Papua New Guinea illustrates another problem associated with the translation of questionnaires. Melanesian Pidgin is not a vernacular language; it is a *lingua franca*, spoken only in some parts of the country and then not by the whole population of the area. There are, in fact, over 700 vernacular languages in Papua New Guinea, many of which have never been written down. Consequently, the use of questionnaires presents some very significant problems, particularly in a nationwide survey. Papua New Guinea is admittedly an extreme example, but in most developing countries there are at least several different vernaculars.

The issue of language is related to that of cultural bias in interviewing. When designing questionnaires, familiarity with the cultural values and attitudes of the interviewees is essential. For example, if one is trying to obtain information about the interviewees' status in the community, one must know what factors are likely to contribute to social status in that particular community. Another sort of cultural problem which sometimes occurs in interviewing is a tendency for the interviewees to give the sort of answers they think the interviewer wants to hear. In Chapter 6 we referred to a survey of the impact of a family planning programme in India, which revealed that people accepted contraceptives and told the organizers of the programme that they were using them, when in fact they were not (Mamdani, 1972).

Finally, brief mention should be made of the use of postal questionnaires. This method of obtaining information is not usually very successful in developing countries because of the relatively high rate of illiteracy and the fact that postal services are not as easily available or as widely used as in developed countries. However, it should not be rejected completely because it is a great deal less expensive than personal interviewing and, in certain circumstances, it can produce useful results. For example, MacPherson used a postal questionnaire to survey village level health workers in the Southern Highlands Province of Papua New Guinea in 1978 and, somewhat to his surprise, obtained an 80 per cent response rate (MacPherson, 1980, Chapter 10). He attributed this success mainly to the fact that the health workers were at that time very dissatisfied with their conditions of service and saw the questionnaire as a possible way of drawing attention to their grievances.

In view of the many problems associated with sample surveys in developing countries, particularly when a written questionnaire is used, we would advise considerable caution in their use. Such surveys should be thoroughly planned and, if a questionnaire is to be used, it should be very carefully designed and (when necessary) translated and it should be pre-tested before use. Furthermore, in view of the high cost of such surveys in terms of time, manpower, and money, the actual benefits which will be obtained should be seriously considered before deciding whether or not to conduct such a survey, and if so what form it should take. In many cases, this sort of cost–benefit calculation may result in a decision to conduct 'unstructured' interviews instead of using a formal questionnaire, or to use some other method of obtaining the information. In the following sections we consider two such alternative methods: interviewing key people and the use of group interviews.

(iv) *Interviewing key people*

It is possible to obtain a considerable amount of information by interviewing certain 'key' people, such as community leaders or extension workers. Such people are particularly useful as a means of obtaining unpublished information or other factual information about a particular area. For instance, if one required more detailed information about local education or health services than was available at the national level, one could visit the local education or health office and interview the staff based there. The information thus obtained would be as reliable as most of the statistics available at the national level because the latter are normally based on information provided by local offices.

In some cases, one may also use key people, such as extension staff, as a means of obtaining more general information about the population of the area in which they work. Thus, one could ask a local medical officer about the standard of living of the local people, their attitudes to disease control, and their more general needs and aspirations. One might also ask similar questions to recognized community leaders, such as traditional chiefs, clan leaders, or councillors. In such cases, the information is rather less reliable because it is 'second-hand' information, which is subject to the personal bias of the person interviewed. We have already discussed in Chapters 6 and 7 some of the problems of using extension staff as a means of communication between 'planners' and 'people' and the difficulty of identifying representative community leaders. Certainly, information obtained in this manner is generally less reliable than that obtained by actually interviewing the people themselves, through either a census or a sample survey.

However, interviewing a small number of key people requires much less time, manpower, and money than conducting a sample survey or census. In view of this and the many problems associated with sample surveys and censuses, we feel that this form of data collection warrants rather more attention than it generally receives, especially if as is often the case—it is a question of obtaining some information in this way or obtaining no information at all. Those using such data should, however, be aware of its limitations and not use it to make decisions which require more detailed or more accurate data.

Two examples from Tanzania will illustrate the possible use of this method of data collection. The first example is a household survey which was conducted in connection with the north-east Nzega planning project described in Chapter 5. In this case, some of the information was obtained not by visiting individual households but by interviewing local political leaders, known as *ten-cell leaders*, and asking them various questions about all the households in their *cell* (Conyers, 1969). The other example is a survey of socio-economic conditions conducted throughout the country in 1970/71. The purpose of the survey was to divide each administrative district into planning zones (known as 'agro-economic zones') on the basis of general information about local conditions obtained by interviewing local agricultural extension officers (Conyers, 1973).

(v) *Group interviews*

Another 'short-cut' method of obtaining information is to hold group interviews. In this case, the people from whom information is required are usually invited to attend a meeting and questions are then asked or a general discussion held, from which the planners or data collectors extract the information they require. This method is particularly useful for obtaining information about the general attitudes and aspirations of a community or other recognizable group of people.

There are some fairly obvious drawbacks of this approach. Firstly, it is often very difficult for the planner to 'steer' the meeting in a direction which will enable him to obtain the necessary information, while at the same time allowing people to speak freely. Secondly, and considerably more important, the meeting tends to be dominated by a few vocal members of the group; other people either do not bother to come to the meeting or come but do not speak. Consequently, the information obtained is biased towards the opinions and attitudes of the more dominant and vocal members. This can be particularly serious if, as often happens, the population of the area is divided along economic, cultural, racial, or other lines, with some individuals or groups clearly dominating others. These problems are very closely related to those of community development programmes described in Chapter 7.

However, as in the case of interviewing key people, this method of data collection is considerably more economic, in terms of the amount of time, money, and manpower required, than more reliable methods and the data obtained are generally better than no information at all. Consequently, it offers considerable potential in developing countries, provided that it is used carefully and that the limitations of the data are fully recognized.

(vi) *Participant observation*

Participant observation is a recognized form of social investigation in which the person seeking information lives and/or works in an area or community and makes observations while doing so. This is potentially one of the most thorough ways of obtaining a wide range of information about the people themselves, their mode of life, and the environment in which they live, because the investigator generally spends a much longer period of time in the area and takes considerable pains to obtain accurate information. We mentioned in Chapter 6 that such a person is unlikely to be accepted as a full member of the community. Nevertheless, provided that he is at least accepted as a fellow resident, this method of investigation is probably least likely to arouse fear, mistrust, or resentment among the local population.

Social planners are unlikely to find themselves in a position to be able to spend sufficient time in an area to adopt this method themselves. However, on many occasions they may be able to obtain some useful information from anthropologists or sociologists who have been, or still are, working in the area concerned and have collected large quantities of data. The problem for the planner is that it is often very difficult to extract the particular information required from the mass of material collected by the participant observer. As we have already indicated elsewhere, anthropologists are not usually interested in the same things as planners and their results are not normally presented in a form which facilitates their use for planning purposes.

One possible answer to this problem which has not been fully exploited in most developing countries is to require anthropologists, sociologists, or any other social researchers to collect specific information required for planning purposes as one of the conditions under which they are allowed to conduct research. Many Third World countries now exert some control over researchers, especially those from overseas, and sometimes this includes directing them into a field of study which is likely to be relevant or useful for the country's development. But very few go as far as to specify particular information which they should collect and the form in which it should be presented. This would not require a great deal of effort on the part of the planners and, as a result, the country would obtain some tangible benefits from the many 'academic' researchers working in the country, many of whom are foreigners and make little or no direct contribution to national development.

Methods of presenting and storing information

The previous section examined various ways of collecting data for social planning purposes. In this section we look briefly at how these data should be presented and stored in order to make the best possible use of them. We look first at methods of presenting statistical and spatial data and then go on to consider data storage and retrieval systems. Finally, we consider briefly the advantages and disadvantages of using computers for the analysis and storage of information. As in other parts of this chapter, it will not be possible to examine any of these topics in any detail. We shall merely indicate those aspects which are particularly relevant to social planners in the Third World and leave the reader to pursue particular topics in more detail as and when required, using the guide to further reading at the end of the chapter.

(i) *Presenting statistical data*

When, as is often the case, the data which have been collected are in a numerical—or *statistical*—form, they usually have to be sorted or analysed in some way before they can actually be used for planning purposes. In some cases, this may involve no more than a simple tabulation of the data. For example, if one has collected information on the provision of various types of health service over a given period of time, this could be presented in the form of a table, showing the provision of each type of health service for each date for which information is available. On other occasions a more complex analysis may be required. Thus, if one has data not only on health services but also on a variety of other indicators of social development, one may wish to see if there is any statistical correlation between the way in which these various indicators change over time.

In either case, some basic knowledge of methods of statistical analysis is required in order to ensure that the significance is not distorted or misrepresented in any way. Such knowledge can be obtained by attending an introductory course in statistics or by reading a basic textbook on the subject. However, since most textbooks are directed towards users in the developed world, a few points particularly related to the use of statistics in developing countries should be mentioned here.

Firstly, when deciding how to analyse or present particular statistics for planning purposes, the quantity and quality of the data should be borne in mind. For example, if one has information about only a very small sample of the population, it is better not to undertake any detailed analysis because the results could be misleading. Even the use of percentages rather than actual numbers in tables is inadvisable if the sample is very small. Similarly, if one has serious doubts about the accuracy of the data, great care should be taken if any form of analysis is attempted because inaccurate data will distort the conclusions drawn from the analysis. These warnings apply in any country, but they are particularly valid in the Third World because the quantity and quality of data tend to be more limited.

The nature of the audience to whom the information will be presented should also be taken into consideration. The average politician or civil servant in a developing country is more likely to comprehend—and therefore to make use of—simple tabulations of data than complex statistical analyses. Experience has indicated that many people find even the concept of percentages difficult to grasp. In many cases it is helpful to present the data in the form of simple charts or diagrams instead of, or in addition to, statistical tables, since they tend to be easier to understand and to have a greater impact.

Finally, because of the lack of resources required for detailed analysis (particularly skilled manpower) and the urgency with which results are so often required, it is important to consider whether the amount of time and effort required to carry out any relatively sophisticated statistical analysis is justified in terms of the additional information likely to be obtained. We do not intend by these comments to imply that statistical analysis is merely a waste of time or to deny that it can be a very useful tool for planning. We merely wish to warn the planner that statistical analysis should be regarded as a means of improving the quality of the information used to make decisions, not as something of value in its own right.

(ii) *Presenting spatial data*

It is often necessary to collect spatial data—that is, data which shows the way in which a particular phenomenon varies from one geographical area to another—and it is important that such data are presented in such a way that it is easy to see not only the spatial distribution of the phenomenon but also the implications of this for planning purposes. This is particularly important for the social planner because of his concern with inequalities, including spatial inequalities.

If the data are available in statistical form they can be tabulated or subjected to statistical analysis, as described in the previous section. However spatial data, whether or not in statistical form, have their own particular mode of presentation—the map. There is a tendency for social scientists to regard maps as something only used by geographers, instead of as a useful tool for presenting any form of spatial data.

Figure 5 illustrates the way in which maps can be used to present social data in a way which facilitates usage in planning. It is a map showing access to health services in the Luapula Province of Zambia, which has been produced by superimposing data on the location of hospitals and health centres on to a map of population distribution. It indicates which areas are most in need of additional services and so can help in making decisions about the location of new hospitals or health centres.

(iii) *Data storage and retrieval*

It is very important that data which are collected for planning purposes are stored in a form in which they can easily be used by anyone involved in planning or decision-making. This includes not only professional planners in a national planning agency but also civil servants in functional ministries at the national level and in regional or local offices, national and local politicians, and community organizations involved in local planning activities.

There are four general principles which should be borne in mind when determining the way in which information should be stored. Firstly, it should be easily accessible. For example, it should not be buried away in an obscure file in some government office; nor should it be stored in a complex computer-based information system to which only a few skilled technicians have direct access.

Secondly, the data should be in a form easily understood or interpreted by any likely user. This means presentation in clear, simple terms, especially for usage by people with limited knowledge of, or experience in, dealing with data—such as local politicians or community groups.

Thirdly, any data which becomes out of date relatively quickly should be stored in such a way as to be easily and regularly updated as new information becomes available. For example, it is much easier to update written information if it is stored on index cards or in loose-leaf files instead of in bound volumes. Similarly, data presented in map form can be easily updated if depicted by movable articles, such as coloured pins, so that the whole map does not have to be redrawn every time new information becomes available.

Finally, the method of storage should be realistic in terms of the input of staff, finance, and other resources available to operate it. Thus, there is no point in establishing a data storage system which requires very large inputs of manpower, since experience suggests that, when there is a shortage of manpower, data storage is one of the first jobs to be neglected. Similarly, it would be pointless to consider an electronic data storage system which has to operate in constant and relatively cool climatic conditions in a tropical environment where air conditioning was unavailable or unreliable.

It is not possible to discuss alternative forms of data storage in any detail here, since a great deal depends on the type of data, the conditions of usage, and the resources available for storage. However, brief mention should be made of what is often known as the *operations room* approach to planning, which was developed in Malaysia in the 1950s and has since been adopted in various forms by a number of other countries. In this approach, the basic data required for planning at both national and local level are stored in the form of maps, charts, and loose-leaf files, which are all displayed in a central meeting room where all discussions on planning matters are held. The data are thus easily accessible whenever needed and, in fact, often become the focus of the meeting. The main drawback of this approach seems to be that, although it is much simpler than many data storage systems, the amount of time required to keep the information up to date and in usable form is still greater than many countries appear able to provide for more than a short period of time.

(iv) *The use of computers*

In developed countries—and increasingly also in developing countries—computers are now used for the analysis of data and also for storage and retrieval. In many cases, this is undoubtedly the most efficient way of handling the data, particularly when there is a large amount. For example, it is obviously much easier to process the data from several thousand questionnaires by computer than it is by hand.

However, it should not be assumed that the computer is always the most suitable method, especially in developing countries, where a number of constraints limit its use. Firstly, it is necessary to consider whether the quantity and quality of the data justifies the use of a computer, either for processing or for storage purposes. If one is dealing with only small quantities of data or data which are notoriously unreliable, it may be much more sensible to use manual methods.

Secondly, computers are expensive to purchase (or hire) and to operate and, in order to operate effectively, they require specially trained manpower and certain environmental conditions, such as a constant temperature and humidity. This means not only that they make heavy demands on scarce resources but also that their effectiveness is very easily impaired if any of these resources or conditions are lacking. Many social research programmes in the Third World are so hampered by problems such as inadequately trained or experienced programming staff and constant breakdowns of the computer that in the end the work could have been done much quicker, if more laboriously, by hand. Furthermore, it should be remembered that one of the main reasons for using a computer in developed countries is to save semi-skilled or unskilled labour, which is much less likely to be in short supply in the Third World.

Finally, access to computer facilities is very limited, especially in countries where there are very few computers or computer terminals and very few skilled programmers and operators. This is particularly important when considering computer-based information systems, since the information would only be

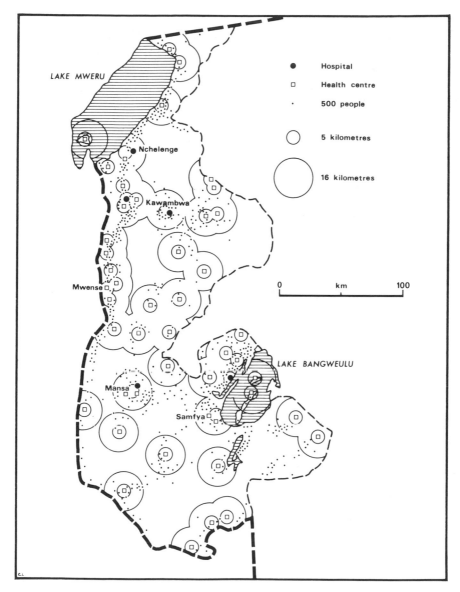

Figure 5   Access to health services: Luapula Province, Zambia.
Source: Adapted from Zambia, 1976, p. 46

available to a few people who have direct access to computer facilities. It will, of course, probably be necessary to store some data (for example, census results) on a computer. But such information should also be made available in other forms (thus each region should have a printed summary of the census data for its own area) and, for many kinds of planning data, a simple operations room approach is likely to be more practicable.

Some general conclusions

We will not attempt to summarize all the points made in this chapter about information needs for social planning. However, there are three general conclusions that can be drawn.

Firstly, decisions made by planners are only as good as the information on which they are based. Consequently, it is important that adequate attention be given to the collection and presentation of information for planning purposes. However, at the same time it should be remembered that data collection and processing is not an end in itself but only a means of making better decisions.

Secondly, the collection and analysis of information for social planning purposes presents particular problems, mainly because much of the information required relates to aspects of development which cannot easily be measured, particularly in quantifiable terms.

And thirdly, when deciding what methods of collecting, analysing, presenting, or storing information, it is necessary to consider the purpose for which the information is required, the users of the information, the quantity and quality of the data available, and the resources available for collection or processing. In the Third World it is often necessary to use simpler methods and to make decisions on the basis of less complete or reliable data; the use of particularly sophisticated methods should not be justified on the basis that it is a desirable end in itself but only if it is likely to improve the quality of the decisions made.

Guide to further reading

Measuring social development

There is a considerable amount of information available on social indicators and their uses. Many works are directed primarily at the developed world; for example, *Social Indicators and Social Policy*, edited by A. Shonfield and S. Shaw (London, Heinemann, 1972) (especially Chapters 1 and 2); and Part Four of *Social Policy Research*, edited by M. Bulmer (London, Macmillan, 1978).

However, there are also a number of books and articles which are specifically concerned with social indicators in the Third World. Two of the most useful are: *Measuring Development*, edited by N. Baster (London, Frank Cass, 1972) (especially Chapters 1 and 2); and *Social Indicators: Definitions, Properties, Uses, Representatives* by R. Apthorpe (University of East Anglia, School of Development Studies, Discussion Paper No. 26, 1978).

There are also a number of United Nations publications in this field. They include *Towards a System of Social and Demographic Statistics*, produced by the Department of Economic and Social Affairs (New York, 1975), and *Contents and Measurement of Socio-Economic Development*, published by the United Nations Research Institute for Social Development (Geneva, 1970). The latter is concerned particularly with the identification of 'core' indicators of development.

Data collection

There are a number of textbooks on social research methods. Unfortunately, most of these are designed for use in the developed world and so, although they are useful as an introduction to general principles and methods, they do not consider the special conditions which exist in developing countries. Three of the most useful texts are: *Social Surveys for Social Planners* by G. Gardner (Milton Keynes, Open University Press, 1978); *Survey Methods in Social Investigation* by C. A. Moser and G. Kalton (London, Heinemann, second edition 1971); and *Research Methods in the Social Sciences* by C. and D. Nachmias (London, Edward Arnold, 1976).

For discussion of the problems of applying these methods in developing countries, the most useful existing books are probably *Comparative Research Methods,* edited by D. P. Warwick and S. Osherson (Englewood Cliffs, NJ, Prentice-Hall, 1973) and *Survey Research in Africa: its Applications and Limits*, edited by W. O'Barr *et al.* (Evanston, Illinois, Northwestern University Press, 1973). A third book, *Social Research Methods in Developing Countries*, edited by M. Bulmer and D. P. Warwick is currently in preparation (Wiley, forthcoming).

The United Nations has also published a number of items on specific social research methods; these are published in a series known as *Studies in Methods*, Series F. A fairly specialized coverage of methods of data collection for planning individual projects is provided in Chapter 6 of *The Cultural Appraisal of Development Projects* by G. Cochrane (New York, Praeger, 1979). A book by S. Pausewang entitled *Methods and Concepts of Social Research in a Rural Developing Society* (Munich, Veltforum Verlag, Afrika-Studien No. 80, 1973) provides a study of research methods in a particular country, Ethiopia, from which some useful general conclusions are drawn. And *Paradise Postponed*, edited by A. Mamak and G. McCall (Sydney, Pergamon Press, 1978) discusses the role and ethics of social research in the Third World, with particular reference to the South Pacific. Finally, a short but useful article on practical methods of data collection is Chambers, R., 'Rapid rural appraisal: rationale and repertoire', *Public Administration and Development,* **1** (1981), 95–106.

Presenting and storing information

Some of the books on social research methods recommended above include some general information on how to analyse and present the data, and for a general discussion of the analysis of social science data a book by J. Silvey entitled *Deciphering Data* (London, Longman, 1975) is recommended.

There are many basic textbooks on introductory statistics, and readers should choose one which is easily available in his own country or educational institution. Some examples include: *An Introduction to Statistics for the Social Sciences* by T. G. Connolly and W. Sluckin (London, Macmillan, 3rd edition 1971); *Elementary Statistics*, by P. G. Hoel (New York, Wiley, 3rd edition 1971); *Facts from Figures* by M. J. Moroney (Harmondsworth, Penguin, 2nd edition 1953); and *Statistics for the Social Scientist* by K. A. Yeomans (Harmondsworth, Penguin, 1968).

There is a lack of basic material on methods of data storage and retrieval for planning purposes. However, for a general introduction to the subject (including a brief discussion of the 'operations room' approach to planning) the reader is referred to Chapter 9 of *Development Planning: Lessons of Experience* by A. Waterston (Baltimore, Johns Hopkins Press, 1965).

CHAPTER 9

GENERAL PLANNING SKILLS

There are many general planning skills and techniques which are relevant to all or most forms of planning, including social planning, and the purpose of this chapter is to examine the relevance of some of these to social planners in the Third World. We shall not attempt to provide a comprehensive coverage of all relevant skills and techniques or to discuss any particular one in any depth. We shall instead focus our attention on those skills which are likely to be particularly useful to the social planner, and the special issues or problems which are likely to arise when trying to adapt general planning skills for use in social planning in the Third World.

There are two main reasons for adopting this approach. One is the sheer impossibility of providing a complete coverage of planning methodology in the space available here, since each particular skill or method really demands a chapter—or in some cases even a book—in its own right. The other reason is that there is already a considerable volume of material available on the general methodology of planning, and the main problem facing readers of this book is likely to be how to adapt this to meet their own needs.

One of the shortcomings of existing literature on planning methods is that most books are written for specialists—such as economists or physical planners—whose main concern is not with the social aspects of planning. There is as yet very little material concerned specifically with the methodology of social planning and, although the basic techniques used are often the same as in other fields of planning, the purposes for which they are used and the particular problems which are likely to arise are different.

Another common cause of confusion or difficulty is the fact that many books on planning methods tend to concentrate on the intricacies of particular techniques—such as alternative ways of calculating the costs of specific items in the case of cost–benefit analysis—instead of more general principles about when such techniques should or should not be used. Consequently, the reader is often unnecessarily confused, particularly if he is unfamiliar with the professional 'jargon' being used—as, for example, when social planners try to read books by economists—and has difficulty in seeing how the particular technique can be adapted to meet his own needs.

Moreover, social planners in the Third World have an additional problem in that most material on planning methods is designed for use in developed countries. Because of the significantly different conditions in the Third World, especially in terms of the quantity and quality of data and the availability of skilled manpower and technical equipment, techniques which are practicable in developed countries are often completely unsuitable in the Third World, or at least can only be applied after considerable modification.

The purpose of this chapter, therefore, is to try to fill some of these gaps and help the reader to make better use of existing literature on planning methods. A guide to some of this literature is provided at the end of the chapter.

There is no universally agreed-upon classification of planning skills and techniques, a fact which also adds to the confusion of someone searching for relevant methods to use in solving a particular problem. We have in this chapter divided the various skills required by the social planner into three main categories:

  (i) decision-making skills;
 (ii) implementation skills;
(iii) management and communication skills.

Although this classification is somewhat arbitrary, it is designed to assist the reader to understand the purposes for which particular skills are used rather than merely to know how to use them.

Decision-making skills

Planning is fundamentally a process of decision-making, and it is therefore not surprising that many planning techniques are designed to help the planner make better—and in particular more *rational*—decisions. Before examining some of these techniques, let us look briefly at what we mean by rational decision-making.

(i) *Rational decision-making*

The concept of rationality has been the subject of a great deal of debate among those concerned with the theory of planning and decision-making. In very simple terms, rational decision-making can be regarded as making decisions by exercising one's reason rather than merely by guessing or reacting to emotional impulses. Carley, in a book entitled *Rational Techniques in Policy Analysis*, provides a more detailed explanation by describing rational decision-making in terms of the following five 'sequential activities':

(1) A problem which requires action is identified and goals, values and objectives related to the problem are classified and organized.
(2) All important possible ways of solving the problem or achieving goals and objectives are listed—these are alternative strategies, courses of action, or policies.
(3) The important consequences which would follow from each alternative strategy are predicted and the probability of these consequences occurring is estimated.
(4) The consequences of each strategy are then compared to the goals and objectives identified above.
(5) Finally, a policy or strategy is selected in which consequences most closely match goals and objectives, or the problem is most nearly solved, or most benefit is got from equal cost, or equal benefit at least cost. (Carley, 1980, p. 11)

The debate arises mainly from the question of how *comprehensive* or thorough one has to be in order to be rational. Does one have to consider all possible alternative strategies or courses of action before making a decision? Does one have to obtain information about all aspects of each of these alternatives before choosing between them? Is it always necessary to find the optimum solution rather than being satisfied with a solution which merely meets certain basic requirements? Most writers on decision-making today would probably agree that the practical planner cannot hope to be entirely comprehensive—but that this does not mean that he (or she) cannot be rational and attempt to arrive at the best possible decision given the practicalities of the environment in which he is working. It is important to bear in mind this pragmatic concept of rational decision-making when we go on to consider the use of alternative decision-making techniques later in this section.

So far we have been talking about rational decision-making in very general terms. What particular implications does it have for the social planner in the Third World? The main role of the social planner in this decision-making process is to ensure that social goals, values, and objectives are given sufficient priority and that the social consequences of alternative strategies are taken into account and given sufficient weight when choosing between them. In other words, he is concerned that the term 'rationality' should not be interpreted merely as economic rationality. Consequently, in the following discussion of particular techniques, one of our main concerns will be to see how these factors can be taken into consideration.

The debate about rational versus comprehensive decision-making has particular significance for planners in the Third World. On the one hand, it could be argued that in many countries of the Third World the scope for comprehensive planning is greater because there is a tendency for goals and objectives to be more clearly articulated and a wider range of alternative strategies to be considered than in developed nations, since the former are concerned to achieve change or 'development' while the latter tend to be preoccupied with maintaining the *status quo*.

But, on the other hand, the practical problems of considering all possible alternatives and choosing between them on the basis of a comprehensive assessment of all possible implications are particularly foreboding in the average Third World country. This is partly because of the difficulty of obtaining adequate data and partly because decisions often have to be made very quickly, thus preventing the planner from undergoing a thorough evaluation process. In many countries, what are generally regarded as 'political' factors also play a major role in decision-making and, although these can be built into the decision-making process, this requires some modification of the concept of rationality and, therefore, of some decision-making techniques. In other words, for planners in the Third World a pragmatic approach to rational decision-making is particularly important.

Let us now turn to the implications of this general discussion for the use of specific decision-making skills. We begin by examining the skills required for two particularly important components of the decision-making process: forecasting likely future trends or events and comparing the merits and demerits of alternative courses of action. We then look briefly at the particular problems of making decisions about the distributional aspects of development, and finally we make some general comments about the use of mathematical models in decision-making.

(ii) *Forecasting*

Since planning involves making decisions about the future, the planner is constantly faced with the task of forecasting what is likely to happen in the future. At what rate is the population likely to grow over the next 10 years? What improvements in health can be expected from the provision of more hospitals? Would more improvement be likely if resources were used instead for primary health care? What social changes may occur if a new mining venture is established in a previously underdeveloped area and what is the probability of each occurring? And so on.

A variety of techniques have been designed to assist the planner to make more accurate forecasts. Many of these are based on the analysis of quantitative data about past or present situations. Thus, future population growth may be predicted by examining past trends and extending these into the future. This approach is generally known as *trend extrapolation*. The most obvious shortcoming of trend extrapolation is that it assumes that the factors affecting future trends are unlikely to be very different—or unpredictably different—from those which determined trends in the past. If this is not the case, it is necessary to use more complex forms of quantitative analysis, which involve the construction of models of the situation which incorporate a variety of inter-related variables. Economists, for example, often use *input–output models* of the national economy to predict what effect an increase in activity in one sector of the economy is likely to have on other sectors.

The main problem with any of these methods is that they are dependent on the existence of reliable quantitative data, often extending back over a reasonable historical period, and such data are frequently not available. This is a particular problem for social planners in the Third World since, as we saw in Chapter 8, the quantity and quality of statistical data is generally more limited in the Third World and data on the social aspects of development are particularly difficult to obtain in quantitative form.

Consequently, it may often be necessary to resort to other methods of forecasting which rely less on quantitative data. One such method is to look for similar situations elsewhere from which lessons can be learned. For example, in Chapter 5 we showed how the Papua New Guinea government has tried to use some of the experience gained in the Bougainville copper-mining project to predict the likely social impact of the new mine to be built at Ok Tedi. Another possible method is to formulate a number of alternative hypothetical pictures (usually known as *scenarios*) about what might happen in the future and to consider which of these is most likely to occur given alternative courses of action. A third approach is to consult a variety of people who, because of their particular experience or expertise, are most likely to be able to predict what will happen in a given situation. Thus, the planner might interview extension officers based in a particular area in order to obtain their views about the likely reaction of the local people to a proposed development project. Various techniques have been devised in order to obtain the maximum amount of information from such consultations, especially when a number of different people are consulted.

These methods all rely to a considerable extent on subjective judgements and so predictions made in this way cannot be assumed to be highly reliable. However, it has to be remembered that no method of forecasting can be completely reliable—especially in the Third World where change tends to be particularly rapid and unpredictable—and given the difficulties of obtaining adequate statistical data, such methods are often no more unreliable than the use of quantitative forecasting techniques, and in most cases they are certainly more practical.

(iii) *Comparing alternative courses of action*

We have already indicated that rational decision-making involves identifying possible alternative courses of action and then comparing these in order to decide which one to follow, and a variety of techniques have been developed to assist the planner in making such comparisons. Most of these techniques are related to the general concept of *cost–benefit analysis*, in which the costs and benefits of each alternative are calculated and priority is given to the one in which the ratio of benefits to costs is highest.

As we mentioned in Chapter 8, cost–benefit analysis is a technique which was originally developed by economists, particularly for use in evaluating projects in order to decide which of a number of projects is likely to be most profitable or whether or not it is economically feasible to go ahead with a particular project. Conventional methods of cost–benefit analysis were, therefore, based on calculating the monetary value of costs and benefits, thus enabling precise comparisons to be made between alternative projects, and research focused on improving methods of calculating the various costs and benefits and taking into account the difference between the present and future values of money.

However, when the concept of cost–benefit analysis is extended to other aspects of planning, the scope and complexity of the problems increase. From the social planner's point of view, the main problem is that most of the social costs and benefits of any particular project or programme cannot be expressed in monetary terms, and some cannot be quantified at all, thus making it very difficult to compare them with economic costs and benefits. Thus, to return to the example of evaluating the likely impact of the Ok Tedi copper mine in Papua New Guinea, the economic benefits—such as mineral production and the creation of jobs—can be fairly easily expressed in monetary terms; but it is very difficult to attach any quantitative, let alone monetary, value to the social disruption which will occur in the area as a result of the mine. As we indicated in Chapter 5, this often means that social considerations are neglected in favour of economic factors, simply because they cannot be quantified, and, in particular, monetarized, and so cannot be incorporated into conventional cost–benefit analysis. This problem is especially acute in developing countries because of the difficulty of obtaining accurate quantitative data on the social—and other—aspects of development.

There is no easy solution to this problem. A number of variations of conventional cost–benefit analysis have been developed to try to deal with the problem of costs and benefits which cannot be expressed in monetary terms. Two possible approaches appear to offer the greatest potential for the purposes of social planning. One is to use other, non-monetary criteria to measure social costs and benefits and then to adopt some sort of weighting system to enable these criteria to be compared with the monetary values used to measure the economic costs and benefits. The other is to use conventional methods of cost–benefit analysis to evaluate the economic aspects of a project, but also to carry out a broader and more qualitative survey of the social implications and to take the results of both studies into consideration when making a final decision. In either case, cost–benefit analysis becomes a much more complex process, fraught with imprecision and value judgements, in which the planner or politician often has to make a choice between financial and social gains. However, surely this is better than making decisions without taking social—and other non-monetary factors—into consideration at all?[1]

In concluding this section, it should be noted that the social planner may need to use cost–benefit analysis either to evaluate alternative social development programmes or projects—such as alternative types of health care programme—or to evaluate the social implications of projects which are designed primarily to achieve economic objectives, as in the case of the copper mines in Papua New Guinea. The fact that social planners are increasingly being called upon to advise on the social implications of economic development projects, makes it particularly important that they are aware of the problems of measuring social factors and of the various ways in which these problems can at least partially be overcome.

(iv) *Making decisions about distribution*

It was pointed out in Chapter 2 that the social planner is particularly concerned with the distributional aspects of development, including the distribution of development between socio-economic groups and the distribution between geographical regions, and the implications of this for specific fields of social planning were demonstrated in Part Two. Because of this concern with distribution and inequality it is necessary to look briefly at its implications for methods of decision-making.

Although it is generally recognized that planners should consider the effects of alternative development programmes and projects on inequalities between socio-economic groups, relatively little attention has been given to the question of how this can be built into the decision-making process. The emergence of a 'basic needs' approach to development policy during the latter part of the 1970s has resulted in some moves in this direction; for example, an international conference held at the University of Sussex in 1977 considered the applicability of macro-economic models for planning the provision of basic needs (Cole and Lucas, 1978). But the specific question of inequalities, which is only one component of a basic needs approach, does not seem to have received a great deal of attention.

The main need is to identify which socio-economic groups are likely to be most affected, positively or negatively, by any proposed policies, programmes, or projects so that their impact on inequalities can be clearly seen. This means that any decision-making techniques—such as models used to predict future trends or methods of comparing the costs and benefits of a project—must be able to incorporate information on different socio-economic groups. And it also means, of course, that the information itself must be disaggregated by socio-economic group. This presents particular problems since, as we saw in Chapter 8, it is often very difficult to obtain meaningful data on inequalities between such groups. Statistical data are seldom disaggregated on this basis, or at least are not available in the form or degree of detail required, particularly in the case of inequalities within communities. For example, it would be difficult to obtain statistical data which would indicate the likely impact of a community development project on inequalities within an Indian village; only an intimate knowledge of the village would enable some predictions to be made.

The social planner, therefore, has two main roles in relation to making decisions about distribution between social groups. First, he should ensure that in any decision-making process the implications for different socio-economic groups are taken into consideration, instead of merely assuming that everyone will benefit equally. And second, he should make every effort to improve the quantity and quality of data available for this purpose.

Rather more attention has been given to the implications of regional inequalities for methods of decision-making, mainly because the distribution and interaction of phenomena in space have for many years been studied by geographers, regional economists, and others involved in the spatial aspects of planning, and special tools have been developed for this purpose. From the social planner's point of view, there are two main aspects of this field of study which are of relevance to methods of decision-making.

Firstly, the social planner should be conscious of the need to identify how different regions are likely to be affected by proposed policies, programmes, and projects so that their impact on spatial inequalities can be assessed. This raises similar issues about the design of decision-making models and the disaggregation of data as in the case of assessing inequalities between social groups—and it raises the same sort of problems, particularly those of obtaining adequate data.

Secondly, the social planner should have a general understanding of the factors which affect socio-economic development within and between regions and he should be aware of some of the methods used by spatial planners to try to distribute such development more evenly. Unfortunately, in many countries the work of spatial planners is not sufficiently coordinated with more general socio-economic planning, particularly if the spatial planners are located in a different ministry or department.

One of the more obvious examples of a spatial planning technique which is relevant to the social planner is the concept of *service centres*, which is concerned directly with the distribution of social services. Service centres are central points at which a variety of social, economic, and administrative services are provided, on the grounds that the concentration of services at a central point is more convenient for the people using them and reduces the cost of their provision. Sometimes, larger service centres are also identified as centres for the development of industry or other forms of economic activity, often as a means of encouraging development outside the main urban centres. In this case, they are often referred to as 'growth centres' or 'development centres'. Figure 6 shows a hierarchy of 'development centres' identified as a basis for planning in Zambia's Third National Development Plan. These development centres range from major urban centres, which should have a wide range of infrastructure, to small village development centres, which should be provided with basic facilities such as a health centre, water supply, agricultural extension services, and so on. Special analytical tools have been developed by spatial planners to assist in the identification of such centres.

(v) *The use of mathematical models*

A model may be described as any attempt to represent reality in some other form. A map, for example, is one kind of model in which the various components are represented in a special kind of graphical form. A *mathematical model* is a model in which the components are represented in the form of quantitative data and relationships between them are expressed in mathematical terms.

Many types of mathematical model are used in planning, particularly—but not only—by economists. They include models of the global situation, models of the economy of one country, and models of a particular sector, region, or project within a country. They include relatively simple models which only represent one aspect or component of the situation, and highly complex simulation models which attempt to represent an entire socio-economic system. And these models may be used for prediction, for comparing alternative courses of action, or merely to describe the present situation.

It is not possible to describe any specific models here. The most important point to note is that, although mathematical models can be very valuable decision-making tools, their use presents serious problems in the average Third World country. The main reasons for this are a shortage of the skilled technical manpower and equipment (such as computers) needed to design and use such models, inadequate quantitative data to feed into them, and the fact that most of the people using the results will not understand how they were obtained. In most countries these problems are such that the situations in which mathematical models can be usefully applied are fairly limited and the planner should thus think carefully before either deciding to apply such a model or using the information obtained therefrom.

The problems of using mathematical models are compounded in the case of social planning by the difficulty of quantifying social data, with the result that social considerations tend to be inadequately represented in such models. The most important role of the social planner, therefore, is to ensure that, if such models are used, every effort is made to incorporate social factors—and if this cannot be done, to warn those using the results that the social implications have been ignored.

Implementation skills

In our discussion of development planning in Chapter 1, we emphasized that planning and implementation must be regarded as two interrelated components of a single process, since the purpose of planning is not to produce plans but to achieve practical results. We have reiterated this every now and again in subsequent chapters, and it is now time to look briefly at some of the techniques which can be adopted in order to strengthen the links between planning and implementation. We shall look first at the general process of making a plan implementable or operational, and then more specifically at budgeting, monitoring and evaluating plan performance, and finally the role and structure of a plan document.

(i) *Making a plan operational*

One of the most critical stages in the process of planning and implementation is deciding how to implement a particular project or programme. For example, once a decision has been made to build a new health centre in a particular area, what actually has to be done before that health centre is ready for use by the local people? More specifically, it is necessary to consider the following kinds of issue: What are the various stages involved in the implementation—from choosing a site to the provision of staff and equipment? Who will be responsible for each stage and how long will it take? How much will each component cost and where will the funds be obtained? Unfortunately, this part of the planning–implementation process is very often neglected because neither the planners nor the implementers consider it to be their responsibility, with the result that the health centre—or whatever else is proposed—never gets further than an idea on paper.

The process of 'operationalizing' a plan is not necessarily very complex. The most important requirements are to ensure that all relevant stages or components of the plan are identified, that sufficient funds and manpower are available, and that someone is actually made responsible for carrying out each stage.

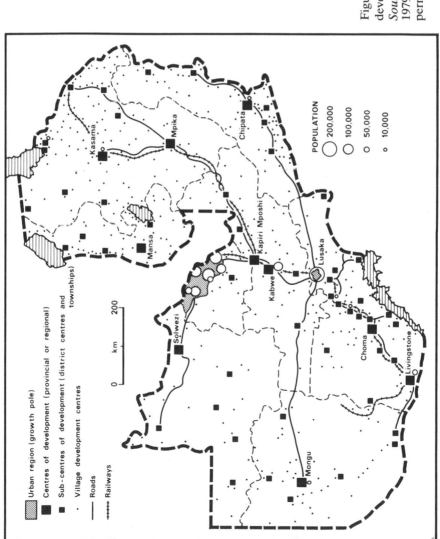

Figure 6 Zambia: hierarchy of development centres.
Source: Adapted from Zambia, 1979, map 9. Reproduced by permission of Government Printer, Zambia

Urban region (growth pole)

Centres of development (provincial or regional)

Sub-centres of development (district centres and townships)

Village development centres

Roads

Railways

POPULATION

200,000
100,000
50,000
10,000

Kasama
Mpika
Chipata
Mansa
Kapiri Mposhi
Lusaka
Kabwe
Solwezi
Choma
Livingstone
Mongu

km
0   200

There are no particular requirements in the case of social planning, except that the social planner is likely to be particularly concerned about any stage where participation by the local people in the project area is required. For instance, in the example of the health centre, the local community may be consulted about the exact site for the centre, expected to contribute labour or money to assist with the construction, or even to provide staff to be trained as community health workers.

Sometimes, however, operationalizing a plan can become a more complex process, especially if there are many different activities and organizations involved. In such cases, there are particular techniques which can be of assistance. Most of these involve what is generally known as *network analysis*, and more specifically a form of network analysis known as *critical path analysis*. The basic aim of these techniques is to identify all the different activities which have to be performed and the interrelationship between them, in order to help the planner to see what has to be done and in what sequence—in other words, to help him to identify the 'critical path' which has to be followed. Sometimes this process of analysis can be undertaken simply with the aid of a large chart which shows all the components of the network; but in more complicated cases it may be necessary to feed all the information into a computer. In either case, it should be remembered that the use of techniques such as critical path analysis is not a substitute for the application of common sense and rational human thought, since the techniques are only useful as a means of analysing the interrelationships between a number of variables; the planner must still identify which variables are important. For example, critical path analysis will not indicate the need to consult the local population about the location of a project unless someone—such as a social planner—has already decided that popular participation is important in such matters.

(ii) *Budgeting*

We mentioned in the previous section the need to ensure that funds are available for implementing a plan. This point is so important that it is necessary to look in more detail at the relationship between planning and budgeting. In recent years considerable attention has been devoted to finding ways of improving this relationship through improvements in what is generally known by economists as *national public expenditure planning*. The main aims of these improvements are to improve plan implementation and to make the budget more effective as a tool for achieving basic national goals and objectives.

Various attempts have been made to design formal systems of planning and budgeting with these objectives in mind. These are generally known as *planning, programming, and budgeting systems* (PPBS) or *planning, programming, and performance budgeting* (PPPB) systems. It is not necessary to describe any of these systems in detail here, since it is unlikely that the social planner will be involved in the detailed design of a planning–budgeting system. However, it is necessary to look briefly at the basic principles involved in any such system because the social planner may be able to use it as a means of indicating the amount of importance which is (or is not) attached to the achievement of social goals and objectives. Moreover, even if he is not in a position to use the system in that way, he is sure at some time or other to have to prepare a budget for a particular project or programme and he will find this easier if he understands some of the basic principles about the relationship between planning and budgeting.

Since efforts to improve national public expenditure planning are concerned with the relationship between planning and budgeting, they generally involve changes in both the preparation of plans and the structure and role of the budget.

On the planning side, the main aim is to prepare plans in a form which takes into account the likely sources of finance for their implementation. This means, firstly, that plans must be realistic in the sense that they do not require much more money than is likely to be available, and secondly, that the various components of the plan must be broken down into components which correspond to the anticipated sources of finance. Thus, if the ministry of education is planning a programme for expanding vocational education, these plans must be realistic in terms of the amount of money the ministry is likely to have and they must be broken down to show how much money is required from each of the main sections of the ministry's budget; for example, how much is required for salaries, how much for equipment, how much for travel, how much for capital works, and so on. And if, as may be the case in something like vocational education, some inputs are required from other ministries or departments, provision must also be made in their budgets.

On the budgeting side, efforts are directed mainly towards making the structure of the budget more relevant for planning purposes and making the actual preparation of the budget an integral part of the general planning process. Changes to the structure of the budget are usually designed to make the various categories into which the budget is divided more relevant as a means of indicating whether or not the budget is achieving the specific goals and objectives specified in development plans. For example, many countries have tried to introduce some form of *project budgeting*, in which at least part of the budget is classified according to particular projects instead of general functions. To return to the example of the expansion of vocational education, the use of project budgeting would mean that the project would be funded as a whole rather than through additions to a number of different functional items (such as salaries, transport, and so on) in the ministry of education's normal budget structure.

A slightly different approach involves efforts to classify budgetary activities according to the extent to which they may contribute towards particular development objectives. In Chapter 4 we saw how Papua New Guinea's national public expenditure plans are broken down in this way (see Table 8, p. 69) and we indicated that this approach can be particularly useful for the social planner, since it can be used to identify which activities are more or less likely to contribute towards social development, or some particular aspect of social development.

Many of the techniques which are used in planning–budgeting systems, especially those which involve changes in the structure of the budget, are also designed to assist in the monitoring and evaluation of plan implementation; it is therefore appropriate that we go on now to look at methods of monitoring and evaluation.

(iii) *Monitoring and evaluation*

Monitoring and evaluating the implementation of plans is an essential component of the process of linking planning and implementation, because it is the only way of discovering the extent to which plan objectives are actually being achieved. This information is needed not only to find out whether planning is having any effect on the course of events but also as a basis for revising existing plans and preparing new ones.

In Chapter 1 we mentioned briefly the importance of regarding planning as a continuous process, rather than something which is done every now and again, and we pointed out that this involves continuous monitoring and revision of plans. Before looking in some detail at methods of monitoring plan performance, it is necessary to consider some more general implications of the concept of continuous planning, since these have a direct bearing on the methods used to monitor performance.

As we suggested in Chapter 1, the concern that planning be a continuous process has resulted in a move away from the preparation of plans for fixed periods of several years—such as three-, five- or even ten-year plans—in favour of more flexible systems. One of the effects of this move has been to give more attention to the preparation of *annual plans*, which are linked to the annual budget. In some countries annual plans are prepared within the longer-term framework of a more conventional plan which covers a period of several years. In such cases, they provide a means of ensuring that the longer-term plans are reviewed and revised regularly in order to take account of changing circumstances. However, in other cases, particularly at times of rapid and unpredictable economic or political change or in countries which do not have the capacity to prepare a medium- to long-term plan, there is no attempt to provide a longer-term framework and the preparation of annual plans constitutes the only form of systematic planning.

Another type of plan which has become popular in recent years is known as a *rolling plan*. A rolling plan is initially prepared for a period of several years, but each year the plan is revised and extended. The system of national public expenditure planning adopted in Papua New Guinea is an example of rolling planning (compare Allen and Hinchliffe, in press). The first plan, which was prepared in 1977, covered the period from 1978 to 1981 (Papua New Guinea, 1977). It included detailed plans for projects to be executed in the 1978 financial year, which were incorporated into the 1978 budget, but only a general outline of projects for subsequent years. During 1978, plan performance was reviewed and the plan was revised and extended. This included the preparation of a detailed plan and budget for 1979 and an outline of projects proposed for the years from 1980 to 1982. And in 1979 the plan was extended another year, and so the process continues. Papua New Guinea's national public expenditure planning system is thus a continuing process of planning and budgeting which involves the continuous monitoring of plan performance and the subsequent revision of the plans themselves.

The concept of continuous planning demands not only that performance in implementing plans is monitored but that this monitoring is undertaken on a more or less continuous basis. In other words, monitoring is not something that can be done once every few years; it has to be built into the regular planning and implementation process. There are a number of ways in which this can be done.

As we indicated in the previous section, most of the systems which have been designed to improve the relationship between planning and budgeting are also designed to facilitate the regular monitoring of plan performance. Thus, for example, it is easier to monitor actual expenditure on a particular project if a system of project budgeting is used, rather than a more conventional system in which expenditure on the project is concealed under a number of different functional headings, such as salaries, transport, or equipment. Similarly, if expenditure is categorized according to the particular objective which it is designed to achieve, it is easier to monitor the extent to which various objectives are actually being achieved.

Other monitoring techniques are concerned with the more detailed process of monitoring the implementation of a particular project, or a series of projects or programmes within a particular government agency or administrative region. We shall examine briefly two types of technique which have been particularly designed for use in developing countries: the *operations room* approach, which we mentioned in Chapter 8 in connection with methods of storing information, and a system known as *programming and implementation management* (PIM), which was originally developed for use in district planning in Kenya (Belshaw and Chambers, 1973).

In both these approaches, the main aim is to establish a management system in which regular monitoring is built into the implementation of projects and programmes and used as a means of improving implementation as well as revising future plans. In the operations room approach, the focus of activity is the operations room, where progress in implementation is regularly recorded in the form of maps, charts, and simple progress reports, which are exhibited around the room, so that they are seen and used by everyone involved in planning and implementation. In the case of PIM, the most important feature is a monthly management meeting, at which those involved in implementation report their progress, using specially prepared reporting forms, and the meeting then discusses any action needed to improve implementation performance and, if necessary, revise plans.

Most countries will find that it is more sensible to devise a system of monitoring to meet their particular requirements rather than to try to reproduce in its entirety a system which has been developed for use elsewhere. However, knowledge of systems such as the operations room and PIM can provide some useful guidelines for anyone responsible for devising such a system. Furthermore, experience with these systems in a number of countries does suggest a few general points which should be borne in mind when designing or operating any kind of monitoring system. Firstly, monitoring should be built into the regular process of planning and implementation so that it occurs more or less automatically. Second, it should fulfil a management role, in the sense that reports on progress in implementing projects or programmes should be used to improve general administrative performance, as in the case of the monthly management meetings in the PIM system. Third, reports on implementation progress should be presented and displayed in a form which makes them easily visible, and therefore usable; this is the main aim of the operations room approach. Fourth, a monitoring system should be as simple as possible, so that it is easily understood and does not require too much time, effort, or money to operate.

In addition to these general points, from the social planner's point of view it is also particularly important that the monitoring system indicates the extent to which social goals and objectives are being achieved and reveals any social problems which may occur during the implementation process. This means that the social planner may have to ensure that, for example, the reporting forms or other procedures used to record progress include information about social factors and that those doing the monitoring have access to appropriate sources of information about these social factors.

In some cases it is necessary not only to conduct a regular monitoring of the implementation of projects or programmes but also to undertake a more thorough evaluation, either on completion of the project or at some appropriate stage (or stages) during the implementation. This sort of evaluation may be needed in order to consider whether the project is actually achieving its objectives or to examine any particular problems which may have arisen during the implementation process. It is likely to be particularly important in the case of large or complex projects or projects which are the first of their kind. The results of such evaluations may be used both to make changes in the implementation or operation of the existing project or to assist in the planning of future similar projects.

We looked in some detail at the role of social planning in this kind of evaluation in Chapter 5, when we examined some case studies of project planning. The case study of copper mining in Papua New Guinea provided a particularly good example of a situation where an evaluation of the impact of a major project—in this case the Bougainville mine—is necessary in order to improve the operation of the existing project and to assist in planning similar projects, such as the Ok Tedi mine. As we indicated in that chapter, the social planner often has a particular role to play in such an evaluation by identifying the social impact of a project which was designed primarily to achieve economic objectives.

The actual methodology used to evaluate the impact of a project or a programme is in some ways similar to that used by planners when deciding whether or not to go ahead with a project or choosing between alternative projects, in the sense that one is again concerned with the relative costs and benefits of the projects. The main difference, of course, is that when evaluating the impact of a project one is concerned with what has actually happened rather than what might happen.

The ideal situation when planning major projects is to be able to conduct both a 'before' and an 'after' study of the project area, in order to see what changes have occurred since the project was introduced. More often than not, however, this does not happen because the need for an evaluation does not arise until the project is well under way, by which time it is too late to do a 'before' study. Furthermore, it should be remembered that, even if it is possible to do a 'before' and an 'after' study, the changes which have occurred cannot necessarily be attributed to the project itself because other extraneous factors may also have had an impact.

As in the case of cost–benefit studies carried out as part of the decision-making process, one of the main problems faced by the social planner when evaluating the impact of projects and programmes is that of measuring social factors and weighing up their importance against economic factors. Thus, in the case of the Bougainville copper mine, it is very difficult to obtain data which indicate the extent of the social and psychological damage caused by the mine and even more difficult to compare this with the benefits in terms of such things as increased government revenue and employment. As we indicated in the earlier discussion of cost–benefit analysis, the only way of tackling this problem is to devise more subjective methods of measurement and comparison which depend very much on the relative importance which planners, politicians, or other decision-makers choose to place on social and economic objectives.

(iv) *The plan document*

We have discussed the role of a plan document on several occasions in previous chapters, and so it is not necessary to consider it at any length here. However, a brief mention is required because the plan document has an important role to play in linking the processes of planning and implementation.

The important point which we have emphasized elsewhere is that a plan document should not be regarded as the be-all-and-end-all of planning but as a link between planning and implementation. More specifically, we can identify two main functions of a plan document. One is to provide a blueprint for those responsible for its implementation and the other is to inform a variety of people, including politicians, aid donors, and the general public, about the type of development activities which are proposed.

This interpretation of the role of a plan document suggests some important points about the nature of such a document and the way in which it should be prepared. Perhaps the most obvious point is that it may be necessary to have more than one plan, or more than one version of the same plan. For example, there may be one plan (or one version of the plan) for the politicians whose approval is required before implementation can begin, another for the aid agency which will be asked to provide the funds, a third for the administrators who will have to implement it, and a fourth for the people whose lives will be affected by it. It is unlikely that the same document will be suitable for all these purposes. This also raises questions about the value of the conventional five-year plan document covering all sectors of the economy. The main value of this sort of document, which is still prepared—at great cost in terms of time and money—in many countries, is probably as a general source of information for politicians and, in some cases, prospective aid donors. It is of very limited value for either the administrators responsible for its implementation or the general public.

Another important question is whether a conventional plan document is actually the best way of presenting the information. Thus, for implementation purposes, the most useful form of presentation is probably a budget, supported by a series of written instructions or operational charts detailing exactly how and when the various components of the plan will be executed. This concept of a 'plan' fits in with the operations room approach to planning and monitoring which we have already discussed.

Similarly, when it comes to conveying information about proposed activities to the local population in the affected area, any form of written document is unlikely to be much help. In such cases it will be necessary to consider other forms of communication, such as making visits to the area, communicating information through extension staff, or using the media or various forms of visual aids. This is something of particular importance to the social planner because of his concern with popular participation in the planning process and it raises many of the issues related to participation which we discussed at length in Chapters 6 and 7.

Management and communication skills

So far in this chapter we have concentrated on the technical skills required by the planner. However, the social planner is not only a technician; he is also an administrator, a manager, and a communicator and a great deal of his work involves dealing with people and managing difficult situations. In this part of the chapter, we therefore consider briefly some of the management and communications skills which he (or she) is likely to require. Since it is not possible to provide a comprehensive guide to the sciences of management or communication, we have selected three particular types of skill which we consider to be of special relevance to the social planner in the Third World. These are coordination skills, methods of writing reports, and the skills required in working with communities.

(i) *Coordination*

We have emphasized on a number of occasions that much of the planner's work involves encouraging and coordinating the planning efforts of others, rather than actually preparing plans himself. We have also pointed out that because of the rather nebulous nature of social planning, it is often difficult to separate it clearly from other forms of planning activity. We shall return to both these points in Chapter 10, when we consider the organizational framework required for social planning. At this point our concern is to consider what skills the social planner needs to assist him in the process of liaison and coordination between a variety of individuals and organizations.

In the first place, there is a need for certain skills which we may refer to as *conceptual* skills. He must accept the concept of planning as part of a complex process of decision-making which involves many individuals and organizations and cannot be considered in isolation from the interrelated processes of policy formulation at one end and plan implementation at the other. It is also important that he is able to view the process of development—and therefore of development planning—as a whole, rather than from the narrow viewpoint of one particular discipline, government agency, or interest group. In other words, he must appreciate the concept of *integrated* development, to which we have referred in previous chapters. An understanding of these concepts will help the planner to see his own role as a coordinator and facilitator.

However, it is not enough to understand concepts; practical skills are also required in order to be able to translate these concepts into reality. Some of these we may refer to as *analytical* skills. The social planner must be able to collect information from a wide range of sources and put it together into some sort of coherent whole. In so doing he will have to weigh up one piece of information against another, see things from many different points of view, decide what to do if certain important pieces of information are missing, and so on.

Others may be more aptly described as *administrative* skills. For example, the planner must be prepared to spend much of his time visiting other offices, collecting information, and discussing plans and progress, rather than merely sitting behind his own desk, as so many civil servants do. He must also expect to spend a disproportionate amount of his time attending meetings and sometimes to find himself in the position of chairing a meeting of people with widely differing views and interests, from which some decision has to eventually emerge.

Finally, and very closely related to the administrative skills, there are what we may call *human relations* skills, which are rather difficult to describe precisely or to learn through formal training programmes. Those human relations skills which are particularly relevant to the planner include the ability to listen to, acknowledge, and—when appropriate—adopt other people's points of view; the ability to convince other people to accept one's own or someone else's views; and the ability to keep on good terms with a wide range of individuals and organizations. In short, what is required is a great deal of patience, tact, and diplomacy.

It should be added that the various coordination skills mentioned here are not required only by social planners. They are essential skills for any planner—and also desirable qualities for most people involved in any form of administrative or management work. They are, however, of special importance to the social planner, partly because of the unusually broad scope of his work which brings him into contact with a particularly wide range of people, and partly because social planning is only just being recognized as a discipline in its own right and so the social planner has to make a special effort to prove his worth. The importance of these qualities will become clearer when we look at the organization of social planning in Chapter 10.

(ii) *Report writing*

Although we have at times emphasized the importance of means of communication other than the written word, the production of written reports is likely to remain an important part of any planner's work. Sometimes the need may be for only a brief report summarizing the results of a meeting or investigation or proposing a particular course of action; on other occasions it may be necessary to produce a more elaborate document, perhaps approaching the conventional concept of a 'plan'. Whatever the type of report required, there are a few important points which the planner working in a developing country should bear in mind. Most of them are simple points and the reader may wonder why it is necessary to mention them at all. However, it is surprising how often they are ignored, even by experienced planners. Four particularly important points are raised briefly in this section.

Firstly, reports should be as short as possible, particularly when they are directed towards politicians, community leaders, or the general public. Long reports require much more time and effort to read, and sometimes the mere sight of a very long report discourages the reader from looking at it at all.

Secondly, reports should be written in the language (or languages) most easily understood by those who have to read them. Sometimes this may mean that considerable time and effort have to be devoted to the translation of reports, and provision should be made for this.

Thirdly, reports should be simply and clearly written and directly relevant to the particular issues under consideration. Problems should be clearly stated and alternative courses of action spelled out in detail, so that the report provides a basis for making and implementing decisions. Too many planning reports are vague and inconclusive and, when a decision is made, a more detailed report has to be prepared before implementation can begin.

And finally, reports should whenever possible be produced on time, even if this means that the quality of the report is not quite as high as one might hope to achieve. This point is particularly relevant to consultants from universities or other academic institutions, who are notoriously bad at producing reports quickly and meeting deadlines, partly because they usually have other commitments—such as teaching duties—but also because they are less accustomed to working to schedules and they tend to be perfectionists in terms of the quality of presentation of their work.

(iii) *Working with communities*

It is important that social planners have some knowledge of the skills required and alternative methods used by people who have to work directly with community groups and organizations. They may not have to use these skills directly, but should have sufficient knowledge to be able to play a meaningful role in planning development programmes which involve work with people. Once again this is an important quality for any planner, or anyone involved in designing or implementing development programmes, but it is of particular significance to the social planner because of his concern with participatory planning and the impact of development programmes on local communities. For example, the social planner may be required to assist in planning community development programmes, improving the quality of extension services, increasing community participation in local planning activities, or devising training programmes for community development workers or other extension staff.

We shall not attempt to discuss community development or extension methods in any detail here, partly because the social planner does not have to be a fully trained community development worker (although a community development worker may well make a good social planner) and partly because the type of methods which are likely to be appropriate in any specific situation will vary considerably. Furthermore, we have already touched upon this subject in the chapters on participatory planning. We shall, therefore, merely make brief mention of a few basic community development or extension skills of which the social planner should be particularly aware.

One of the most basic skills required by community workers is some understanding of what is meant by a 'community', how to identify community groups, and how to encourage and strengthen community identity and solidarity. This will depend to a great extent on the nature of communities and community organization in any particular country or region, since—as we saw in Chapter 7—there is no simple definition of what constitutes a community. However, the discussion in that chapter should have provided some indication of the factors which the social planner or community worker should consider when attempting to define or strengthen any form of community structure.

Another fundamental skill is the ability to encourage and assist local initiative without playing too great a role or having too much direct influence. This is commonly known as the *non-directive* approach to community work (compare Batten, 1967). The extent to which a non-directive approach is actually adopted and the methods used will again vary considerably, depending on the role which the community worker is supposed to play—or sees himself playing—in any particular situation.

There is also a group of related skills and techniques which are concerned with how to deal with particular situations which may arise when working with communities. For example, it is important to have some idea how to identify community leaders and to appreciate the advantages and disadvantages of working through one leader rather than another. Equally important is knowing how to recognize and deal with conflict and disunity within communities, bearing in mind that many efforts to involve local communities in planning and development succeed only in involving—and therefore benefiting—the more affluent members of the community.

One of the roles of the community worker or other form of extension worker is to act as a liaison between the community and relevant government and non-government organizations at the regional or national level. He should be able not only to communicate information about local conditions, needs, and views to regional or national authorities but also to provide information and, when necessary, obtain financial assistance for the local community. This means that he must know where to find such information and assistance and must be prepared to fight his way through considerable bureaucratic 'red tape' in order to obtain it. This is especially important in the case of a general community development worker who has no particular technical skills (such as agriculture, business organization, or construction) which he himself can offer the community, since his 'success' is likely to depend to a considerable extent on his ability to obtain outside assistance when it is needed.

Finally, it is necessary to consider the personal qualities of the community worker himself. In most situations it is important that he is able to live and work as far as possible as a member of the community. This means that he must not be of a social group (for example, tribe, caste, or class) which is unacceptable to the community in which he will work, he must be able to speak—or prepared to learn—the local language, and he must be prepared to adopt a life style which is not too different from that of the majority of the community. The importance of these qualities has implications for the methods of recruitment and conditions of employment of community workers, as well as for the design of training programmes, since only some of these skills can be instilled in the community worker by training.

In conclusion we may quote from the author of a number of books on community development training written in the 1960s, who points out that:

Although the community development worker may need to acquire some technical skills . . . his basic and primary skill is working with people. This is a particularly difficult and complex skill to learn. No one community or community group is quite the same as any other, and therefore the worker cannot ever be sure that what he has succeeded in doing in one community he can do with equal success in another: and one lesson that all the cases teach is that in this field of work it is the people, not the worker or his agency, who are in control (Batten, 1965, p. 181)

This is an important reminder not only for the community development worker but also for the social planner, who may be proficient in a wide range of technical planning skills but will not get very far unless he remembers that it is ultimately the people who have the power to determine the success or failure of many development programmes.

Notes

1. In writing this section considerable assistance was obtained from discussions with Majid Rasoolzadeh, an MA student at the Institute of Planning Studies, University of Nottingham, who was engaged in a dissertation on this topic.

Guide to further reading

It is not easy to find useful reading material on planning methods. As indicated in the introduction to this chapter, there are no comprehensive textbooks on the planning skills required by social planners in either developed or developing countries and, although there is a wealth of material on some specific planning techniques, most of it is directed towards planners in developed countries, and a large part of it is too technical or too specific for the general reader. In this section we attempt to identify some of the more useful material for those particularly concerned with social planning in the Third World.

Decision-making skills

One of the most useful and up-to-date general texts on decision-making skills is *Rational Techniques in Policy Analysis* by M. Carley (London, Heinemann, 1980). It includes a discussion of the general concept of rational decision-making and most of the specific techniques mentioned in this chapter and, although it is written primarily for readers in the developed world, its relatively straightforward and practical approach make it reasonably suitable for use in the Third World. Another advantage of Carley's book is that it adopts an interdisciplinary approach to the subject. For details of decision-making techniques used particularly by economists, the reader is referred to Part Two of *Planning Development* by K. B. Griffin and J. L. Enos (London, Addison-Wesley, 1970); or a similar text on economic planning.

The debate about rational decision-making is summarized in Chapter 2 of Carley's book. However, readers may also like to consult a text on the theoretical basis of planning; see for example Chapters 6 and 8 of *Planning Theory* by A. Faludi (Oxford, Pergamon Press, 1973).

There are a large number of books on cost–benefit analysis, including a few directed specifically to the Third World. Two of the more useful ones are: *The Appraisal of Development Projects* by M. Roemer and J. J. Stern (New York, Praeger, 1977) and the *Guide to the Economic Appraisal of Projects in Developing Countries* produced by the Overseas Development Administration of the United Kingdom government (London, HMSO, revised edition 1977).

For a discussion of some of the problems of incorporating social factors—including the distributional aspects of development—into project appraisal, some useful articles can be found in *World Development,* 6 (1978), No. 2 (which is the report of a symposium on the employment and distributional aspects of project appraisal organized in 1977 by the Kuwait Fund for Arab Economic Development) and in *Models, Planning and Basic Needs,* edited by S. Cole and H. Lucas (University of Sussex, Institute of Development Studies Research Report, 1978).

There is a considerable amount of literature on a spatial approach to decision-making, including the application of growth centre and service centre theories. Three books which provide a useful introduction to this field and are specifically concerned with developing countries are: *Development Planning and Spatial Structure* edited by A. Gilbert (London, Wiley, 1976); *The Organisation of Space in Developing Countries* by E. A. J. Johnson (Cambridge, Mass., Harvard University Press, 1970); and *Underdevelopment and Spatial Inequality* edited by D. Slater (*Progress in Planning,* Vol. 5, 1975, Part 2). The application of spatial techniques to the analysis of development problems is also illustrated in *The Development Gap* by J. P. Cole (Chichester, Wiley, 1981).

The use of various mathematical models in decision-making is described in many of the books already mentioned. However, for a discussion of their application in the Third World the most useful is probably *Models, Planning and Basic Needs*; although concerned particularly with global models, much of the discussion is relevant to the use of any type of mathematical model.

For a shorter discussion of the use of models, see 'Notes on the use of models in development planning' by H. B. Chenery in *The Crisis in Planning*, edited by M. Faber and D. Seers (London, Chatto and Windus, 1972), pp. 129–135. And for more limited usage, a report by R. Mohan entitled *Urban Economic and Planning Models: Assessing the Potential for Cities in Developing Countries* (World Bank, 1979) may be of interest to some readers.

Implementation skills

There is a considerable amount of material on the implementation of plans and, in particular, on the relationship between planning and budgeting. The following are recommended as general sources:

Caiden, N. and A. Wildavsky, *Planning and Budgeting in Poor Countries* (New York, Wiley, 1974).

Beenhakker, A., *A System for Development Planning and Budgeting* (Farnborough, Hants, Gower, 1980).

Waterston, A., *Development Planning: Lessons of Experience* (Baltimore, Johns Hopkins Press, 1965), Chapter 9.

Waterston, A., 'An operational approach to development planning' in Faber, M. and D. Seers (eds.), *The Crisis in Planning* (London, Chatto and Windus, 1972), Chapter 4.

Useful articles on planning and budgeting also appear from time to time in a journal called *Finance and Development*, which is published (and issued free) by the International Monetary Fund.

The programming and implementation management (PIM) system is described in a number of papers produced by the Institute for Development Studies (IDS) at the University of Nairobi, particularly *PIM: a Practical Management System for Implementing Rural Development Projects and Programmes* (IDS Discussion Paper, 1973). The operations room approach is described briefly in Chapter 9 of Waterston's book *Development Planning: Lessons of Experience*.

Management and communication skills

There are various books and manuals on general administration and management, many of which are designed for use in a particular country. The reader is therefore advised to consult the most appropriate ones available in his or her own university or training institution. Unfortunately, however, coordination skills—which are particularly important for the planner—receive very little attention in most of these manuals.

Working with communities requires more specific skills, and there are a number of books in this field. The best-known writer on this subject in the Third World is T. R. Batten, whose books include: *Training for Community Development* (1962); *The Human Factor in Community Work* (1965); and *The Non-Directive Approach in Group and Community Work* (1967). All these books are published by Oxford University Press. They are, however, now rather dated, and when using them readers should bear in mind changes which have occurred in attitudes towards community development and in the socio-economic and political status of most Third World nations. Many countries produce their own handbooks on community development or extension methods and these are likely to be of more direct value to readers in these countries.

For a more recent discussion directed particularly towards the training needs of social planners, the reader may also find useful an article entitled 'Training social planners for social development' by J. Midgley (*International Social Work*, 22 (1980), 2-15). And finally, for more general references on community development and extension he should consult the reading list at the end of Chapter 7.

CHAPTER 10

ORGANIZATION FOR SOCIAL PLANNING

This chapter is concerned with the organizational framework within which social planning occurs: the type of people who are involved in social planning, the organizations in which they work, their roles and functions, and their relationship with others involved in the planning process. We have already examined in some detail in earlier chapters the organizational framework required for specific aspects of social planning. For example, in Chapter 3 we looked at the organization of planning for social services, with particular reference to education and health planning, and in Chapters 4 and 5 we considered the types of organization needed to ensure that social factors are taken into account in both national and project planning. The purpose of this chapter is to bring together the appropriate sections of the previous chapters in order to obtain a picture of the organizational structure required for social planning as a whole. This will necessitate some repetition of earlier sections, but we consider this justified in view of the importance of seeing social planning as a whole rather than merely as a number of separate activities.

Since social planning is a relatively new discipline and its importance is only just being fully recognized in the Third World, many countries do not as yet have a fully developed social planning structure. Consequently, in this chapter we shall find ourselves considering what sort of organizational structure *should* exist, rather than what actually *does* exist. In other words, the approach adopted in this chapter tends to be prescriptive rather than descriptive. It will also be necessary to generalize to a fairly high degree, and it is important that readers realize that the generalizations made here must be adapted to meet the specific needs and conditions of each country. For instance, the size of a country, its political organization, the relative importance of planning, and the type of social policies will all have a major impact on the type of social planning structure which is required.

The rest of the chapter is divided into four sections. The first section looks in more detail at a question which has been raised on several earlier occasions: what sort of person is a social planner? The next section considers the types of organization in which social planners may be located and their role in these organizations, and this is followed in the third section by an examination of the relationship between social planners and others involved in planning. Finally, the last section returns to the broader issues raised in the first two chapters about the role of social planning and the relationship between social planning, social policy, and socio-political change.

Who is the social planner?

The first question which may be raised at this point is whether 'the social planner' is in fact one person or many. We have seen how the term 'social planning' is used to refer to many different—although related—activities, and it is possible for each of these activities to be carried out by a different sort of person. Thus, education planning may be done by educational administrators, the social evaluation of projects may be conducted by a sociologist or anthropologist, and responsibility for ensuring local participation in planning may be placed in the hands of a local government administrator or community development worker. In some cases, these people may perform such tasks as only one part of a much wider set of duties. The sociologist who examines the social impact of a project, for example, may actually be a university lecturer who does such work only in his vacations.

However, there does seem to be an increasing need for what we might call a *professional social planner*. The professional social planner might be described as both a generalist and a specialist. He is a generalist in the sense that he can turn his hand to many different types of social planning; and he is a specialist because he is concerned only with social planning—he is not a general administrator, an economic planner, or a sociology lecturer who carries out social planning functions in addition to his other duties.

There are two main advantages in having a professional social planner. Firstly, he is likely to have a broader view of the issues and problems involved in any aspect of social planning. For example, a professional social planner in an education planning unit will introduce a wider perspective to education planning than someone who has been trained only in education. He should be more aware of the role of education in social development and of the existence of general social policies which may affect education planning. And secondly, he is more likely to have access to a set of analytical skills or techniques which, as we saw in the two previous chapters, are common to many forms of social planning.

What sort of person might become a professional social planner? There are several possibilities. One possibility is a person who begins his (or her) career by specializing in one particular form of social development or social planning—for example, education, health, social welfare, or community development—and then decides to extend his interests to other aspects of social planning. Another possibility is a generalist administrator or development planner who develops a special interest in the social aspects of development and planning. A third type of social planner is the university-trained sociologist or anthropologist who decides to put his academic skills to more practical use. And finally there are those people who have been educated or trained specifically as social planners.

Until recently nearly everyone involved in social planning fell into one of the first three categories, and the majority would probably not have looked upon themselves, or have been officially classified, as 'social planners'. However, with the growing interest in social planning there are now more positions officially classified as social planning positions, and an increasing number of courses on social planning at various levels are available for those who wish to become professional social planners.

In view of the increasing popularity of social planning training, it is worth giving some attention at this point to the content of such training programmes. The content of each course will obviously depend very much on its particular purpose, its level and length, and the background and previous training of the course participants. However, it is possible to identify four main components which should be incorporated into most courses on social planning. These are: an introduction to the study of development in general, and social development and social policy formulation in particular; an introduction to the structure of government and administration and the role and methods of development planning; an analysis of the role of social planning and the different forms which it may take; and instruction in the basic skills and techniques required by social planners, as outlined in Chapters 8 and 9. In addition, students may be given the opportunity to specialize in particular aspects or forms of social planning if appropriate.

In conclusion, it should perhaps be emphasized that, as in so many other occupations, the attitude of the person concerned is more often than not as important as his professional education or training. In the case of a social planner, it is important that he not only have the general qualities of a good administrator or planner—such as industriousness, integrity, tact and diplomacy, an analytical mind and an ability to express himself clearly orally or on paper; but also that he is aware of the importance of social goals and social development and is committed to their achievement.

We have seen elsewhere that, on many occasions, the social planner has to withstand considerable opposition. He may have to oppose cuts in social services at a time when overall government expenditure has to be reduced or recommend that a major economic development project be abandoned, or at least significantly modified, because it will have an undesirable social impact. Similarly, he may find himself advocating a policy which is unpopular with politicians or senior civil servants because of its redistributive implications or insisting that the local community be involved in planning a project, even though this will increase the cost of the planning process in terms of time and money. He cannot do this unless he understands, and is fully committed to, the social and ideological premises on which social planning is based.

The location of social planners

Having given some thought to the question of who is a social planner, we may now consider in what sort of organizations social planners should be located and what their role should be in these organizations. In this section we examine the role of social planners in a national planning agency, in other ministries or agencies at the national level, and at the regional or local level; and we also look at the possible role of social planning consultants.

(i) *Social planners in a national planning agency*

We have indicated elsewhere that it is not our intention in this book to examine the advantages and disadvantages of having a national planning agency or to consider in any detail the size, status, role, or internal organization of such an agency. We shall simply assume that most Third World countries do have some sort of national planning agency—whether it be a ministry or department in its own right, part of another ministry or department (such as the ministry of finance), or some special body such as a planning office or commission, responsible perhaps to the president or prime minister—and confine our attention to the role which social planners should play in such an organization.

We may identify three main roles for social planners in a national planning agency, corresponding to the three broad categories of social planning which we have defined in this book. Firstly, they should assist in the formulation of policy and preparation of plans for the social services—education, health, social welfare, housing, and so on. This involves close liaison with the various ministries, departments, or other agencies directly involved in providing these services, in order to encourage planning in these agencies and to ensure that their plans are in line with overall national policy and with the policies and plans of related organizations.

Secondly, they should try to ensure that social factors and social considerations are taken into account in all forms of planning. As we indicated in Chapters 4 and 5, this is a rather broader and more complex role. The persons concerned must be aware of the many different interpretations or manifestations of the word 'social' and they must be familiar with all aspects of the planning process.

Thirdly, social planners have a role to play in ensuring that there is adequate participation in the planning process. This is also a rather vague responsibility, which may involve a variety of activities; for example, developing channels of communication between the national and village levels, ensuring that the local community is properly consulted when planning a particular development project, and encouraging or liaising with community development organizations.

It is difficult to generalize about the number of people required to carry out this work and their role within the national planning agency, since much will depend on the size and internal organization of the planning agency. There are several advantages in having a special social planning section, responsible for all of the activities described above, since this emphasizes the importance of social planning and the links between different aspects of social planning. It also means that there is a group of people involved in social planning on a full-time basis, thus increasing the likelihood that social considerations will receive adequate attention.

However, in some situations it may be better to distribute social planners—particularly those responsible for ensuring that social factors are taken into consideration in all aspects of planning and that there is adequate popular participation—among other sections of the planning agency. In this case, the impact of the social planner is likely to be less obvious, but it could in the long run be more effective because he will be working side by side with other planners and may thus be able to influence their attitudes more easily. The main disadvantages of this approach are that the views of the social planner may be overshadowed by those of his colleagues or his efforts may be diverted into other activities not directly related to social planning.

Whatever structure is adopted, it is important that, in addition to the appointment of full-time social planners, all staff of the planning agency are made aware of the importance of the social aspects of planning. If this is done, social planners will find not only that their views are more readily accepted by their colleagues but also that the latter begin to take social factors into account more or less automatically, without having to be continuously reminded of the need to do so.

Before going on to look at the role of social planners in other organizations, it should be pointed out that planners in a national planning agency do not have an easy role to play. They have to provide leadership, guidance, coordination, and sometimes direction to all other agencies involved in planning, and yet they have to do this without appearing to be dictatorial or unsympathetic towards the other agencies. They must also have sufficient understanding of the various agencies with which they are dealing to be able to coordinate their activities, without actually being specialists in these fields themselves. These problems face social planners just as much as any other staff in a national planning body.

(ii) *Social planners in other ministries or agencies*

Social planners also have an important role to play in other ministries, departments, or agencies at the national level. The most obvious need for social planners is in those agencies specifically responsible for the provision of social services. In Chapter 3 we discussed in some detail the organization of planning in ministries responsible for social services, with particular reference to the ministries of education and health. We pointed out that, especially in larger ministries, the planning units should, if possible, include a 'professional' social planner as well as specialists in the particular field concerned, such as education or health. The professional social planner will provide a broader view of planning issues and assist in liaison with the national planning agency.

However, social planners are needed not only in those agencies responsible for the provision of social services. They also have an important role to play in the planning units of most other ministries, departments, or agencies, where their job is to ensure that social factors receive adequate attention in planning and that local communities are involved in the planning process as much as possible. This is probably the area where, in most countries, a great deal of progress still has to be made. It is generally accepted that planning units in ministries responsible for activities such as agriculture, industrial development, mining, forestry, and so on should include economists and statisticians as well as technical staff; but it can still be very difficult to persuade those in charge of such units that they should also have a social planner. This reflects the fact that economic and technical considerations still tend to dominate planning decisions in such organizations.

It may not always be necessary or possible to employ full-time social planners in all other ministries. In some cases, the shortage of funds and of suitable social planning staff may make it more practical merely to ensure that at least some members of the planning staff appreciate the need to take account of social factors and are specifically responsible for ensuring that this is done, even if they may have to perform other duties as well.

These people need not be trained specifically as social planners; for example, in a ministry of agriculture someone who has worked for some length of time at the local level and proved to be a capable and sympathetic extension worker may be a suitable choice. What is important is not that there are large numbers of people officially classified and trained as professional social planners, but that the social aspects of planning receive adequate attention. For this reason, it is equally important that all planning staff, whatever organization they are in, are educated about the importance of social planning.

(iii) *Social planners at regional or local level*

It is very difficult to generalize about the role of social planning at regional or local level, since so much depends on the size of the country and the degree of decentralization in its political, administrative, and planning structure. In a large country with a federal system of government, for instance, each state or province may have a fully developed planning organization, including a central planning unit and planning sections within each functional department or agency. In this case, social planners obviously have a major role to play. However, at the other extreme, a very small country with a relatively centralized system of government may have no full-time planning staff at regional or local level.

In general terms, however, two points may be emphasized. Firstly, in any country considerable effort should be made to decentralize planning as much as possible, within the limits imposed by the lack of resources and the need to retain overall national control of the planning process. We do not intend here to discuss the advantages and disadvantages of decentralized planning or regional planning. We have already considered this issue in some detail, at least from a social planning point of view, in Chapters 6 and 7. It should, however, be mentioned that decentralized planning is desirable not only as a means of facilitating local participation but also as a way of increasing flexibility and coordination at the local level.

The other important point to note is that the social aspects of planning are just as important at the regional or local level as they are at the national level. In fact, in some respects they are even more important, since this is the level at which the interaction between 'planning' and 'people' is most likely to occur. Consequently, it is very important that social factors are taken into account in any form of planning or decision-making which occurs at regional or local level.

In practical terms, this does not necessarily mean that a full-time social planner should be employed in every province, region, or district. This may be desirable, but in most countries it is unlikely to be possible, at least in the short run. It may not even mean that full-time planners of any sort should be based at regional level in the immediate future. What is important is that those who are involved in decision-making at this level—whether they be professional planners, administrators, politicians, or community leaders—are fully aware of the importance of social considerations and ensure that they are taken into account when making decisions. One of the tasks of professional social planners at the national level should be to educate people at the local level in this regard.

(iv) Social planning consultants

So far we have confined our attention to permanent or full-time planning staff, even though these staff may not always spend all their time on activities related to social planning. However, there are occasions when it is either necessary or desirable to employ social planners on a short-term basis to undertake specific tasks. The most obvious case is when it is necessary to evaluate the social impact of an existing or proposed development project, and this evaluation requires a special survey. A similar need may arise if any other social issue requires particular attention; for example, if the national planning agency is asked to make a special investigation into the causes of urban crime or the ministry of health requires information on the social implications of a proposed family planning programme. In all these cases it is necessary to employ additional staff because the existing planning staff either are fully occupied on other duties or lack the specialized skills needed to undertake this particular task.

On such occasions there is often a role for what may be called 'social planning consultants'. These people may be professional consultants, who earn their living from such projects, or they may be those who are normally employed in another capacity but do occasional consultancy work. The most obvious example of the latter group are university staff, who are often employed as consultants in their vacations or other spare time, sometimes with the assistance of a team of university students, for whom the project provides useful practical experience.

Social planning consultants may be employed individually or as part of an interdisciplinary team, depending on the nature of work to be done. The growing importance of social planning is reflected in the fact that an increasing number of interdisciplinary planning teams now include a social planner. For example, when Papua New Guinea advertised in 1978 for consultants to prepare a plan for the development of the Simbu Province, in preparation for the establishment of a World Bank funded integrated rural development project in the area, it specified the fact that the planning team must include someone with social planning skills.

The employment of consultants inevitably has some disadvantages and social planning consultants are no exception in this respect. The most obvious disadvantage is that consultants are generally less familiar with local conditions and needs than permanent planning staff. Consequently, they have to spend considerable time familiarizing themselves with the local situation and their conclusions or recommendations are sometimes unrealistic. Furthermore, when they have prepared their plans or proposals their role is over and so there is no continuity between planning and implementation. Many plans prepared by consultants are never implemented for these reasons.

Another problem in the case of professional consultants is that they normally charge high fees. In this respect it is usually more economical to employ non-professionals, such as university staff. But university staff also present problems, because their approach often tends to be too 'academic' and, partly because of other commitments such as teaching, they are frequently unable to complete projects on time.

There is no easy or universal answer to these problems. However, as a general guide it may be said that consultants should probably not be employed unless absolutely necessary and, if they are employed, the terms of reference should be clearly specified. The problems may also be reduced by utilizing local research institutions, which are now found in many developing countries, sometimes attached to universities but engaged in research on a full-time basis. There is considerable scope for the expansion of social planning skills in such institutions, and for their use by governments when consultants are required.

The relationship between social planners and other people

We have emphasized throughout this book that planning should be regarded as a complex decision-making process involving many different kinds of people—not merely professional planners. Consequently, it is important that the planners work very closely with everyone else involved in the planning process. This is perhaps particularly important in the case of social planners because it is very difficult to separate social planning, either from other forms of planning or from other related activities in the field of social development. In this section we therefore examine the relationship between social planners and others involved in the planning process, notably other professional planners, administrators, politicians, and the general public.

(i) *Social planners and other planners*

Although social planning is becoming increasingly important as a discipline in its own right and there is an increasing demand for professional social planners, we have seen in previous chapters that it is very difficult to draw a clear distinction between social planning and other forms of planning. One reason for this is that the word 'social' is used very broadly to mean many different things, and there is often considerable overlap between what is loosely referred to as the 'social' and the 'economic' aspects of development. For example, we have seen that although education is normally regarded as a social service, it has major economic implications; consequently, it is important that economic planners are involved in education planning. Another reason is that much of the work of the social planner consists of influencing the activities of other planners, rather than carrying out separate planning exercises. Thus, the social planner may be responsible for ensuring that social factors are taken into consideration in planning a major economic development project, evaluating the effects which a new agricultural development strategy is likely to have on social inequalities, or devising means of popular participation in the preparation of a national or local plan. In all these cases, the social planner cannot work in isolation.

Consequently, it is very important that planning organizations are designed in such a way that social planners can interact easily with other professional planning staff. For example, if there is a separate social planning section in a national planning agency, steps should be taken to ensure frequent interaction between this and other sections. Similarly, if a social impact study is required as part of the planning of a specific development project, a social planner should be involved and he should work as part of an interdisciplinary planning team, not on his own.

The type of planners with which social planners are most likely to have to work are economists, since most planning offices are still staffed largely by economists. However, relationships with other planners are also important. For example, it is now accepted that physical or spatial planners (that is, planners concerned primarily with land use and the physical layout of urban or rural areas) should take social—and also economic—factors fully into account in their work. In the past there was a tendency for physical planners to operate in isolation from other planners; in most countries they were—and often still are—based in a separate department or ministry and trained in their own professional training institutions. However, it is now generally recognized that there is a need for much closer coordination between physical planners and their colleagues in the fields of social and economic planning, even if they remain in separate ministries or departments.

Unfortunately, social planners cannot expect their relations with other planners always to be easy. As a relatively new discipline, social planning is not always held in high regard by economists, physical planners, or other professionals, especially when—as often happens—the social planners raise issues and problems which make the work of the other planners more difficult or complicated. As we have indicated elsewhere, it is not easy to convince other planners that more money should be allocated to 'unproductive' social services, that a major industrial development project should be shelved because of the social implications, that urban housing should be redesigned to resemble traditional housing styles more closely, or that the commencement of a new project should be delayed for six months while the people in the area are properly consulted. However, social planners should not be discouraged by such opposition or confine their activities to projects which do not involve cooperation or conflict with others. They should regard it as a challenge to be met with courage and enthusiasm.

(ii) *Social planners and administrators*

In this section we shall not confine ourselves specifically to social planners since, in terms of their relationship with administrators, social planners face very similar problems to other professional planners. The relationship between planners and administrators is particularly important. We have mentioned elsewhere that, although for convenience we have talked about 'planners' (or more specifically 'social planners') as a distinct category of people, it is not always necessary—or desirable—to have a special cadre of professional planners. In many cases it may be more practical to combine the roles of planner and administrator; and where the two roles are officially separated it is very important that they work closely together.

The relationship between planners and administrators is clearly allied to the relationship between planning and implementation. Theoretically, planners prepare the plans and administrators implement them. However, as we pointed out in the initial discussion of planning in Chapter 1, in practical terms they cannot be regarded as entirely separate activities. We prefer to regard them as different components of a complex process of decision-making, which extends from the formulation of policies to the preparation and implementation of specific programmes or projects, and their continuous monitoring and revision as implementation proceeds. Throughout this process planners and administrators must work very closely together.

It is important that administrators are involved in the preparation of plans as well as in their implementation. One reason for this is that they can provide much useful information which should be incorporated into the plans. For example, an education planner based either in the ministry of education or in a national planning agency will need information on existing education services, future needs and priorities, and the resources available for meeting these needs; and most of this information can be obtained more easily from administrative staff in the various divisions of the ministry of education than from any other source. The other reason why administrators should be involved is that, if they are involved, they are much more likely to be committed to the plans and therefore to play an active part in their implementation. Many plans are never implemented because they are imposed upon those responsible for implementation without any prior consultation or discussion. Whether or not the administrators actually agree with the content of the plans, they are likely to be uncooperative simply because they were not consulted.

This suggests that more often than not the main role of the planner is to stimulate and coordinate the planning activities of others, rather than to actually do all the 'planning' himself. Consequently, it is in some ways misleading to call him a 'planner', although we have used the term in this book for want of any better nomenclature. In Papua New Guinea, for example, the National Planning Office opposed the appointment of people actually called 'provincial planners' since it felt this would give a misleading impression of their role. However, in this case its views were overridden by those of provincial politicians, who liked the prestige associated—in their eyes—with the term 'planner'.

Once again social planners cannot expect that their relationship with administrators will be easy. There is a natural tendency for administrators to resent professional planners, regarding them as interfering generalists who try to impose their views without adequate understanding of the professional or technical matters involved. Similarly, there is a tendency for planners to dismiss administrators as being conservative, bureaucratic, and narrow-minded. There is a need for more give and take on both sides in an effort to develop a mutual understanding, and the planner may often find that he has to take the initiative in this respect.

(iii) *Social planners and politicians*

The relationship between planners and politicians depends to some extent on the political structure and organization of any particular country. It is perhaps useful to distinguish three different ways in which politics and politicians can influence the planning process. Firstly, there are the situations where individual politicians try to influence planning decisions in order to obtain benefits for themselves or their electorates. For example, the minister responsible for education insists that the next secondary school be built in his home area or the members of cabinet refuse to restrict private health services because they benefit directly from them. These situations occur in every country, although they do tend to occur more frequently and have more serious implications in some countries than others.

Secondly, there are the situations where planning decisions are highly influenced by clear policy directives prescribed by the political leadership. For example, there may be policy directives about the way in which social services should be distributed between rural and urban areas or between different social groups, there may be directives about the relative mix of private and public enterprise or about the priority to be given to social as opposed to economic development, and so on. The planners have to accept these policy directives and plan accordingly. This sort of political influence is likely to be more important in the so-called 'second' and 'third' worlds—that is, in the socialist bloc and the developing countries—than it is in the 'first' world of Western Europe and North America.

The third type of political influence is what might be called 'politicization' of the planning process. In this case, planners are not merely given clear political directives but are subject to more or less continuous political influence or control. This may occur in a number of ways. For example, senior officials in the national planning agency may be political appointees or the planning agency itself may be located in a strategic political position, such as the office of the president or prime minister, or subject to almost day-to-day control by a political committee. This kind of influence is more likely to occur in one-party states, where the division between politicians and civil servants is to some extent blurred and the whole civil service is in a sense politicized. It is closely related to the second type of influence which we have distinguished, but there is a difference in that it is possible to give strong policy directives to planners while at the same time maintaining a clear distinction between politicians and civil servants.

Whatever the political situation in a particular country, it is impossible to separate planning from politics completely. In theory, one may say that the politicians are responsible for formulating policy and the planners' job is to translate this policy into specific programmes or projects. But in practice, as we have pointed out several times in previous chapters, it is not possible to make such a clear distinction between policy-making and planning. Planners inevitably find themselves involved in some way or other in policy-making, and the question of where their role stops and the politicians' role begins can really only be answered on an individual case-by-case basis.

There is a tendency in many countries for planners to resent politicians in much the same way as administrators often resent planners. They feel that politicians make unrealistic demands and refuse to approve their plans or distort them to meet their own personal ends. In other words, they regard political influence as political interference. This attitude is unfortunate since it is both unrealistic and unconstructive. Planners and politicians have to be able to live and work together, just like planners and administrators. This is not easy and it can really only be achieved by encouraging frequent dialogue between the two, so that each learns to understand the other's priorities and point of view.

Until now we have been talking in general terms about all planners. There is not a great deal of difference between social planners and other planners in this respect. There are some areas in which social planners are likely to be particularly affected by political influences or to be affected in a particular way. For example, plans for the location of social services—such as schools and health facilities—are highly susceptible to the influence of individual politicians who wish to see such services provided in their own areas. Less obvious but much more important is the very strong influence which politics has on attempts to change the social structure of society and in particular to reduce inequalities and, to the extent that social planners are particularly concerned with these issues, they are likely to be more affected than other planners by political attitudes towards them. We shall return to this topic in the last section of the chapter. However, in terms of the general relationship with politicians, social planners—like all planners—have to face up to the realities of political influence and try to develop a good working relationship with politicians.

(iv) *Social planners and the general public*

We have discussed the relationship between planners and the general public in considerable detail in Chapters 6 and 7, and here we shall only attempt to summarize the main points. Participation by the general public in the planning process is—or at least should be—a matter of concern to all planners. However, it is of particular concern to social planners because one of the main roles of the social planner, as defined in this book, is to ensure that people's needs and views are taken into account in the preparation of plans and that they are given a chance actually to participate in the planning process as much as possible.

The advantages and disadvantages of various methods of popular participation were discussed in Chapter 6. It was concluded that there is no easy way; any reasonably effective method is likely to be expensive and time-consuming and the results are often confusing and frustrating. However, this does not mean that all attempts to achieve popular participation should be abandoned. For both practical and political or ideological reasons it is very important that ordinary people be involved in planning, and this means that the planning machinery must facilitate dialogue between the planners and the general pub lic. Such dialogue will not be achieved easily because of the 'communication gap' between planners and people. This gap tends to be greater, especially in developing countries, than the gaps between planners and politicians or planners and administrators. However, the effort must be made. All planners—and social planners in particular—should constantly remember that the purpose of planning, like the purpose of development, is to benefit people; people should not be regarded as a means of achieving 'better' plans.

The social planner's role in society

So far in this chapter we have talked about social planning in terms of organizational structures and relationships. We have perhaps given the impression that if the 'right' kind of people are employed in the 'right' positions in the 'right' organizations and that there is adequate communication between these people and others involved in the planning process, then all will be well.

However, the reader will hopefully realize from the content of previous chapters that the situation is actually far more complex. The role of social planning and the achievements of social planners depend much more on the social, economic, and political environment in which they operate than on organizational structures. We touched upon this issue in the section on planners and politicians, but let us now look at it in more detail.

In the first place, before one can start thinking about what sort of people should be employed as social planners and where they should be located, the government of a country has to accept that there is a need for social planning. This means not merely acknowledging the need to plan education, health, and other social services but recognizing that social factors and social goals have a very important role to play in development; in other words, it means recognizing that development must be, to use President Kaunda's terminology, 'man-centred' (Kaunda, 1974). It is no coincidence that those countries where social planning has begun to emerge as a discipline in its own right tend to be those which attach greater importance to social aspirations and goals.

Secondly, the actual work in which social planners find themselves engaged will depend on both the existing structure of society and its problems and on the types of social policies formulated by the political leadership. This is particularly obvious in the case of the social planner's role in trying to change the structure of society. For example, in a country like India the social planner is bound to devote much of his attention to looking for ways of reducing the gross social inequalities which exist in the country; and yet at the same time, the various approaches which he can consider are limited by the fact that, although the government acknowledges the need to reduce inequalities, it lacks either the ability or the political will to introduce extreme measures (such as a complete reform of the land tenure system) to overcome them. On the other hand, in some other countries, for example Tanzania, although inequalities such as those in India are unknown, the government has resolved to take much more drastic steps to try to prevent their occurrence in the future. In fact, Tanzania has at times received criticism for going too far in promoting social considerations at the expense of economic development.

However, the social, economic. and political environment also affects the more mundane tasks of the social planner. For example, we saw in Chapter 3 how the development of plans for the education and health sectors is limited very much by the existing education or health situation, the types of policies the government is prepared to introduce, the availability of funds, and the attitudes of the people themselves towards the provision of education and health services. Similarly, the social planner's role in encouraging popular participation in planning and development is constrained by the existing political and administrative structure in the country, traditional systems of decision-making and the attitudes of political leaders, other planners, administrators, and the people themselves towards participation.

Finally, the actual achievements of social planners are, in the same sort of way, highly influenced by the environment in which they operate. In fact, it is perhaps here that the most effective constraints—and consequently often the greatest frustrations—occur. The main cause of frustration is the gap which so often exists between policies and plans on the one hand, and what is actually achieved on the other. This gap may be due to a number of factors: the inability or unwillingness of administrators to implement plans; the lack of basic resources, such as personnel, money and equipment; opposition from individuals or groups with vested interests in maintaining the *status quo*; the reluctance of people to accept or adapt to change; or the failure of politicians to follow through in translating vague policies into concrete action, often because of their own vested interests. All these factors limit the achievements of the social planner and make his work challenging but often very frustrating.

In some situations the gap between what a social planner feels should be done and what he can actually achieve may be so great that he decides that he cannot work within the official planning system. One example of such a situation is the case of a planner who is committed to egalitarian development policies, but lives in a country where gross inequalities exist and are condoned or even encouraged by the government in power. A similar situation would be that of someone committed to participatory planning in a country where planning is highly centralized and authoritarian.

In such cases, the planner may choose to work in non-government organizations which are trying to bring about social and political change from outside the system. These organizations may take a variety of forms, including voluntary agencies, community organizations, and political groups. We have mentioned some examples of such organizations in previous chapters, especially in the section on community development, where we considered the role of community development in bringing about social change.

However, although many problems undoubtedly exist in most Third World countries, this does not mean that all attempts to establish an organizational structure which facilitates social planning should be abandoned—or that the social planner should give up the struggle to achieve social goals. We conclude with a quotation from a recent study of Mozambique and Tanzania conducted by the Institute for Food and Development Policy in the United States, which emphasizes this point.

In 1972, I. F. Stone, the indefatigable American journalist and publisher of his own anti-war newsletter was asked: 'Mr. Stone, why do you keep going? How can you continue to work so hard when no-one is listening? The Vietnam war is escalating.' 'Well,' responded Mr. Stone, 'I see it this way. If you expect to see the final results of your work, you have not asked a big enough question.'
     I. F. Stone's response came to mind as we were evaluating our impressions of Mozambique and Tanzania. Their problems are enormous and their mistakes, no doubt, many. Only the future can reveal the concrete lessons their experience has to teach. While final judgements are out of place, what can accurately be said of the people of both countries is that they *are* asking the biggest questions. That fact is a challenge to us all. (Lappé and Beccar-Varela, 1980, p. 120)

Further reading

We have not attempted to provide a comprehensive list of material related to this chapter. One reason for this is that many of the points raised in this chapter have already been mentioned in earlier chapters and where additional reading is available this has already been indicated. The other reason is that there is, in fact, no general material on the organization of social planning in developing countries. There are books and articles on the organization of certain forms of social planning—for example, education and health planning or project planning—and these have been indicated in the appropriate chapters. But, apart from brief references in a few United Nations publications (for example, pages 10–12 of the *Report on the Symposium on Social Policy and Planning, Copenhagen, 1970*, published in 1971) there has not, at least to the author's knowledge, been any real attempt to outline the type of organization required for social planning as a profession in its own right.

LIST OF WORKS CITED
IN THE TEXT

Note: Books and other sources of information referred to only in the guides to further reading at the end of each chapter are not listed here, since full references have already been provided.

Adelman, I., and C. T. Morris, 1978. *Economic Growth and Social Equity in Developing Countries* (Stanford, Stanford University Press).

Allen, W., and K. Hinchcliffe, in press. *Planning, Policy Analysis and Public Expenditure: Theory and the Papua New Guinea Experience* (Farnborough, Hants., Gower Publishing Company).

Apthorpe, R. (ed.), 1970. *People Planning and Development Studies* (London, Frank Cass).

Apthorpe, R., 1978. *Social Indicators: Definitions, Properties, Uses, Representations* (University of East Anglia, School of Development Studies, Discussion Paper No. 26).

Baster, N. (ed.), 1972. *Measuring Development* (London, Frank Cass).

Batten, T. R., 1965. *The Human Factor in Community Work* (London, Oxford University Press).

Batten, T. R., 1967. *The Non-Directive Approach in Group and Community Work* (London, Oxford University Press).

Beenhakker, A., 1980. *A System for Development Planning and Budgeting* (Farnborough, Hants., Gower Publishing Company).

Belshaw, D., and R. Chambers, 1973. *PIM: a Practical Management System for Implementing Rural Development Programmes and Projects* (University of Nairobi, Institute for Development Studies Discussion Paper).

Brokensha, D., and T. Scudder, 1968. 'Resettlement' in Rubin, N., and W. M. Warren (eds.), *Dams in Africa* (London, Frank Cass), pp. 20–62.

Bureau of Resource Assessment and Land Use Planning, 1970. *Northeast Nzega Planning Project: Final Report* (University of Dar es Salaam, BRALUP Research Report 6/10).

Carley, M., 1980. *Rational Techniques in Policy Analysis* (London, Heinemann).

Chambers, R., 1969. *Settlement Schemes in Tropical Africa* (London, Routledge and Kegan Paul).

Cochrane, G., 1979. *The Cultural Appraisal of Development Projects* (New York, Praeger).

Cole, J. P., 1981. *The Development Gap* (Chichester, Wiley).

Cole, S. and H. Lucas (eds.), 1978. *Models, Planning and Basic Needs* (University of Sussex, Institute of Development Studies Research Report).

Colson, E., 1971. *The Social Consequences of Resettlement* (Manchester, Manchester University Press).

Conyers, D., 1969. *Report on the Methodology Used in the General Household Survey of Northeast Nzega* (University of Dar es Salaam, Bureau of Resource Assessment and Land use Planning Research Report 6/5).

Conyers, D., 1973. *Agro-Economic Zones of Tanzania* (University of Dar es Salaam, Bureau of Resource Assessment and Land Use Planning Research Paper).

Conyers, D., 1976. *The Provincial Government Debate* (Port Moresby, Papua New Guinea Institute of Applied Social and Economic Research, Monograph 2).

Conyers, D., 1977. 'Administration in China: some preliminary observations', *Journal of Administration Overseas,* **16**, 98–113.

Conyers, D., 1981a. 'Decentralization and regional development: a comparative study of Tanzania, Zambia and Papua New Guinea', *Public Administration and Development,* **1**, 201–229.

Conyers, D., 1981b. 'Development from the middle: decentralisation in Papua New Guinea' in Taylor, D. R. F., and W. Stohr (eds.), *Development from Above or Below? Radical Approaches to Spatial Planning in Developing Countries* (London, Wiley).

Conyers, D., and D. R. Simpson (eds.), 1978. *The Future of local Government in Papua New Guinea,* special issue of *Yagl-Ambu* (Papua New Guinea Journal of the Social Sciences), **5**, No. 1.

Deutscher, I., 1973. 'Asking questions cross-culturally: some problems of linguistic comparability' in Warwick, D. P., and S. Osherman (eds.), *Comparative Research Methods* (Englewood Cliffs, New Jersey, Prentice Hall), Chapter 8.

Djukanovich, V., and E. P. Mach, 1975. *Alternative Approaches to Meeting Basic Health Needs in Developing Countries* (Geneva, World Health Organization).

Dunn, P. D., 1978. *Technology with a Human Face* (London, Macmillan).

Esman, M. J., 1974. 'Administrative doctrine and developmental needs' in Morgan, E. P. (ed.), *The Administration of Change in Africa* (New York, Dunellen), pp. 3–26.

Foster, P., 1965. 'The vocational school fallacy in development planning' in Anderson, C. A., and M. J. Bowman (eds.), *Education and Economic Development* (Chicago, Aldine).

Foster, P., 1966. 'A rebuttal' in Hanson, J. W., and C. S. Brembeck (eds.), *Education and the Development of Nations* (New York, Holt Rinehart and Winston).

Frank, A. G., 1969. *Latin America: Underdevelopment or Revolution* (New York, Monthly Review Press).

George, V., and P.Wilding, 1976. *Ideology and Social Welfare* (London, Routledge and Kegan Paul).

Ghai, D. P., 1977. 'What is a basic needs approach to development all about?' in Ghai, D. P., *et al.* (eds.), *The Basic Needs Approach to Development* (Geneva, International Labour Organization), Chapter 1.

Ghai, D. P., E. Lee, and S. Radwan, 1979. *Rural Poverty in the Third World: Trends, Causes and Policy Orientations* (Geneva, International Labour Organization, World Employment Programme Research Working Paper 23).

Gish, O., 1970. 'Health planning in developing countries' in Apthorpe, A. (ed.), *People Planning and Development Studies* (London, Frank Cass), Chapter 5.

Gish, O., 1977. *Guidelines for health Planners* (London, Tri-Med.).

Honey, M., 1980. 'Tanzania tallies up its triumphs and tribulations', *The Guardian,* 8 December 1980.

Hicks, U. K., 1961. *Development from Below* (Oxford, Clarendon Press).

Hyden, G., 1980. *Beyond Ujamaa in Tanzania: Underdevelopment and an Uncaptured Peasantry* (London, Heinemann).

Independent Commission on International Development Issues (Brandt Commission), 1980. *North–South: a Programme for Survival* (London, Pan Books).

India, Planning Commission, 1961. *Third Five Year Plan* (New Delhi, Government Printer).

Intergovernmental Council of Copper Exporting Countries (CIPEC), 1980. *Statistical Bulletin 1979* (Neuilly sur Seine, France, CIPEC Documentation Centre).

Jones, J., 1980. 'An assessment of community development activities in Senegal and Nigeria', *Development Studies Association Annual Conference,* Swansea.

Joy, J. L., 1968. 'What an economist wants to know about dams' in Rubin, N., and W. M. Warren (eds.), *Dams in Africa* (London, Frank Cass), pp. 13–19.

Kandeke, T. K., 1977. *Fundamentals of Zambian Humanism* (Lusaka, National Education Company of Zambia).

Kapteyn, R. C. E., and C. R. Emery, 1972. *District Administration in Zambia* (Lusaka, National Institute of Public Administration).

Kaunda, K., 1974. *Humanism and a Guide to its Implementation, Part 2* (Lusaka, Government Printer).

Lappé, F. M. and A. Beccar-Varela, 1980. *Mozambique and Tanzania: Asking the Big Questions* (San Francisco, Institute for Food and Development Policy).

Leys, C., 1972. 'A new conception of planning' in Faber, M., and D. Seers (eds.). *The Crisis in Planning* (London, Chatto and Windus), Chapter 3.

Long, N., 1977. *An Introduction to the Sociology of Rural Development* (London, Tavistock).

Lipton, M., 1977. *Why Poor People Stay Poor: Urban Bias in World Development* (London, Maurice Temple Smith).

MacPherson, S., 1979a. 'The political development of health in Papua New Guinea', *Australia and New Zealand Association for the Advancement of Science Annual Conference,* Canberra.

MacPherson, S., 1979b. 'Social policy in Papua New Guinea' (Port Moresby, University of Papua New Guinea, Department of Anthropology and Sociology, mimeo).

MacPherson, S., 1980. 'The development of basic health services in Papua New Guinea with particular reference to the Southern Highlands Province' (University of Nottingham, Department of Social Administration, Ph.D. thesis, unpublished).

Mamak, A., and R. Bedford, 1974. *Bougainvillean Nationalism: Aspects of Unity and Discord* (Christchurch, New Zealand, Bougainville Special Publication No. 1).

Mamdani, M., 1972. *The Myth of Population Control: Family, Caste and Class in an Indian Village* (New York, Monthly Review Press).

Mayer, R. H., 1972. *Social Planning and Social Change* (Englewood Cliffs, New Jersey, Prentice-Hall).

Mehmet, O., 1978. *Economic Planning and Social Justice in Developing Countries* (London, Croom Helm).

Molteno, R., 1977. 'Zambian humanism: the way ahead' in Kandeke, T. K., *Fundamentals of Zambian Humanism* (Lusaka, National Education Company of Zambia), pp. 212–239.

Mulasa, T., 1970. 'Central government and local control' in Hyden, G. *et al.* (eds.), *Development Administration: the Kenyan Experience* (Nairobi, Oxford University Press).

Mwansasu, B. U., and C. Pratt (eds.), 1979. *Towards Socialism in Tanzania* (Tanzania Publishing House and University of Toronto Press).

Myrdal, G., 1968. *Asian Drama: an Enquiry into the Poverty of Nations* (Harmondsworth, Penguin Books) (originally published by Twentieth Century Fund).

Nyerere, J. K., 1967. *Education for Self-Reliance* (Dar es Salaam, Government Printer) (reproduced in various publications, including Nyerere, 1968).

Nyerere, J. K., 1968. *Freedom and Socialism: Uhuru na Ujamaa* (Nairobi, Oxford University Press).

Nyerere, J. K., 1977. *The Arusha Declaration Ten Years After* (Dar es Salaam, Government Printer).

Papua New Guinea, 1974. *National Health Plan 1974–78* (Port Moresby, Government Printer).

Papua New Guinea, 1975. *Constitution of the Independent State of Papua New Guinea* (Port Moresby, Government Printer).

Papua New Guinea, 1976. *Papua New Guinea Education Plan 1976–80* (Port Moresby, Government Printer).

Papua New Guinea, 1977. *The National Public Expenditure Plan 1978–81* (Port Moresby, Government Printer).

Papua New Guinea, 1978. *The National Public Expenditure Plan 1979–82* (Port Moresby, Government Printer).

Papua New Guinea, 1979. *National Education Strategy: Papua New Guinea Education Plan Review and Proposals* (Port Moresby, Institute of Applied Social and Economic Research).

Pearse, A., 1980. *Seeds of Plenty, Seeds of Want: Social and Economic Implications of the Green Revolution* (London, Oxford University Press).

Robinson, J., 1975. *Economic Management in China* (London, Anglo-Chinese Education Institute).

Saul, J. S., 1974. 'Planning for socialism in Tanzania: the socio-political context' in Rweyemamu, J. F. *et al.* (eds.), *Towards Socialist Planning* (Dar es Salaam, Tanzania Publishing House).

Schaffer, B., 1970. 'Social planning as administrative decision making' in Apthorpe, R. (ed.), *People Planning and Development Studies* (London, Frank Cass), Chapter 3.

Seers, D., 1969. 'The meaning of development', *International Development Review,* **6** (Dec.), 2–6.

Slater, D. (ed.), 1975. *Underdevelopment and Spatial Inequality,* Vol. 4, Part 2 of *Progress in Planning* (Oxford, Pergamon Press).

United Nations, 1970. *Social Welfare Planning in the Context of National Development Plans* (New York).

United Nations, 1971. *Popular Participation in Development: Emerging Trends in Community Development* (New York).

Warren, N., and W. M. Rubin (eds.), 1968. *Dams in Africa* (London, Frank Cass).

Waterston, A., 1965. *Development Planning: Lessons of Experience* (Baltimore, Johns Hopkins Press).

Watson, J., 1980. Verbal communication, University of Nottingham.

West, R., 1972. *River of Tears: the Rise of the Rio Tinto-Zinc Corporation Limited* (London, Earth Island).

Williamson, W., 1979. *Education, Social Structure and Development* (London, Macmillan).

World Bank, 1980a. *World Development Report 1980* (Oxford University Press).

World Bank, 1980b. *Education: Sector Policy Paper* (Washington, DC, 3rd edition).

World Bank, 1980c. *Health: Sector Policy Paper* (Washington, DC, 2nd edition).

World Bank, 1980d. *The World Bank and the World's Poorest* (Washington, DC).

Zambia, 1971. *Second National Development Plan* (Lusaka, Government Printer).

Zambia, 1976. *Luapula Province: Some Development Indicators* (Lusaka, Ministry of Development Planning).

Zambia, 1979. *Third National Development Plan* (Lusaka, Government Printer).

Zambia, 1980. *Health by the People* (Lusaka, Ministry of Health).

AUTHOR INDEX

SUBJECT INDEX

224

Southern Highlands Province, Papua New Guinea 164

Spatial analysis 25–27, 168–169, 180

Spatial (physical) planner 181, 205

State, role in providing social services 48

Statistics
 presentation of 167–168
 problems of collection 146, 154–155
 social statistics 71, 146, 161

Sussex University 180

Tabora Region, Tanzania 88–89, 90

Tanzania
 data collection 165
 decentralization 108
 development policy 59, 63–64, 72, 75, 76, 77, 210, 211
 education 45, 47
 further reading 78–79
 health services 48
 local government 113, 114
 socialist planning in 77
 ujamaa villages 63–64, 72, 91, 98, 127

Technology, appropriate 46, 66

Third World, definition of 16–17

Tobacco, in Zambia 93–95

Tobacco Board of Zambia 93, 94, 95

Trend extrapolation 177

Urbanization 73, 117

Unemployment 14, 30, 117

United Nations 126–128, 146, 215–216, 217

Universities 1, 192, 203, 204

Vanuatu 113

Voluntary agencies 48, 52–53, 119–120, 211

Water supply 37, 46, 89, 116

Welfare services 8–10, 37, 42, 46

Women, role of 117

World Bank 22, 77, 147, 155, 204

World Health Organization 52

Zambia
 decentralization 108–109
 development centres 181, 183
 development policy 60, 61, 72
 education 38–39, 45
 health services 45, 169, 171
 local government 113, 114
 participatory planning in 137
 tobacco schemes in 93–98, 100